Impeachment in U.S. History

This book offers the most comprehensive study yet of the history behind impeachment in the United States, considering its use against presidents, judges, justices, and members of the cabinet.

Although the Founding Fathers intended for the impeachment of federal officials to take place rarely, and only for the most egregious instances of malfeasance, calls for impeaching members of the U.S. government seem today to be almost routine. Presenting their arguments in a manner engaging to laypersons and specialists alike, authors Bolt and Kaufman describe the precolonial and colonial origins of impeachment in the United States, how the Founding Fathers intended for the process of impeachment to occur, the changes that have taken place to that process since the country's founding, and why one hears the word "impeachment" used so often at present. Incorporating dozens of cases, including many that are oftentimes forgotten, this book demonstrates that partisanship is not new when it comes to trying to remove federal officers from their post and that unseating those officers via impeachment proceedings has proven very difficult.

Accessibly written and featuring a number of primary source documents and tools for student learning, *Impeachment in U.S History* is ideal for students of American history and American political history in particular.

William K. Bolt is Professor of History at Francis Marion University, USA. He is the author of *Tariff Wars and the Politics of Jacksonian America*.

Scott Kaufman is Professor of History and Board of Trustees Research Scholar at Francis Marion University, USA. He is the author, editor, or co-editor of twelve books on U.S. diplomatic, military, and political history.

Seminar Studies

Each book in the Seminar Studies series provides a concise and reliable introduction to a wide range of complex historical events and debates, covering topics in British, European, US and world history from the medieval period to present day. Written by acknowledged experts and including supporting material such as extracts from historical documents, chronologies, glossaries, guides to key figures and further reading suggestions, Seminar Studies titles are essential reading for students of history.

Almost half a century after its launch, the series continues to introduce students to the problems involved in explaining the past, giving them the opportunity to grapple with historical documents and encouraging them to reach their own conclusions.

Series Editors:

Independence and Nation-Building in Latin America
Race and Identity in the Crucible of War
Scott Eastman and Natalia Sobrevilla Perea

Capitalism and Individualism in America
Gavin Benke

Woodrow Wilson
The First World War and Modern Internationalism
Michael R. Cude

The Mexican Revolution
Robert Weis

The Reagan Revolution
Prudence Flowers

Impeachment in U.S. History
William K. Bolt and Scott Kaufman

For more information about this series, please visit: https://www.routledge.com/Seminar-Studies/book-series/PEASSH

Impeachment in U.S. History

William K. Bolt and Scott Kaufman

Routledge
Taylor & Francis Group
LONDON AND NEW YORK

Designed cover image: The impeachment trial of President Andrew Johnson. Everett Collection / Bridgeman Images

First published 2026
by Routledge
4 Park Square, Milton Park, Abingdon, Oxon OX14 4RN

and by Routledge
605 Third Avenue, New York, NY 10158

Routledge is an imprint of the Taylor & Francis Group, an informa business

British Library Cataloguing-in-Publication Data
A catalogue record for this book is available from the British Library

Library of Congress Cataloging-in-Publication Data
Names: Bolt, William K., 1977– author | Kaufman, Scott, 1969–- author
Title: Impeachment in u.s. history / William K. Bolt, Scott Kaufman.
Other titles: Impeachment in US history
Description: Abingdon, Oxon [UK] ; New York, NY : Routledge, 2025. | Series: Seminar studies | Includes bibliographical references and index. | Contents: English Precedents and the Constitution—Impeachment in the Early Republic—Impeachment in the Antebellum Period—Impeachment in the Era of Reconstruction—New Rules, New Challenges—Rule XI and Judicial Review—Partisanship and the Demand for Reform—Judges, Justices, and Justiciability—Presidents and (Bi)Partisanship—Flexing the Impeachment 'Muscle'—Assessment.
Identifiers: LCCN 2025036690 (print) | LCCN 2025036691 (ebook) | ISBN 9781032933924 hardback | ISBN 9781032933917 paperback | ISBN 9781003565680 ebook
Subjects: LCSH: Impeachments—United States—History
Classification: LCC KF4958 .B65 2025 (print) | LCC KF4958 (ebook) | DDC 342.73/068—dc23/eng/20250827
LC record available at https://lccn.loc.gov/2025036690
LC ebook record available at https://lccn.loc.gov/2025036691

ISBN: 978-1-032-93392-4 (hbk)
ISBN: 978-1-032-93391-7 (pbk)
ISBN: 978-1-003-56568-0 (ebk)

DOI: 10.4324/9781003565680

Typeset in Sabon
by codeMantra

Contents

Figures

Acknowledgements

Will would like to thank his wife, Megan, his daughter Delaney, and his mother Marie Linda Bolt for their patience, support, and encouragement during this process. He would also like to express his thanks to his co-author and friend, Scott Kaufman, who gently prodded him to complete his chapters in a timely manner and who made sure that this project made it across the finish line.

Scott would like to thank his wife, Julie; his father and stepmother, Burton Kaufman and Jane Bloom; and his sister and brother-in-law, Heather Kaufman and Steve Moore for their love and support. He cannot forget his and Julie's 'dog-ster,' Lexi, whom he sometimes had to skip walking to work on the manuscript. Finally, he wants to thank his co-author, Will Bolt, not only for the time he put into this book, but who, as department chair, consistently has supported his research.

Together we would like to thank our colleagues in the History Department at Francis Marion University for their encouragement and support. We would be remiss if we did not acknowledge the staff at the Rogers Library at Francis Marion University who tracked down numerous obscure books for us.

Chronology

1376 William Latimer becomes the first person in England to be impeached
1386 Michael de la Pole is first person in England impeached for committing 'high crimes and misdemeanors'
1635 The governor of the Virginia colony, John Harvey, becomes the first official impeached in the British colonies
1669 Maryland becomes the first British colony to use term 'impeachment' in punishing an official
1774 Massachusetts Superior Court Judge Peter Oliver becomes the last official impeached in the colonial era
1787 Constitutional Convention held
1788 28 May, *Federalist Papers* published
21 June, U.S. Constitution ratified
1799 Case of Senator William Blount establishes the precedent that impeachment does not apply to members of Congress
1803 Judge George Pickering becomes the first federal officer impeached by the House of Representatives
1804 2 March, Judge Pickering becomes the first federal official convicted by the Senate, which removes him from office
12 March, Samuel Chase becomes the only Supreme Court justice impeached by the House of Representatives
1805 Senate acquits Justice Chase
1830 House of Representatives impeaches Judge James Peck
1831 Senate acquits Judge Peck
1862 19 May, House of Representatives impeaches Judge West Humphreys
26 June, Senate convicts Judge Humphreys and removes him from office
1868 24 February, Andrew Johnson becomes the first president impeached by the House of Representatives
16–26 May, Senate acquits President Johnson
1876 2 March, House of Representatives impeaches former Secretary of War William Belknap
1 August, Senate acquits Secretary Belknap
1904 House of Representatives impeaches Judge Charles Swayne

1905 Senate acquits Judge Swayne
1912 House of Representatives impeaches Judge Robert Archbald
1913 Senate convicts Judge Robert Archbald, removes him from office, and votes to disqualify him from holding a future federal post
1926 1 April, House of Representatives impeaches Judge George English
4 November, Judge English resigns; Senate drops further proceedings against him
1932 House of Representatives impeaches Judge Harold Louderback
1933 Senate acquits Judge Louderback
1935 Senate revises its impeachment proceedings by adopting Rule XI
1936 2 March, House of Representatives impeaches Judge Halsted Ritter
17 April, Senate convicts Judge Ritter and removes him from office
ca. late May, Judge Ritter appeals Senate conviction to the U.S. Court of Claims
7 December, In *Halsted Ritter v. United States*, U.S. Court of Claims denies Judge Ritter's appeal
1962 In *Baker v. Carr*, U.S. Supreme Court clarifies that political questions are not reviewable by the judiciary
1972 Break-in at the Democratic Party's national headquarters at the Watergate building in Washington, D.C. sets the stage for the Watergate scandal
1974 President Richard Nixon, all but assured of impeachment and conviction by Congress, resigns
1980 President Jimmy Carter signs into law the Judicial Councils Reform and Judicial Conduct and Disability Act
1986 22 July, Judge Harry Claiborne becomes first federal official impeached by the House of Representatives in half a century
9 October, Using Rule XI for the first time in its proceedings, Senate convicts Judge Claiborne
1988 After receiving a case brought to it via the Judicial Councils Reform and Judicial Conduct and Disability Act, House of Representatives impeaches Judge Alcee Hastings
1989 10 May, House of Representatives impeaches Judge Walter Nixon
20 October, Using Rule XI in part of its proceedings, Senate convicts Judge Hastings and removes him from office
3 November, Senate convicts Judge Nixon and removes him from office
1993 U.S. Supreme Court declares in *Nixon v. United States* that Senate impeachment proceedings are not subject to judicial review and that Rule XI was constitutional
1998 House of Representatives impeaches President Bill Clinton
1999 Senate acquits President Clinton
2010 11 March, House of Representatives impeaches Judge Thomas Porteous, Jr.
8 December, Senate convicts Judge Porteous and removes him office

2019 House of Representatives impeaches President Donald Trump
2020 Senate acquits President Trump
2021 13 January, House of Representatives impeaches President Trump for the second time
13 February, for the second time, Senate acquits President Trump
2024 13 February, House of Representatives impeaches Homeland Security Secretary Alejandro Mayorkas
17 April, Senate adjourns trial of Secretary Mayorkas

Who's Who

Agnew, Spiro T. (1918–1996) Agnew was the governor of his home state of Maryland from 1967 to 1969 and then became vice president under Richard Nixon. In 1973, the U.S. public learned that he was the target of a federal investigation for accepting bribes and evading tax payments. Facing the likelihood of impeachment, he resigned in October 1973.

Archbald, Robert W. (1848–1926) Born in Pennsylvania, Archbald served simultaneously on three courts: the U.S. District Court for the Middle District of Pennsylvania (1911–1913), the U.S. Court of Appeals for the Third Circuit (1911), and the United States Commerce Court (1911–1913). In July 1912, the House of Representatives impeached him on charges of corruption. The Senate found him guilty in January 1913 and afterward made him only one of three judges disqualified from holding another federal office.

Ashurst, Henry (1874–1962) An Arizona native, Ashurst represented his state in the Senate from 1912 to 1941. In 1934, he recommended, as had George Hoar thirty years earlier, that the Senate establish a small commission to hear evidence in an impeachment trial. That proposal eventually became Rule XI.

Bayard, James A. (1767–1816) A member of the Federalist Party who hailed from Delaware, Bayard represented his state in both the U.S. House (1797–1803) and the Senate (1804–1813). He was one of the House managers during the trial of Senator William Blount.

Belknap, William (1829–1890) After allegations of his corruption became public, Belknap resigned his position as secretary of war in 1876 but was then impeached by the House via a unanimous vote. The Senate subsequently acquitted him on the grounds that a former officeholder could not be convicted. He remained the only cabinet secretary to be impeached until Alejandro Mayorkas in 2024.

Biden, Joseph, Jr. (1942–) A senator who represented his home state of Delaware from 1973 to 2009, Biden also served as vice president of the United

States during Barack Obama's two terms in office. Elected to the White House in 2016, Biden became a repeated target of conservatives who accused him of impeachable crimes.

Blount, William (1749–1800) Blount was a North Carolinian who was one of the signers of the Constitution and later served as a U.S. senator from Tennessee. In the mid-1790s, he participated in a conspiracy that would have allowed the British to occupy large areas of the Old Southwest, particularly New Orleans. President John Adams learned of his scheme and notified Congress. The House impeached Blount, and the Senate expelled him. In a subsequent trial conducted from 1798 into 1799, the Senate refused to convict, citing lack of jurisdiction. Blount remains the only member of Congress to be impeached.

Burr, Aaron (1756–1836) The third vice president of the United States, Burr was born in the colony of New Jersey and served in the American Revolution. After the war, he worked for the New York State government as attorney general (1789–1791) and U.S. senator (1791–1797) before his election as vice president in 1800. In 1804, he killed former Treasury secretary Alexander Hamilton in a duel, and went on the run both for Hamilton's murder and a later plot to invade Mexico. Acquitted of treason in 1807, he spent some time in Europe, and returned to the States, where he practiced law. A series of strokes eventually took his life.

Bush, George H. W. (1924–2018) Born in Connecticut, Bush served in the U.S. Navy during World War II and settled in Texas a few years after that conflict ended. Between 1967 and 1989, he held a number of government positions, including member of the House of Representatives, ambassador to the United Nations, head of the Central Intelligence Agency, and vice president under Ronald Reagan. Elected president of the United States in 1988, he served one term in office. During his tenure in the White House, there was talk of impeaching him for involving the United States in the Persian Gulf War (1990–1991) without seeking a congressional declaration of war.

Bush, George W. (1946–). One of former president George H. W. Bush's sons, the younger Bush was born in Texas, where he sat as governor starting in 1995. He was elected president of the United States in 2000. His decision to have U.S. forces invade Iraq in 2003 and his response to the damage caused to the U.S. Gulf Coast by Hurricane Katrina in 2005 led to talk of impeaching him.

Chase, Samuel (1741–1811). A lifelong resident of Maryland, Chase signed the Declaration of Independence and then served as an associate justice on the Supreme Court starting in 1796. On partisan political grounds, the House of Representatives in 1804 impeached him for misbehavior. The Senate acquitted him the following year, and Chase continued to serve on the Court until his death. He remains the only member of the Supreme Court to be impeached.

Claiborne, Harry E. (1917–2004) An Arkansan by birth, Claiborne took up residency in Nevada after serving in World War II. There, he was a judge of the U.S. District Court for the District of Nevada from 1978 to 1980 and chief judge of the same from 1980 to 1986. A jury found him guilty of tax evasion in 1984, and two years later, he became the first sitting judge sent to prison. Because he refused to give up his post, the House of Representatives unanimously impeached him—making him the first of only three federal officers impeached without a dissenting vote. The Senate convicted him in October 1986 and removed him from his post.

Clayton, Henry, Jr. (1857–1929). Born in Alabama, Clayton served as one of his state's representatives in the House of Representatives from 1897 to 1914. From 1914 until his death, he sat simultaneously on the U.S. District Courts for the Middle District and Northern District of Alabama.

Clinton, William (Bill) (1946–) A native Arkansan, Clinton served as his state's attorney general (1977–1979) and governor (1979–1981 and 1983–1992). In 1992, he was elected president of the United States. Six years later, he became only the second president impeached by the House of Representatives, which charged him with perjury and obstruction of justice. The Senate acquitted him in 1999.

De La Pole, Michael (c. 1330–1389) The first Earl of Suffolk and England's Lord Chancellor, de la Pole in 1386 became the first person in his country impeached for having committed 'high crimes and misdemeanors'. Found guilty, he was removed from office.

Delahay, Mark (circa 1817–1879). Born in Maryland, Delahay moved to Kansas in the 1850s, where he served as a judge for the District Court for that state. In 1873, the House of Representatives impeached him for repeated intoxication while sitting on the bench. He resigned before the Senate began its trial. He is the only person impeached without any articles drawn up against them.

Douglas, William O. (1898–1980) Born in Minnesota, Douglas was a member of the Securities and Exchange Commission (SEC) from 1936 to 1937, and then chaired the SEC from 1937 to 1939. In 1939, he became an associate justice on the U.S. Supreme Court. Republican Representative Gerald Ford made an abortive attempt to impeach Douglas, accusing him of misbehavior. Douglas continued to serve on the Court until his resignation in 1975.

English, George W. (1866–1941) An Illinois native, English sat on the U.S. District Court for Illinois' Eastern District starting in 1918. In 1926, the House of Representatives impeached him for corruption and denying individuals the right to legal counsel. Rather than face a Senate trial, English resigned that same year.

Fortas, Abe (1910–1982) A native of Tennessee, Fortas served twice as undersecretary of the Department of the Interior in the 1940s. In 1965, he joined the Supreme Court as an associate justice. Four years later, he became embroiled in an ethics scandal that prompted Republican Senator Robert Griffin to call for his impeachment in 1969. Under pressure from Chief Justice Earl Warren, Fortas resigned his post in 1969.

Hamilton, Alexander (1755?–1804) Born in the Caribbean, Hamilton was a brilliant financier who by age 14 worked as a chief clerk for a trading company. Ambitious to a fault, he became a leading advocate of independence from Great Britain and fought in the American Revolution. He participated in the drafting of the Constitution and wrote many of the essays in the *Federalist Papers* that urged ratification of the new document. He later served as President George Washington's secretary of the Treasury, became a leader in the new Federalist Party, and made an unsuccessful bid to succeed Washington as president. In 1804, he died in a gun duel with then-Vice President Aaron Burr.

Hastings, Alcee L. (1936–2021) Born in Florida, Hastings was a judge on the 17th Judicial Circuit Court of Florida from 1977 to 1979, and on the U.S. District Court for Florida's Southern District from 1979 to 1989. In 1988, the House of Representatives impeached him on charges that included involvement in a conspiracy and perjury; a Senate conviction followed the next year. Hastings appealed his conviction on the grounds that the Senate's use of Rule XI during his trial was unconstitutional. That appeal was rejected following the Supreme Court's 1993 decision *Nixon v. United States* that upheld Rule XI.

Hoar, George (1826–1904). A native of Massachusetts, Hoar represented his state in the House of Representatives from 1869 to 1877 and the Senate from 1877 until his death in September 1904. Shortly before his passing, Hoar suggested a small Senate committee rather than the full Senate hear evidence in impeachment cases. That suggestion later became Rule XI.

Humphreys, West (1806–1882). A lifelong resident of Tennessee, Humphreys served as his state's attorney general from 1839 to 1851. Two years later, he began serving on Tennessee's three U.S. district courts. In 1862, the House of Representatives impeached Humphreys for his support for the Confederacy during the Civil War. The Senate later that year convicted him and barred him from holding another public office.

Jackson, Andrew (1767–1845). Born somewhere near the North Carolina–South Carolina border, Jackson eventually settled in Tennessee, which he represented in the House of Representatives (1796–1797) and Senate (1797–1798 and 1823–1825). In between, he won fame for his military leadership during the War of 1812. He ran for and won the presidency in 1828 as the nominee of the new Democratic Party. During his second term in office, the opposition Whig Party sought to impeach him for removing federal deposits from the Bank of the United States but lacked the votes. Instead, the Senate censured him in 1834.

Johnson, Andrew (1808–1875) Born in North Carolina, Johnson moved to Tennessee, representing that state in the House of Representatives (1843–1853) and Senate (1857–1862 and 1875); in between he was Tennessee's governor. He was elected as Abraham Lincoln's vice president in 1865 and entered the Oval Office later that year following Lincoln's assassination. In 1868, the House of Representatives impeached him for violating the Tenure of Office Act. He survived a Senate conviction by one vote.

Latimer, William (1330–1381) Generally considered the first person impeached in England, Latimer, also known as the Fourth Baron Latimer, had served his nation as a soldier, diplomat, and chamberlain to King Edward III. Parliament impeached and convicted him in 1376, and removed him from office. Edward afterward pardoned him.

Louderback, Harold (1881–1941) Born in California, Louderback sat on the U.S. District Court for the Northern District of his home state from 1928 to 1941. In 1933, the House of Representatives impeached him for misconduct, including corruption, but the Senate found him not guilty. He continued to serve as a judge until his death.

Mason, George (1725–1792) One of the country's Founding Fathers, Mason was born in Virginia, sat in his colony's legislature from 1758 to 1761, and supported independence from Great Britain. At the constitutional convention held in Philadelphia, he had suggested including in the Constitution a reference to 'maladministration' as a justification for impeaching the president. The majority of delegates rejected that suggestion, finding it too vague. In turn, Mason proposed, and the delegates accepted, including the language 'other high crimes and misdemeanors'.

Mayorkas, Alejandro (1959–) Only the second cabinet member to be impeached—the first being William Belknap—Mayorkas is the son of a family that fled Cuba for the United States. He eventually settled in California, where he worked as a private and federal attorney. He was the director of the U.S. Citizenship and Immigration Services from 2009 to 2013, and, starting in 2021, the head of the Department of Homeland Security. In 2024, the House of Representatives impeached Mayorkas for failing to stem the flow of undocumented immigrants across the U.S.–Mexican border. The Senate subsequently acquitted him.

Mueller, Robert (1944–) A native New Yorker, Mueller served in the U.S. Marine corps, followed by work as both a private and federal lawyer from the mid-1970s until 2001. From 2001 to 2013, he was the director of the

Federal Bureau of Investigation. In 2017, he served as a special counsel in the Department of Justice, during which he investigated President Donald Trump for allegedly conspiring with the Russian government to influence the outcome of the 2016 election.

Nixon, Richard (1913–1994) Nixon served as a representative (1947–1950) and senator (1950–1953) of his home state of California before becoming vice president of the United States under Dwight Eisenhower. He lost a bid for the presidency in 1960 but won the White House in 1968 and reelection in 1972. His involvement in the Watergate scandal, including clear-cut evidence that he had obstructed justice, made his impeachment and conviction all but certain. Having the choice of being removed from office or resigning, Nixon chose the latter course in August 1974.

Nixon, Walter L. (1928–) A Mississippian by birth, Nixon served as a judge for the District Court for the Southern District of his home state from 1968 to 1982 and chief judge of the same from 1982 to 1989. In 1986, a jury found him guilty of perjury, but he refused to resign. The House of Representatives subsequently impeached him without a dissenting vote—the second time the House had done that. The Senate convicted him in November 1989 and removed him from office. Nixon appealed his conviction to the U.S. Supreme Court, which rejected it in January 1993.

Obama, Barack (1961–) The first African American president, Obama was born in Hawaii and moved several times, including to Illinois in 1991. He represented Illinois in the Senate starting in 2005. Three years later, he became president of the United States. During his two terms in the White House, he faced repeated calls for his impeachment from conservatives, who leveled numerous charges against him.

Peck, James (1790–1836) Originally from North Carolina, Peck moved to Missouri, where he served as a judge for the District Court of Missouri starting in 1822. The House of Representatives impeached him in 1830 on the grounds that he abused his power. Exonerated by the Senate, he continued to serve on the district court until his death.

Pickering, John (1737–1805) A lifelong resident of New Hampshire, Pickering served as the judge for the district court of his state. His bouts of insanity and alcoholism led the House of Representatives and Senate to impeach and convict him in 1803 and 1804, respectively.

Porteous, G. Thomas, Jr. (1946–2021) Born in Louisiana, Porteous served as a judge for the U.S. District Court for the Eastern District of his home state from 1994 to 2010. The House of Representatives began to investigate him in 2008 on charges of perjury and obstruction of justice. Two years later, members of the House voted unanimously to impeach him, making him the third and most recent federal official impeached without a dissenting vote. The Senate convicted him later that year and disqualified him from holding another federal office.

Reagan, Ronald. (1911–2004) Originally from Illinois, Reagan moved to California in the 1930s, where he became an actor and, from 1967 to 1975, governor of that state. He unsuccessfully ran for president in 1976 but won the White House in 1980. During his second term in the Oval Office, there was talk of impeaching him because of his administration's involvement in the Iran-Contra scandal.

Rehnquist, William (1924–2005) Born in Milwaukee, Rehnquist had worked in the office of the U.S. Attorney General from 1969 to 1971. In 1972, he became an associate justice on the Supreme Court, followed by chief justice in 1986. The author of a history of the Supreme Court, Rehnquist wrote the opinion in the 1993 case *Nixon v. United States* that upheld the Senate's use of Rule XI in impeachment proceedings.

Ritter, Halsted R. (1868–1951) Born in Indiana, Ritter moved to Florida in 1925, where, four years later, he became a judge on the U.S. District Court for the Southern District of that state. In 1936, the House of Representatives impeached him for corruption, tax evasion, and harming his court's reputation. The Senate found him guilty later that year and removed him from office. Ritter appealed his case to the U.S. Court of Claims, which rejected his claim that same year. In 1937, he tried but failed to have the U.S. Supreme Court hear his appeal.

Swayne, Charles (1842–1907) Born in Delaware, Swayne moved to Florida in the mid-1880s, where he became a judge on the U.S. District Court for the Northern District of Florida. In 1904, the House of Representatives impeached him for misbehavior, including corruption. The Senate acquitted him the following year. Swayne continued to serve on the district court until his death.

Taylor, Zachary (1784–1850) A Virginian by birth, Taylor became well-known for his military service during the Mexican War. Elected president of the United States in 1848, he came under suspicion for a series of shady deals from which members of his cabinet profited. His death settled the issue.

Trump, Donald (1946–) Trump was the first president of the United States who had no governmental or military experience, the second to serve two non-consecutive terms, and the only chief executive impeached twice. Born in New York State, he won fame as a businessman, author, and television celebrity. In 2019, the House impeached him for abusing his power and obstructing Congress; two years later, it impeached him for trying to overturn the outcome of the 2020 presidential election. Both times, the Senate exonerated him.

Turner, George (c. 1750–1843). Born in England, Turner migrated to Britain's American colonies and fought in the American Revolution. He later became a judge in the Northwest Territory. Residents there sought to impeach him for his toughness, but the House of Representatives saw no reason to proceed with what otherwise would have been the first impeachment in U.S. history.

Tyler, John (1790–1862) A lifelong resident of Virginia, Tyler served his state as a U.S. representative (1816–1821), governor (1825–1827), and U.S. senator (1827–1836). Elected in 1840 as William Henry Harrison's vice president, he succeeded to the presidency upon Harrison's death in 1841. His numerous vetoes of measures supported by his Whig Party led to talk among Whigs of impeaching him. However, the opposition Democratic Party refused to assist in that effort.

Warren, Earl (1891–1974) A native Californian, Warren had served as attorney general and governor of his state before becoming chief justice of the Supreme Court in 1953. In 1961, the John Birch Society sought but failed to have Warren impeached on the grounds that his opposition to racial segregation was part of a broader communist conspiracy to destroy the United States.

Welch, Robert W., Jr. (1899–1985) A U.S. businessperson, Welch was a devout anticommunist who founded the far-right-wing John Birch Society in 1958, and who tried to have Supreme Court Justice Earl Warren impeached by Congress. Welch's conspiracy-laden theories warning of communist infiltration of the U.S. government and armed forces drew him a rebuke from both liberals and other political conservatives.

Part I

Analysis and Assessment

Preface

In February 2025, two Republicans in the U.S. House of Representatives proposed articles of **impeachment** against judges who had issued decisions blocking efforts by President **Donald Trump** to reduce federal spending and the size of government. One of their targets, District Court Judge Paul Engelmayer, had prohibited the administration's newly created Department of Government Efficiency from accessing Treasury Department systems that oversaw trillions of dollars in expenditures. The other target, District Court Judge John J. McConnell, Jr., had declared unconstitutional a spending freeze that would have affected programs such as Head Start and grants offered by the Labor Department. Representative Eli Crane of Arizona justified removing Engelmayer from office on the grounds that he had engaged in 'judicial overreach' (Covarrubias, 2025). Meanwhile, said Crane's Georgia colleague, Andrew Clyde, McConnell had proven himself 'a partisan activist weaponizing our judicial system to stop President Trump's funding freeze on woke and wasteful government spending' (Solender, 2025).

Two months later, Shri Thanedar, a Democratic representative from Michigan, submitted a resolution to impeach Trump. Thanedar charged the president with a variety of crimes, including obstruction of justice and abuse of power. Finding little support, including within his own party, he ended his impeachment bid.

These efforts to impeach the individuals in question were the latest examples of a process the Founding Fathers had intended to be used rarely, and only for those cases where a federal official endangered the welfare of the United States either through lawbreaking or malicious, gross, or corrupt misconduct. In developing the impeachment process, they turned in part to Great Britain, which since the fourteenth century had given Parliament the power to try private individuals or public officials for 'high crimes and misdemeanors' that jeopardized the well-being of the government or society. Those who settled in London's North American colonies adopted elements of the British system. But there were two key differences. First, in the colonies, impeachment applied only to public officeholders, namely, colonial officials. Second, in Great Britain impeachment could be political or criminal in nature, and involve punishments ranging from a fine to removal from office,

DOI: 10.4324/9781003565680-2

jail time, or even execution. In the colonies, though, those convicted only lost their government job. Put another way, impeachment practiced in the colonies was political in nature as opposed to criminal.

Following independence, most of the new states included in their constitutions impeachment procedures that could oust an officeholder if found guilty. Hence, when the Founders wrote the Constitution, they brought with them a deep understanding of what impeachment was, that the process of impeaching an individual was political rather than criminal in character, and that the ultimate penalty was deprival of one's federal post. After intense debate, they ruled out having the Supreme Court oversee impeachments, choosing instead to assign that power to the legislative branch. They placed the start of the process in the hands of the House of Representatives, which could impeach a federal officeholder through a simple majority vote. If that happened, then the case fell into the arms of the Senate, where two-thirds of its members needed to vote in the affirmative to convict and remove the accused from office. It was the provision for a supermajority in the Upper House that the Founding Fathers believed offered the best protection against impeachment's use for partisan ends. Instead, senators from different political viewpoints would have to find common ground for conviction to succeed.

Since the founding of the republic, the impeachment process has undergone changes. Early on, members of Congress reached the conclusion that impeachment did not apply to themselves, as they had the option of expelling members if necessary. Hence, only those who sit in the executive and judicial branches are impeachable. Lawmakers had to grapple with the question as to whether a person who resigned from office could still face impeachment. With rare exception, those on Capitol Hill have exhibited a reluctance to pursue former officeholders on the grounds that, because they no longer sit in government, they are private individuals for whom impeachment is not applicable. The House of Representatives used to impeach a person even before submitting articles, but now does the opposite. Starting in the first half of the twentieth century the Senate passed Rule XI, by which it relies on a small committee rather than the entire body to hear evidence regarding a government official's malfeasance. The Supreme Court has weighed in as well, declaring that the judiciary has no right under the Constitution to review convictions issued by the Senate of individuals impeached by the House. Moreover, the justices determined that while in office a president cannot face criminal proceedings that in and of themselves might justify their removal. Consequently, impeachment provides the only means of dismissing the nation's highest officer.

In *Impeachment in U.S. History*, we provide the reader with an understanding of the British and colonial underpinnings of the impeachment process and the changes that have taken place. Additionally, we provide numerous instances of those who have been targeted for removal as well as how they reacted to the effort to oust them from office. Importantly, we do not limit ourselves to just those people whose cases reached the Senate. Instead, we include dozens proposed by members of Congress (and even sometimes non-members) that did not get out of committee or did not receive consideration by the full House. In so doing, we offer the reader a number of observations. The first is that trying to remove a person from office is exceptionally difficult. Over the country's 250-year history, 46 people have served as president, over 110 as Supreme Court justices, and literally thousands of others as ranking members of the executive branch or lower-court judges. Yet only 20 people have had their case reach the Senate, and, of them, only eight have been found guilty.

Second, the bar for impeaching a president is higher than that for a judge or justice. While one expects any federal official to act morally, Article I, Section 3 of the Constitution specifically refers to jurists needing to maintain 'good Behavior' if they wished to retain their posts. Hence, whereas a president may engage in an immoral act, such as having an extramarital affair or punching someone in the face, it would be less likely to lead to that individual's conviction as would be the case for a jurist.

Finally, there is the issue of partisanship. In 1797, just nine years after the Constitution's ratification, Senator **William Blount** became the first person impeached by the House. Within six years, two more individuals, Judge **John Pickering** and Supreme Court Justice **Samuel Chase**, also were impeached. Partisan politics was a key driving force in all three cases. And while only Pickering ultimately received a Senate conviction, so many impeachments in such little time suggested that impeachment was likely to receive regular use by one party to force political opponents from office. In one respect, that observation proved incorrect. Between Chase's impeachment and the year 1868, when **Andrew Johnson** became the first president impeached, there were numerous calls to boot individuals from their government positions. Yet prior to Johnson, the Senate received only two other impeachment cases, those of judges **James Peck** and **West Humphreys**. In both instances, senators exhibited non- or bipartisan sentiment, acquitting Peck and convicting Humphreys. Johnson's impeachment and near-conviction, though, longed for by Radical Republicans, suggested a return to partisan politics.

In fact, though, partisanship declined following Johnson's acquittal by the Senate in 1868. For almost the next century, talk of impeaching one person or another came up numerous times. Yet of them, only seven were impeached by the House: Secretary of War **William Belknap**, and judges **Mark Delahay**, **Charles Swayne**, **Robert Archbald**, **George English**, **Harold Louderback**, and **Halsted Ritter**. Delahay and English resigned before their cases could receive a Senate hearing. The Upper House found Archbald and Ritter guilty, and it acquitted the others. And while partisan politics sometimes played a part in these impeachments, the outcomes time and again reflected bipartisan or nonpartisan support for guilt or innocence.

Partisanship, however, began to reappear starting in the 1960s. In fact, by the second decade of the 2000s, calls for the impeachment of this person or that for purely partisan reasons were, in the words of one professor, 'as common as a Taylor Swift concert' (Most, 2023). In 2023 alone, members of the House called for ousting President **Joe Biden**, Vice President Kamala Harris, Supreme Court Justice Clarence Thomas, and Homeland Security Secretary **Alejandro Mayorkas**. That Biden was on that list pointed to the fact that the president was no longer immune from impeachment. Granted, the Founding Fathers never intended for the legislature to exempt the Oval Office's occupant from possible removal, and, prior to President Johnson's impeachment, there had been talk of removing from office **Andrew Jackson** and **John Tyler**. But until 1998, Andrew Johnson was the only chief executive impeached by the House. Since then, two presidents, **Bill Clinton** and Donald Trump, have had their cases reach the Senate—in the case of Trump, twice. And without fail, every chief executive starting with **Ronald Reagan** has been the target of impeachment resolutions. Other executive branch officers also have been foci of demands for their ouster, whether they be Ambassador to the United Nations Andrew Young in 1977, Vice President Dick Cheney in 2007, or, in 2015, Environmental Protection Agency head Regina McCarthy and Internal Revenue Service Commissioner John Koskinen.

With judges, the situation is more nuanced. There are instances of interparty agreement favoring their removal. Such was true with Harry Claiborne, who in 1986 became the first judge impeached by the House in 50 years. Bipartisanship held as well when the Senate convicted **Alcee Hastings** and **Walter Nixon** in 1989, and **G. Thomas Porteous** in 2014. Yet there are many instances, including those of Supreme Court justices **Earl Warren**, **Abe Fortas**, and **William Douglas** in the 1960s–1970s, and the above-mentioned cases of judges Engelmayer and McConnell, where calls for their dismissal had obvious partisan undertones.

In addition to looking at the development of the impeachment process, the standards held for presidents and jurists, and the role partisanship plays in efforts to remove officeholders, our book has a final purpose. Honing the process of impeachment was not without disagreements, and even today scholars do not see eye-to-eye on all matters related to it. Accordingly, we point out in the text where the experts are divided, and we provide the reader with a sizeable number of primary documents that take opposing viewpoints on the same issue. Consequently, we give those who read our book and those who use it in their classes an opportunity to think more deeply about these matters, and to encourage discussion and debate. Judges tend to be held to a higher bar than presidents when it comes to impeachment, but is that fair? Does it make sense that a sitting president is largely immune from criminal proceedings that might warrant their removal from office? Is Rule XI just, or even constitutional? Should the judiciary have the right to review the cases of individuals convicted by the Senate? Ought a federal officer who has resigned their position still be subject to impeachment? Has bipartisanship today disappeared from the impeachment process? Has the political polarization taking place currently made impeachment all but a meaningless endeavor? These are just a few of the questions we hope that professionals and laypersons alike will think about as they peruse the pages that follow.

1 English Precedents and the Constitution

Writing on 10 October 1787, less than a month after the Constitutional Convention had drafted the Constitution that year, an unknown individual using the pseudonym 'The Federal Farmer' discussed the new document. He referenced impeachment, but hinted that the American people would have nothing to worry about that doctrine being abused. 'The right of impeachment in the house, can be of but little importance; the house cannot expect often to convict the offender; and, therefore, probably, will but seldom or never exercise the right' (Ford, 1888: 300). To put it bluntly, 'The Federal Farmer' erred. Impeachment has been deployed dozens of times and is constantly discussed in contemporary America.

It is sometimes said that good writers borrow and great writers steal. The people of the United States did not invent the doctrine of impeachment. A leading authority on impeachment, Jonathan Turley, perhaps said it best when he wrote, 'American impeachments stand on English feet'. In fact, by the time the first colonists arrived in North America, impeachment had become an integral part of the political lexicon in England and had a long history tracing back to the medieval period. While there is some dispute about the date (Turley, 1999: 9), it appears that the first impeachment took place in England in 1376, exactly 400 years before the establishment of the United States. That event had a profound and lasting impact on American history.

William Latimer and Impeachments in England

What occurred in 1376 related directly to the Hundred Years' War that began in the 1330s and pitted England against France. Although England did well initially, it suffered a number of defeats in the field starting in 1373 that forced it to agree to a truce that took a toll on the reputation of an aging King Edward III. Worse, his son was dying, meaning that the throne would fall into the lap of his grandson, who was still a child. Pessimism thus clouded the minds of the members of Parliament when they met in 1376. Though created by the crown in the thirteenth century, Parliament by this time had, in the words of one scholar, 'developed to serve as a mouthpiece for the nation's 'political community' (Monaghan, 2024: 19). Asked to agree

DOI: 10.4324/9781003565680-3

to taxes to cover the war's costs, members of the English legislature realized that they lacked the strength to overthrow the king. But they could go after Edward's aides, whose financial corruption they tied to England's setbacks on the battlefield.

Among those targeted was **William Latimer**, Fourth Baron Latimer, who served as Edwards's chamberlain and oversaw some of England's ports. Members of Parliament's lower house, the House of Commons, charged him with accepting bribes from the French in return for ceding to France two French towns. Several others, including two alderman, Richard Lyons and John Peeche, joined Latimer as defendants, accused too of using their positions for personal economic gain. Latimer, the first to receive what later became known as impeachment, insisted that the Commons had no right to prosecute him. Sir Peter de la Mere, who in essence became the first Speaker of the Commons, made sure that, in the name of fairness, Latimer received a hearing in Parliament's upper house, the House of Lords, which conducted a trial, found him guilty, and removed him from office. Lyons and Peeche received the same punishments. Although Edward pardoned all three, an important precedent had been set: Corrupt officials, even if they enjoyed the support of the monarch, could be removed from office. In essence, no one remained above the law.

Latimer's impeachment triggered others. In 1386, Parliament impeached **Michael de la Pole,** Lord Suffolk and England's Lord Chancellor. It was during his case that the term 'high crimes and misdemeanors' was applied for the first time. The sitting monarch, Richard II, declared this impeachment void, but the next year, a faction in Parliament, styled the Lords Appellant, impeached five advisers to the king, including de la Pole. The so-called 'Merciless Parliament', as it became known, convicted the five men and sentenced four of them to death without a trial. Only two, Nicholas Brembre and Robert Tresilian, lost their heads, while the others, including de la Pole, fled into exile. In 1388, the House of Commons impeached six judges, including Robert Belknap, for responding to 'certain questions submitted to them, as judges, wrongfully' (Feerick, 1970: 6). The House of Lords thereafter convicted them, removed them from office, and had them sent to Ireland.

A weakening of Parliament's influence saw impeachment largely disappear starting in the mid-1400s. But a heightening of tensions between Parliament and the crown starting in 1620, which led to civil war in England in 1642, witnessed impeachment return with a vengeance and continue well after the war ended in 1651. The House of Commons impeached more than 100 people during just the years 1620 and 1649. One of them was the jurist Sir Robert Berkeley, whom the Commons in 1641 accused of treason. Specifically, he had tried 'to subvert the laws of the kingdom by traitorous words, opinions, judgments, and practices' (Feerick, 1970: 7). The House of Lords convicted him and removed him from office. In 1667, the Commons charged Chief Justice of the King's Bench John Keeling for imposing fines on juries that made decisions he did not favor. However, after listening to his defense, Parliament decided to drop the matter.

These cases in England elicit three important observations. The first is that they established the foundation for a two-step process by which the House of Commons leveled against someone what could be broadly worded charges of malfeasance that threatened the welfare of the nation. Apparently, it sometimes only used the threat of impeachment to try to force what it regarded as potential troublemakers into line. If deemed necessary, the Commons could turn to the House of Lords and ask it to try that individual. Second, before they offered to hear a case, the House of Lords demanded detailed evidence proving the accused had engaged in 'serious and willful wrongdoing, negligence, or betrayal of public trust'. Consequently, of the 57 impeachment cases that took place between 1626 and 1715, only five made it to the Lords (Kyvig, 2008: 12; Turley, 1999: 13). Finally, while the accusations themselves had political overtones, the determination of guilt was judicial in nature and included penalties that ranged from fines to removal from office and even execution.

Impeachment in the Colonies

The process of impeachment practiced in Great Britain's American colonies reflected similarities to that of the homeland when it came to who drew up the charges and who convicted. However, the penalties the colonists imposed were more limited in nature. In 1635, members of the Virginia legislature, known as the House of Burgesses, charged the colony's governor, John Harvey, with having negotiated a bad treaty with Native Americans. Moreover, he allegedly had plotted with the people in Maryland against the interests of the people of his colony. Virginians impeached Harvey and sent him back to England, where they expected him to receive a punishment. Instead, King Charles I promptly sent Harvey back to Virginia, where he held his post until 1639. Though Harvey's case is considered the first impeachment in the British colonies, it took years before what happened to him was referred to as such (Bowman, 2024: 22–49).

The differences between the impeachment of de la Pole and his co-conspirators on the one hand and Harvey on the other are stark. In England, impeachment was treated as a criminal offense that necessitated a harsh punishment, including death. Harvey's opponents in the House of Burgesses, however, regarded his crimes as political in nature. In England, impeachment could lead to legal consequences such as execution or forfeiture of land and titles. In America, the only outcome of impeachment would be the inability to hold office again. A subsequent court can prosecute someone impeached and convicted in America, but even the Congress established under the Constitution cannot impose a penalty. Harvey's actions, whether or not they constituted an impeachment, revealed that he had been forced from his office not due to corruption but for political differences with members of the House of Burgesses.

The colony of Maryland became the first to employ the term 'impeachment', though no statute for it existed in the colony. In 1669, Robert Morris, an influential businessman, circulated a petition in the Maryland Assembly calling for the impeachment of one of its members, John Morecroft, who convinced his accusers that the case should be resolved in a legal court and not in a deliberative body. The legislature agreed, and the proceedings against Morecroft ended. Seven years later, Maryland impeached Thomas Truman, a politician and military officer who botched an expedition against the Susquehannock Indians. To cover his failures, Truman ordered the execution of five chiefs. Afterwards, the Maryland legislature impeached and convicted him. Instead of jail time, he was only fined and released. In 1681, Marylanders went after Jacob Young, a Native American interpreter who some colonists believed cared more about the well-being of the Susquehannocks than his fellow colonists. Though it appeared Young might face the charge of treason, he instead was impeached and convicted. Some of the colonists wanted to use a bill of attainder against him, but they banished him instead.

Whereas Maryland had no explicit clause in its charter for impeachment, the same cannot be said of its neighbor to the north, Pennsylvania. Established as a proprietary colony in 1682 under the auspices of William Penn, Pennsylvania's charter made an explicit reference to impeachment. The General Assembly under Article 19 had the power to 'Impeach Criminals,' while Article 20 noted that impeachments would take place before a 'provincial council' (Bowman, 2024: 46). Pennsylvanians first used this power just three years after their colony's establishment when they impeached Chief Justice Nicholas Moore. The ten articles of impeachment charged him mainly with procedural errors. Before a trial could occur, Penn, who had a close relationship with Moore, gave him another office. The matter subsequently died.

In 1707, the Pennsylvania legislature went after another close friend of Penn, James Logan. After serving in a variety of positions, including as Penn's secretary, Logan secured a seat on the Provincial Council, which was the upper house of the colony's two-house legislature (the other being the General Assembly). Logan's loyalty to the colony's founder and his determination to advance Penn's interests aroused the hostility of other members of the council. In response, they drafted thirteen articles of impeachment against him. It is important to note that Logan was neither a part of the executive branch nor a judge, but rather a legislator. In the end, Logan escaped conviction because of a technicality. In 1702 a new Charter of Privileges had been established. This charter specifically allowed for the Assembly to impeach officials but never specified where a trial would take place.

Pennsylvanians craved further impeachments, and got their wish in the late 1750s when William Moore ran afoul of them. A judge in Chester County, he won the ire of some of his fellow colonists for questionable decisions. Further upsetting them was the Seven Years' War—also known as the French and Indian War—that lasted from 1756 to 1763, and that pitted Great Britain against France and France's Native American allies in North America. The conflict had divided the colony, with many Quakers refusing to support any military efforts and other Pennsylvanians opposing some of the fiscal measures to pay for the war. Moore, however, was an unabashed defender of Great Britain's efforts to defeat the French. Pennsylvania officials conspired with British officials to remove Moore, but the British balked. Moore found out about these maneuvers, erupted in anger, and defended himself in a pamphlet. In this battle of wills, the legislature did not back down, opting instead to prosecute the judge for libel. Upon his conviction, Moore secured his release from jail because he could only be detained while the legislature sat. With legislators out of session, Moore resumed his judicial duties.

When Pennsylvania's lawmakers returned to work, they tried to pressure Lieutenant Governor William Denny into trying Moore, even though no official articles of impeachment had been drawn up. Denny responded by saying he had no power to do so. The legislators favoring Moore's removal pointed out that under Pennsylvania's colonial charter, the Assembly could impeach. They added that if someone was impeached in England, a trial took place in the House of Lords. Since there was no equivalent to the House of Lords in Pennsylvania, they suggested that the governor or Denny himself assume that role. Denny again balked, insisting he had no legal authority to conduct a trial. The matter ended in 1759 when officials in London ordered the Assembly to cease and desist.

William Moore's offenses probably were not worthy of impeachment. Instead, it appears he had alienated too many powerful people in Pennsylvania. The judge perhaps survived because by this time impeachment had fallen into disuse back in England. Although Parliament had the power to remove judges using impeachment, the monarch could do the same by revoking what was known as the jurist's 'patent'—that is, a document that set the judge's term in office. Hence, if England's ruler for some reason developed a distaste for the person sitting on the bench, booting him from office necessitated only revoking his patent. In 1701, Parliament decided to restrict that power by passing a bill allowing jurists to serve 'during good behavior'. From that point on, the English legislature had to ask the king to remove the offending judge, which it did not do prior to the colonists' Constitutional Convention in 1787. As historian Gordon S. Wood wrote, 'Since impeachment in England had not been used since the early years of the eighteenth century, many of the colonists had retained only a vague sense that their legislatures possessed the power' (1969: 141).

The colonies of Maryland and Pennsylvania did not have a monopoly over impeachment. The people of Massachusetts used it as well, impeaching in 1706 Samuel Vetch and three of his associates for trading with the enemy. Vetch was basically a soldier of fortune who secured a diplomatic post from the Massachusetts governor to negotiate with French officials in present-day Quebec, Canada. He probably abused his position to line his own pockets.

When he returned to Massachusetts, bureaucrats there wanted to prosecute Vetch and his friends for treason, but backed off and settled on impeachment for 'high misdemeanors'. After conviction in the upper chamber, known as the Council, Vetch appealed to the government back in London, which had qualms about the whole sordid affair, and ordered Vetch and his friends released. Vetch may have escaped justice in this instance but, ironically, he died in a debtors' prison in 1732.

The last colonial impeachment occurred one year before the opening shots of the American Revolution were fired at Lexington and Concord. The setting was once again Massachusetts, and the issue that triggered impeachment was that of judicial independence. Colonial legislatures attempted to make judges sensitive to colonial matters by voting them a salary each year. If a jurist seemed willing to do only the bidding of the crown, then the legislature could withhold his salary. In 1773, the British government sponsored a bill that would pay colonial judges from the coffers in London. The people of Massachusetts believed that those who sat on the bench should be paid from funds raised in the colony and not in London. The legislature subsequently asked five Superior Court judges if they would accept the lower salary that it appropriated or the higher one sent from London. Four of the five judges responded in the affirmative. Only Peter Oliver, the chief justice, said he would take London's offer. He explained that he needed the higher salary to offset economic hardships he had suffered as a result of what the colony had paid him. Just like in Pennsylvania, the members of the Assembly asked the governor, Thomas Hutchinson, to intervene and remove Oliver. And, just like in Pennsylvania, Hutchinson refused. Enraged, the legislature impeached him for 'high crimes and misdemeanors'. They equated the chief justice's acceptance of the higher salary as tantamount to a bribe. After the lower chamber impeached Oliver, the matter ended because Hutchinson dissolved the legislature. Oliver afterward left the country when the British evacuated Boston in March 1776. One of the leading authorities on impeachment, Frank Bowman, wrote of this matter: 'Oliver's impeachment was in the purest sense political' (2024: 54).

These impeachments of William Moore in Pennsylvania and Peter Oliver in Massachusetts must have been in the minds of some of the Founding Fathers when they met in Philadelphia in 1787 to draft the new constitution. Indeed, nearly twenty men who participated in the Massachusetts ratifying convention of 1788 took part in the Oliver impeachment. In another irony, the president of that ratifying convention was William Cushing, who had been one of the four judges who accepted the lower salary offered by Massachusetts's legislators.

Post-Independence

After the colonies proclaimed their independence in July 1776, many of them quickly drafted new state constitutions. These constitutions tended to be hastily written and suffered from an excess of democracy. Several states rewrote their constitutions multiple times during and immediately after the Revolution. Nine of these early state constitutions (Delaware, Massachusetts, New Hampshire, New Jersey, New York, North Carolina, Pennsylvania, South Carolina, and Virginia) had some method to impeach either officeholders, judges, or both. Even Vermont, which had proclaimed its independence from New York in January of 1777, included a method of impeachment in its constitution written later that year. From 1776 until 1787, it appears the people frequently used impeachment to get rid of an officeholder who remained loyal to the crown. When not impeaching Tories or Loyalists—interchangeable terms that referred to those who had wanted to remain a part of the British Empire—the states used impeachment to root out corrupt officials. But impeachment continued to have political overtones. In 1781, the state of Virginia broached removing Governor Thomas Jefferson after he evacuated Charlottesville during a British invasion and failed to notify the members of the legislature who had come to the city to meet there. Jefferson survived, but his actions cast a dark shadow that haunted him for the rest of his political career.

These state constitutions differed over who could be impeached, for what and when, and, if impeached, where the trial would take place. The states of Virginia and Delaware declared that the chief executive (governor in Virginia, president in Delaware) could only be impeached once out of office. Virginia also said that an official would be impeached in the House of Delegates, but the trial would take place before the General Court. The states of Pennsylvania and Vermont allowed for the impeachment of 'state criminals'. In Maryland, New York, and South Carolina, the House of Delegates (Maryland), the Assembly (New York), or the House of Representatives (South Carolina) could impeach state officials, but only if two-thirds of the members supported it. New York and South Carolina created special courts comprised of judges and senators to conduct the trial. In all three states, a two-thirds majority was required to remove an official from office (Bowman, 2024: 58–65).

The Massachusetts State Constitution of 1780 is usually regarded as the high-water mark in the era of state constitution making [*Doc 1*]. Mostly the work of one of the country's Founding Fathers, John Adams, a specially called convention drafted this constitution and then sent it to the people for ratification. In addition to devising a new framework as to how the people wrote their constitutions, the Massachusetts state constitution strengthened the office of the governor. The people elected the governor, and, once in office, that person had the power to veto legislation. That veto, though, could be overridden. Massachusetts's constitution influenced other states. In fact, New Hampshire's constitution largely plagiarized that of its southern neighbor. In both cases, the language regarding impeachment was essentially the same. Like the two-step process used in England, impeachment in Massachusetts and New Hampshire began with their representatives impeaching the person accused of malfeasance. A trial then took place in the Senate. No longer were state judges involved. If someone was convicted in either state, they would be removed from office and not allowed to hold an office in the future. Many of the ideas broached and discussed in the state constitutions of Massachusetts and New Hampshire reappeared at the Constitutional Convention in May of 1787.

Impeachment at the Constitutional Convention

The delegates to the Constitutional Convention of 1787 confronted impeachment on multiple occasions. All the original drafts and plans for a new form of government mentioned impeachment in one way or another. Thus, a consensus existed that at least some or all government officials could be impeached. On 25 May the debates commenced, and as soon as 2 June the delegates discussed the process for removing officials from office. James Dickinson of Pennsylvania proposed that the president could be impeached. This minor motion tested the consensus on impeachment because Dickinson suggested that a president could be drummed out 'on the request of a majority of the legislature of individual states' (Elliott, 1836, IV: 149). The consensus began to disappear as the delegates tried to hammer out exactly who could be impeached and what might constitute an impeachable offense. Once that had been resolved, the process of impeachment had to be debated and resolved.

The delegates must have sensed that they had begun to tread on dangerous ground because most of them knew that George Washington was going to serve as the first president, and any talk of impeachment could be seen as a slight against Washington's integrity. But the delegates had not yet determined how long a president would serve. If they followed the idea that tyranny begins when annual elections end and confined the president to a single one-year term, then impeachment would be unnecessary since the people would be able to vote the president out of office within a year. If, however, the delegates allowed the president to serve a much longer term, or perhaps even serve for life as **Alexander Hamilton** recommended, then impeachment would be required. Simply put, instead of being a simple stand-alone issue, impeachment had become entangled with other topics in Philadelphia. Those other matters required resolution before addressing impeachment. After a brief debate, the delegates rejected Dickinson's motion, with only Delaware supporting it.

Solving the issues that led to the Great, or Connecticut, Compromise—which had to do with the makeup of Congress—consumed most of the delegates' attention in the following weeks. Impeachment reappeared on 13 June when the delegates debated a National Judiciary. Edmund Randolph and James Madison of Virginia co-sponsored a resolution giving jurisdiction to the national legislature for impeachments. This elicited no debate, however. At the end of the day, Massachusetts' Nathaniel Gorham presented a report clarifying what the delegates had already agreed. The ninth article mentioned 'impeachment and conviction of malpractices or neglect of duty' of the National Executive. The thirteenth article muddied the waters by claiming that the National Judiciary would handle impeachments for 'any national officers' (Farrand, 1966, I: 230–31).

Impeachment faded into the background for over a month. On 20 July, the delegates tackled impeachment for an extended period, but this debate related solely to the president. The topic of discussion centered on when the country's leader could be impeached. Would it be during his term or after? North Carolina's William Davie argued that the president had to be impeachable while in office. Otherwise, he 'will spare no efforts or means to get himself reelected'. New York's Gouverneur Morris added, 'He can do no criminal act without "coadutors", who may be punished. In case he should be reelected, that will be a sufficient proof of his innocence.' When the debate shifted to eliminating impeachment entirely, Benjamin Franklin said it had to be available to the people because, if it was not in the new constitution, the only alternative would be assassination, which deprived a suspected official of his life without a trial. Future vice president Elbridge Gerry echoed Franklin. 'A good magistrate will not fear [impeachments]. A bad one ought to be kept in fear of them', Gerry announced. Finally, by a vote of eight states to two, the delegates concurred that the president could be impeached (Farrand, 1966, II: 64–66, 69).

By the end of August, with the temperature and tempers soaring, the delegates had established a framework for impeachment. On 27 August, they agreed that a president could be impeached in the House of Representatives for 'treason, bribery, or corruption' but would then be tried before the Supreme Court. The proverbial dam finally broke on 8 September. After making progress on how treaties would be ratified, the delegates returned to impeachment. Virginia's **George Mason** believed that presidents should be liable for impeachment for treason, bribery, and 'maladministration'. Mason perhaps used this word as a backdoor method to broaden impeachment. Gouverneur Morris objected to the use of 'maladministration', and said that an election every four years would prevent 'maladministration'. Mason therefore withdrew 'maladministration' and added instead a near-facsimile of the language long used in England: 'other high crimes and misdemeanors'. This convention adopted this new phrasing by a vote of eight states to three (Farrand, 1966, II: 550).

Having resolved what a president or official could be impeached for, the delegates next addressed where the trial should take place. Madison objected to it occurring in the Senate, favoring instead the Supreme Court. Morris countered that it had to be before the Senate because the House had already impeached the president, and the Supreme Court was too small to conduct a trial [*Doc 2*]. Roger Sherman of Connecticut seconded Morris by reminding the delegates that since the president would appoint members to the Supreme Court, they might be beholden to the chief executive in the case of a presidential impeachment. Convinced, the delegates rejected Madison's motion and agreed to have the trial take place in the Senate. It appears that the convention's attendees spent little time debating the threshold required to convict an impeached president. Parliament had required a simple majority in the House of Commons and the Lords to impeach and convict. The convention delegates accepted that threshold for impeachment in the House but, without any recorded debate, settled on a two-thirds majority in the Senate to find someone guilty. They then finalized the language for the impeachment clause, and the matter rested on 8 September. Nine days later, the convention concluded its business, and the Constitution went to the states for ratification.

After nearly four months of debate, the final text of the Constitution of 1787 referred to impeachment in four different places. They are as follows:

- Article I, Section 2: The House of Representatives shall chuse their Speaker and other Officers; and shall have the sole Power of Impeachment.
- Article I, Section 3: The Senate shall have the sole Power to try all Impeachments. When sitting for that Purpose, they shall be on Oath or Affirmation. When the President of the United States is tried, the Chief Justice shall preside: And no Person shall be convicted without the Concurrence of two thirds of the Members present.
- Judgment in Cases of Impeachment shall not extend further than to removal from Office, and disqualification to hold and enjoy any Office of honor, Trust or Profit under the United States: but the Party convicted shall nevertheless be liable and subject to Indictment, Trial, Judgment and Punishment, according to Law.
- Article II, Section 4: The President, Vice President and all civil Officers of the United States, shall be removed from Office on Impeachment for, and Conviction of, Treason, Bribery, or other high Crimes and Misdemeanors.

Impeachment at the Ratifying Conventions

Impeachment became a topic of discussion in a few states during the ratification process. That it received sparse attention probably stemmed from the fact that Washington would be the first president, and most considered him beyond reproach. Accordingly, few felt it necessary to consider this part of the Constitution, as it would not be invoked while Washington led the nation. The **Federalists**, who supported the Constitution, were better organized and outflanked their opponents, the **Antifederalists**. By the time many Americans in rural parts of the country had received a copy of the Constitution, the Federalists had already scored victories by large margins in Delaware, Pennsylvania, New Jersey, Georgia, and Connecticut. (In fact, ratification was unanimous in Delaware, New Jersey, and Georgia.) Only in Pennsylvania, which approved the new constitution, did impeachment warrant what turned out to be a very brief discussion.

The Federalists encountered their first real test in Massachusetts. Given the importance of that state's constitution to the practice of impeachment, it is surprising that the subject elicited little discussion there. The delegates went through the Constitution line by line but did not deliberate over the process of impeachment either in the House or the Senate. Still, the Massachusetts convention ratified the Constitution by a close vote of 187 to 168.

After the people of Rhode Island rejected the Constitution by an overwhelming majority, which had been expected, the debate shifted south, with Maryland and South Carolina holding their conventions. Federalist fears of a rejection or adjournment without ratification—which most deemed to be tantamount to non-acceptance—proved to be unfounded. Maryland approved the Constitution by a vote of 63 to 11. South Carolina followed suit a month later, endorsing it by the wide margin of 149 to 73. This meant that eight states had now ratified the document. Only one more was needed.

Impeachment began to surface in the subsequent ratifying conventions. The states of Virginia, New York, and New Hampshire had dueling conventions. The New Hampshire gathering, which commenced after New York and Virginia had started their own, ended first. The convention in New Hampshire was a continuation of an earlier one that had adjourned in February without ratifying or rejecting the Constitution. When it reconvened on 18 June, one delegate grumbled over the repetition of 'dry arguments'. This became ironic because, after just four days of debate, New Hampshire voted for ratification. Not wanting to take any chances, one Federalist invited some of his Antifederalist friends to lunch, where he offered them alcoholic beverages. When the vote began after lunch, the inebriated Antifederalists failed to respond when their names were called, and New Hampshire endorsed the Constitution by a vote of 57 to 47 (McDonald, 1965: 223).

While impeachment did not figure in the debates in New Hampshire, it appeared in New York and Virginia. Most Federalists realized the fates of New York and Virginia had become intertwined. If Virginia went first and ratified, New York would follow the example. If New York went first and rejected the constitution, Virginia would do the same. Though the Constitution was now the law of the land, the stakes were high enough for Federalists and Antifederalists in both states to ride their horses nearly to death to keep their friends informed of what was happening.

The Virginia convention began on 2 June. There, George Mason and James Madison, who had their disagreements over the Constitution at the Philadelphia convention, clashed over whether a president could be impeached for misusing presidential powers such as the pardon. Mason did not think the president should have pardoning power because he might abuse it and lead the nation down the path to a monarchy. Madison responded by saying the House could impeach the president if he perverted the pardoning power. Therefore, the people had little to fear from the country's leader because impeachment would act as a check against potential abuses. In the end, Virginia ratified the Constitution by the close vote of 89 to 79. It then submitted twenty proposed changes. One of these called for 'some tribunal other than the Senate be provided for trying impeachments of Senators' (Maier, 2010: 308).

The New York convention commenced on 17 June. Antifederalists attacked the aristocratic Senate, insisting, as had some in Virginia, that an impeached official should be tried before a unique tribunal instead of the Senate. Otherwise, a senator could be impeached in the House and then face trial in the same body in which they served. This argument elicited sparse debate. Little did the attendees realize that the question regarding the impeachment of a senator would soon come before Congress.

The supreme legacy of the constitutional era turned out to be the *Federalist Papers*, which was a series of 85 essays written by Alexander Hamilton, James Madison, and John Jay in support of the new constitution. Although written to tell the people of New York that they had hardly any reason to fear the government they proposed, these documents became sacrosanct for Americans. The *Federalist Papers* analyzed just about every section of the pending constitution. *Federalist 65* [*Doc 3*] covers impeachment in great detail. Written by Hamilton, this essay discussed the 'judicial character' of the Senate. The author sought to demonstrate that the Senate was a much better venue for a trial than the Supreme Court. In Great Britain, and in many of the recently adopted state constitutions, the lower chamber impeached, and then the upper chamber tried the impeached individual. The new constitution continued that principle.

In the next essay, *Federalist 66* [*Doc 4*], Hamilton rejected the idea that the process envisioned would intrude on the Constitution's separation of the new government's powers among judicial, legislative, and executive branches. Rather, impeachment by the legislature stood the best chance of inhibiting the executive from abusing its authority. Opponents, he added, worried that the impeachment procedures established gave too much power to the Senate, which had as well the job of ratifying treaties. If senators liked a treaty signed by the president, what incentive would they have to convict that same individual for wrongdoing? Hamilton replied that critics failed to take note of the fact that only the House could impeach someone. And just because members of the Senate approved a treaty did not mean they would refuse to convict an impeached president who had engaged in obvious malfeasance.

Hamilton—and, indeed, the Constitution's writers—gave far more attention to the president's position when it came to impeachment than to members of the judiciary. After all, the president was the nation's leader. However, whereas the chief executive had to answer to the voters every four years, federal judges and justices, once confirmed, had life tenure. Article III, Section 1 of the Constitution, in language similar to that adopted by the British Parliament in 1701, specifically stated, 'The Judges, both of the supreme and inferior Courts, shall hold their Offices during good Behavior.' But what if they acted improperly? Hamilton answered that question in *Federalist 78* [*Doc 5*], pointing out that the Constitution's 'good behavior' clause was the best way to prevent 'despotism'. Left unclear was whether 'good behavior' meant something more than avoiding the acts spelled out in Article II, Section 4.

Writing in March of 1788, Publius, the pseudonym used by the authors of the *Federalist Papers*, predicted that impeachment would have political undertones. In the end, Hamilton was proven correct. But this was an audacious statement to make in 1788. A strong sense of unity remained among the American people because their revolution had only ended five years earlier. Hamilton emphasized that impeachments were political in nature,

> as they relate chiefly to injuries done immediately to society. The prosecution of them, for this reason, will seldom fail to agitate the passions of the whole community, and to divide it into parties, more or less friendly or inimical, to the accused.

He observed that how senators reached their conclusions 'will be regulated more by the comparative strength of parties than by the real demonstration of innocence or guilt' (Cooke, 1961: 439–40).

After a protracted debate, New York ratified the Constitution by a vote of 30 to 27 on 26 July, leaving only North Carolina and Rhode Island. Antifederalists dominated both of these states. In the former, which commenced its convention five days before New York voted to approve the new document, impeachment received the most extensive discussion in all of the ratifying conventions. James Iredell, a Federalist, called the impeachment clause 'one of the greatest securities for a due execution of all public offices'. He continued,

> If this power were not provided, the consequences might be fatal. It will be not only the means of punishing misconduct, but it will prevent misconduct. A man in public office who knows that there is no tribunal to punish him, may be ready to deviate from his duty; but if he knows there is a tribunal for that purpose, although he may be a man of no principle, the very terror of punishment will perhaps deter him. (Elliott, 1836, IV: 32)

North Carolina adjourned its convention on 2 August and did not reconvene it until November of 1789. By this time, twelve amendments had passed through the U.S. Congress and had been sent to the states for ratification. Congress passed ten in 1789—the Bill of Rights—which the states ratified in 1791. The passage and pending ratification of these amendments assuaged the fears of many in North Carolina, who approved the Constitution by a vote of 194 to 77. Still, North Carolinians included nearly thirty more changes they wanted to see made to the document. Rhode Island proved more stubborn, not holding its second ratifying convention until March of 1790. The delegates adjourned after debating the Constitution for nearly a week. They reconvened in late May and finally endorsed the document by the close vote of 34 to 32. Like many other states, Rhode Island included suggested changes.

Questions Unanswered

Impeachment had ebbed and flowed throughout the process of writing and approving the new constitution. In Philadelphia, the Framers had grappled with that subject on numerous occasions. While impeachment appeared sparingly at the ratifying conventions, it was not nonexistent. Indeed, Hamilton, Madison, and Jay felt compelled to write the *Federalist Papers* to win support for the document they had played such an important part in writing. Moreover, Hamilton specifically devoted a fair amount of attention explaining how the Constitution envisioned impeachments taking place so that the American people could anticipate their elected officials would be held accountable if they did not remain above board.

The Founding Fathers, though, were men of their time who lacked crystal balls. There were questions that they left unanswered. Antifederalists had raised the potentially sticky problem of a senator facing impeachment in the House and then trial before their peers. In such a situation, could their fellow senators act impartially? What did 'good behavior' for members of the judiciary mean? Finally, what about partisanship? The Framers of the Constitution had assumed, as Madison explained in *Federalist 10*, that the new United States would have multiple factions—or, for lack of a better term, political parties—thereby preventing one faction from dominating the others. But within the Founders' lifetime, a two-party system developed. Given that Hamilton himself argued that impeachment was political in nature, could impeachment become a weapon used by one party against the other for political ends? In the coming years, Americans found themselves confronting this very question.

2 Impeachment in the Early Republic

Few Americans discussed impeachment during the early 1790s. After all, President George Washington, his advisers, and his appointees all seemed above reproach, and the American people appeared more interested in getting the new government off the ground and securing a viable economic infrastructure. But by the mid-1790s, impeachment entered political discourse. This more than likely stemmed from the rise of partisanship in America at the time. The unity brought on by the American Revolution had disappeared, with Americans increasingly identifying as either Federalists or Democratic-Republicans. From the late 1790s until the early 1800s, three impeachment trials occurred. Senator **William Blount**, Judge **John Pickering**, and Associate Justice **Samuel Chase** were all impeached. Blount and Chase escaped conviction, but Pickering was not so fortunate. These impeachments all had political undertones. And, while these early impeachments failed to set a clear precedent about impeachment moving forward, they did establish one thing: impeachments, for the most part, would tend to be partisan.

The actions of Judge **George Turner** prompted the earliest talk of impeachment under the Constitution of 1787. Born in England around 1750, Turner had emigrated to the colonies, fought in the Continental Army, and purchased property in the Northwest Territory—a large body established in 1787 by the federal government under the Articles of Confederation that today includes parts of the states of Michigan, Ohio, Indiana, Illinois, Wisconsin, and Minnesota. Appointed a judge of the Northwest Territory by President Washington in 1795, Turner ran afoul of the settlers there, who charged him with ruling over his courtroom with an iron fist. To Turner's foes, impeachment became their only course of redress. They therefore sent a petition requesting as much to the federal government, which, at that time, met in Philadelphia. On 10 May 1796, Attorney General Charles Lee referred the petition to the House of Representatives, cryptically calling for 'a certain mode of prosecution' (*Annals of Congress*, 4th Cong., 1st sess., 1796: 1338). The petitioners certainly expressed a veiled hope that Congress would impeach and remove Turner. The House referred the matter to a select committee of five members, which decided to take no action. Turner resigned his judgeship soon thereafter.

DOI: 10.4324/9781003565680-4

William Blount

The attempt to impeach Turner became merely a curious footnote in American history. Without a vote and subsequent trial, no precedents had been set other than that Congress could refuse to act on a call to remove a federal official. The next attempt at impeachment, however, became one that received extensive scholarly attention. A day before the United States celebrated its twenty-first year of independence, the Senate learned of a conspiracy allegedly orchestrated by Tennessee senator William Blount. Born in North Carolina, Blount had fought against the British during the Revolution, became one of the signatories of the Constitution in 1787, and played a leading role in getting Tennessee admitted as a state in 1796. According to the charges leveled against him, the same year Tennessee secured statehood, Blount asked an intermediary named John Chisholm to contact Robert Liston, who served as Great Britain's minister to the United States. What concerned the Senator was the Treaty of San Lorenzo, also referred to as Pinckney's Treaty, which U.S. and Spanish officials had signed in 1795. Spain at the time controlled both Louisiana—which was then a large swath of land between the Mississippi River and the Rocky Mountains—and Florida, and had denied Americans the right either to use the Mississippi River or the port of New Orleans. Under Pinckney's Treaty, Spain removed those restrictions.

What worried Americans by 1796 was that the Spanish monarchy might surrender its holdings to France, which might proceed to reverse what Madrid had granted them. Through Chisholm, Blount proposed to lead an American force to take over Florida and Louisiana, with London offering financial assistance in support of this gambit. Since the British at that time had begun fighting Spain, an American attack would aid the British militarily because it would distract the Spanish and force them to allocate resources to another front. Once the United States drove the Spanish out of those territories, the British could then move in and mop up. In return, London would guarantee the U.S. free access to the Mississippi River and New Orleans.

Blount also had a personal economic motive for trying to secure this area. The Tennessean, like many other Americans, had speculated on millions of acres of land in what was then referred to as the 'Old Southwest'—the area that today includes Kentucky, Tennessee, Alabama, Mississippi, Florida, and West Virginia—but with the uncertainty surrounding the Mississippi River and New Orleans, the value of that acreage had declined and threatened the senator with bankruptcy. If the French indeed won control of the Mississippi, then Blount's fortunes would plummet further, and he would be ruined. In the end, westerners like Blount, who had despised the British because of the Revolution, now began turning to them because they seemed to be the only people capable of stopping the French.

Liston sent Chisholm back to Britain to discuss the scheme with Foreign Secretary Lord Grenville, only to have Grenville scoff at the idea. Undeterred, Blount pressed on. In April 1797, he wrote a letter to his friend James Carey outlining his plans in detail. Like any good conspirator, Blount, in writing, urged Carey to destroy the correspondence, only to have Carey fail to follow those explicit instructions. In fact, Carey compounded his error by showing Blount's letter to a friend, who stole it and sent it to government officials in Philadelphia.

In June 1797, news of Blount's actions reached President John Adams. After delaying for several weeks, Adams submitted to the Senate on 3 July the incriminating letter. When confronted by Vice President Thomas Jefferson before the entire Senate, Blount absented himself, twice requested postponements to examine his files, and then, on 5 July, packed his belongings and absconded from the capital. As investigators trailed the senator, members of both political parties submitted statements condemning him, with many referring to his actions as treasonous. The president's wife, Abigail, even called him a 'Judas'. In the Senate, talk of expulsion became commonplace. Across the hall in the House of Representatives, impeachment became the topic of discussion (Melton, 1998: 105–11, Clayton, 1996: 158).

Though disgraced, Blount knew that Congress would be adjourning any day, and he thought that perhaps the matter might be forgotten during a congressional recess. Therefore, he reversed course and reappeared at his Senate desk, acting as if nothing had happened. His colleagues, though, would not be as accommodating as he had hoped. Instead, on 7 July, a unanimous House of Representatives endorsed a resolution calling for Blount's impeachment. The House, however, had not yet drafted articles of impeachment, thereby setting a precedent for over a century by which it impeached first and drafted articles later.

The next day, the Senate, perhaps not wanting to be outdone by the House, voted to expel Blount by a margin of 25 to 1. Only Henry Tazewell of Virginia voted against the expulsion. Even Blount's Tennessee colleague, William Cocke, endorsed his banishment.

Lawmakers now faced two questions. First, could they impeach a member of Congress? Second, since Blount had become a former member via expulsion, could impeachment still be applied? Congress adjourned on 10 July without resolving these questions. Instead, it created a committee headed by Samuel Sitgreaves, a Federalist from Pennsylvania, to gather evidence on Blount's activities and, apparently, to discover who else might have been involved in the Tennessean's plan. In essence, Blount's pending trial in the Senate was no longer about convicting him, since most believed him guilty, but how impeachment could be used to unravel a conspiracy. Figuring out who knew what and when could also have political benefits for the accusers.

Sitgreaves' committee had the power to issue subpoenas, and over the summer began to flex its muscles. Secretary of State Timothy Pickering, himself a staunch Federalist, assisted the committee throughout the summer. That a member of the executive branch offered to aid a legislator in an impeachment proceeding was to become an exception to the rule: In future impeachments, it was members of the executive branch who oftentimes became the target, and who, in turn, attempted to stonewall Congress. In 1797, though, the Federalists controlled the executive branch of government, and they relished the prospect of embarrassing Blount, a member of the opposition.

On 4 December, shortly after Congress had returned, Sitgreaves presented his lengthy report to the House, taking two days to deliver it. The report, however, included no articles of impeachment. Not until 25 January did the Pennsylvanian submit five articles, all related to statements Blount had made in his incriminating correspondence to Carey. By this time though, the Federalists had begun to have second thoughts about proceeding. While their reasoning is unclear, it was the case that the Federalists in the 1790s had been highly pro-British, while the Democratic-Republicans had leaned in favor of France. Yet the Blount conspiracy involved a Democratic-Republican conspiring with the British. This muddied the political waters, and perhaps prompted the Federalists to reevaluate their stance because the whole matter might turn some Americans against Great Britain and into the arms of the French, which would benefit the Democratic-Republicans.

On 29 January the House approved the articles without a recorded vote. Just before the House took up the articles of impeachment, it agreed to move forward with the articles by a vote of 42 to 41. The Senate shared that lack of eagerness. Its members dispatched the sergeant-at-arms, Rhode Island's Joseph Wheaton, to Tennessee with a writ to bring William Blount back to Philadelphia for his trial. The emissary located Blount in Knoxville, the state's capital, but the former senator made it clear that he had no intention of returning to Philadelphia. Wheaton then tried to raise a posse to help him bring Blount back, but Blount remained too powerful a force politically in eastern Tennessee for anyone to answer the call. Not only did the ex-senator remain in Knoxville during the Senate trial, but he also won an election to the Tennessee state senate and prevailed on his fellow state senators to appoint him their speaker. Ironically, while serving in the Tennessee senate, Blount became a judge in an impeachment trial of a state judge!

In an era before cars or railroads, it took time for lawmakers to travel between the capital and their home states. Consequently, the Senate did not commence the first impeachment trial in U.S. history until 7 December 1798. As onlookers packed the galleries, **James A. Bayard** of Delaware and Maryland's Robert Goodloe Harper delivered most of the oral arguments on behalf of the House managers. Bayard, a Federalist, toed the party line and embraced a broad definition of impeachment. Just because Blount had been expelled from the Senate, he contended, it could still convict him and disqualify him from holding another federal post [*Doc* 6]. These statements offer strong evidence that Bayard envisioned the impeachment process as political in nature; or, if Federalists could impeach and remove from office their political rivals, even if they no longer held a federal position, then they (the Federalists) could ensure their supremacy in the capital.

Although nearly bankrupt, Blount had secured the legal services of two distinguished lawyers, Jared Ingersoll and Alexander Dallas, to present his defense. They argued that Blount could not be convicted for multiple reasons. First, noted Dallas, the senator no longer served as a United States senator [*Doc 7*]. Second, elected officials could not be impeached because they were civil officials. Since Ingersoll had served at the Constitutional Convention as a delegate from Pennsylvania, his arguments perhaps carried extra weight. He cautioned that the Federalist majority endeavored to abuse the power of impeachment and would set a bad precedent. 'This is the first and last opportunity to pause and consider before the irretrievable step is taken', he warned (Gerhardt, 2000: 50). While the Senate's deliberations have been lost to history, it appears they focused on Blount's status as a senator. The conclusion reached was that, as a member of the Upper House, the Tennessean could not be considered a civil official and, consequently, could not be impeached and then convicted. Later that month, members of the House learned through the presiding officer of the Senate, Vice President Jefferson, that the Senate had approved a resolution by a 14–11 vote, declaring it lacked jurisdiction in the case and had dismissed the charges. Thus, on a technicality, the impeachment of William Blount came to an end. But the Senate had established an important precedent—impeachment did not apply to the legislative branch.

Prosecuting Pickering

In 1800, the country endured a bitterly contested election. Due to a quirk in the Electoral College, the House had to decide between Thomas Jefferson and **Aaron Burr** as to who would be the nation's third president. Jefferson and Burr both belonged to the Democratic-Republican Party, but since each elector got to cast two votes, the two men received the same number, producing a tie. On the thirty-sixth ballot, the House finally chose Jefferson. The new president and his supporters then passed and convinced the states to ratify the 12th Amendment, which clarified a presidential ticket for electors. From then on, presidential candidates and their running mates would be chosen together. Although Jefferson and his party dominated the executive and legislative branches, the Federalists made a hasty retreat to the courts, determined to prevent the new chief executive from undoing all the work of the 1790s. Yet, by pinning their hopes on the judiciary, the Federalists paved the way for a new round of impeachments. Although these impeachments involved a district judge and then an associate justice of the Supreme Court, they created divisions within Jefferson's political organization, with some members championing the efforts at removal and others trying to pump the brakes.

Just before Jefferson's inauguration, the outgoing Federalist majority in Congress passed and then lame-duck President Adams signed the Judiciary Act of 1801. This created sixteen new circuit courts, which Adams promptly filled with Federalist judges. When Supreme Court Chief Justice John Jay retired at the end of 1800, Adams nominated John Marshall to fill the vacant slot so Jefferson would not have the opportunity. Not surprisingly, the incoming head of state and his followers cried foul over what they called the 'Midnight Judges'.

In 1802, Democratic-Republicans repealed the Judiciary Act of 1801. Many Federalists argued that, in so doing, their political opponents had undermined the young republic because there would be no check against Jefferson. Some Federalists predicted the Supreme Court would declare what the Democratic-Republicans had done unconstitutional, only to see it do just the opposite in the case of *Stuart v. Laird*. For Federalists, the country's highest tribunal had opened the door to the destruction of the federal judiciary, for the courts now would bend to the will of the majority. The Federalists were certain that their nightmares had become reality when the Democratic-Republicans commenced impeachment proceedings against New Hampshire District Court Judge John Pickering in 1804.

Born in New Hampshire in 1737, Pickering attended Harvard University, went into law, and became a luminary in his home state for his service as an attorney, judge, and state legislator. He won the attention of President George Washington, who appointed him to his federal judgeship in 1795. In that post, Pickering began to find solace in the bottle, suffered bouts of insanity, and engaged in profanity-laced tirades from the bench. He had clearly become unfit to discharge his duties, with many suspecting he had truly gone insane. The problem was that the Constitution offered no remedy

Figure 2.1 Judge John Pickering, whose mental illness became central to his impeachment. From *The Pickering Genealogy* (1897), courtesy of HathiTrust.

for a member of the judiciary who was mentally incapable of carrying out his or her responsibilities.

Through intermediaries, Jefferson initially tried to persuade Pickering to retire, but his effort stalled thanks to New Hampshire state politics. Once it became known that the president wanted Pickering off the bench, several candidates in the Granite State began pressing their claims for the soon-to-be-vacant office. Jefferson now found himself on the horns of a dilemma: if he authorized an effort to remove Pickering, he would then have to decide who would fill the vacant judgeship. Whomever he selected would curry favor with one faction in New Hampshire but anger others. Complicating Jefferson's decision was that some members of his party, while realizing Pickering had become an embarrassment, did not believe impeachment to be a constitutionally viable recourse. Other Democratic-Republicans wanted to make an example of Pickering and use that as a springboard to go after other Federalist judges, including Chief Justice Marshall. Like a good politician, Jefferson played for time hoping Pickering might relent. But, since Pickering refused a gentleman's courtesy, the president concluded he had no alternative but impeachment.

Was insanity, however, a constitutionally permissible justification for impeachment? Article II, Section 4 made reference to 'Treason, Bribery, or other High Crimes and Misdemeanors', but did that clause include mental illness? When discussing the potential impeachment of associate justice **William O. Douglas** 160 years later, Representative Gerald Ford famously defined 'High Crimes and Misdemeanors' as 'whatever a majority of the House of Representatives considers them to be at a moment in history'. Jefferson decided to have Congress make that determination by asking lawmakers on 4 February 1803 to commence impeachment proceedings. The House would have to determine whether a mental disability could be considered a 'high crime or misdemeanor'.

A month later, following little debate, the House impeached Pickering by a tally of 45 to 8. As with William Blount, its members informed the Senate that they would, in due time, offer impeachment articles against the judge. The four articles the House managers sent to the Senate cited Pickering for drunkenness while on the job and violating the law in his decisions.

Many Democratic-Republicans in the Upper House had reservations about convicting and removing an insane judge from the bench, and the House managers, led by John Randolph of Virginia, tried to prevent Pickering's attorneys from raising his mental status. After a three-day debate behind closed doors, the Senate agreed to hear testimony regarding Pickering's psychological well-being. Pickering's attorneys breathed a sigh of relief, certain that the Senate would not vote to convict and remove from office a mentally unstable man. They erred. Democratic-Republicans resolved to remove Pickering because the Constitution offered them no other choice. In doing so, Democratic-Republicans, arguably, set a bad precedent, for they had lowered the bar for what could be considered to be a 'high crime or misdemeanor'.

John Quincy Adams, who served as a senator at the time and belonged to the Federalist party but would soon join the opposition, noted in his diary that the administration had put pressure on Democratic-Republicans to convict Pickering (Ellis, 1971: 73).

With Jefferson's supporters determined to convict a mentally ill judge, Federalist senators made several attempts to postpone the trial, thinking a delay would benefit Pickering. Perhaps the people, if given more time to comprehend what the Democratic-Republicans were plotting, might pressure their senators into acquitting Pickering, or maybe Pickering could still be convinced to resign. Perhaps even, the judge might die of old age. Democratic-Republicans, under increasing pressure from the administration, beat back these efforts. To assuage their consciences over convicting a mentally ill man, they adopted a resolution, asking simply whether Pickering was 'guilty as charged in the article of impeachment exhibited against him by the House of Representatives' (*Annals of Congress*, 8th Cong., 1st sess., 1803: 364). The wording offered senators a rationale to convict an insane individual, for they could argue that, if they convicted Pickering, it was only because of the evidence presented to them by the House. Along party-line votes, the Senate voted 19–7 to convict Pickering on the first article and 20–6 on the second, with seven senators refusing to respond. The entire affair suggested that the impeachment of judges would be a partisan affair. Just thirteen months after his conviction, Pickering died. Democratic-Republicans would soon have a second chance to establish a clear precedent.

Chasing Chase

As soon as he secured a conviction of Pickering in the Senate, Randolph commenced impeachment proceedings against Associate Justice Samuel Chase. A prominent figure in Maryland politics, Chase had served in the Continental Congress, signed the Declaration of Independence, and participated in the Maryland ratifying convention of 1788, where he joined Antifederalists in opposing the Constitution. He subsequently reversed course and became an ardent Federalist. He held a variety of judgeships in Maryland until 1796, when Washington nominated him to sit on the U.S. Supreme Court. Following Senate confirmation, he began his service as an associate justice that February.

Chase had a stormy career on the bench. It appears he often allowed his political views to influence his rulings and, on multiple occasions, delivered politically motivated charges to juries before they deliberated. At this time, Supreme Court justices still had to ride the circuit and participate in a variety of federal cases in addition to hearing cases as members of the Supreme Court. A partisan charge to a Baltimore jury in May of 1803 became the tipping point, when Chase all but instructed the jury to convict the defendant, Thomas Cooper, who supported Thomas Jefferson. 'Ought this seditious and official attack on the principles of our Constitution, and on the

Figure 2.2 Samuel Chase, the only Supreme Court Justice impeached. Courtesy of the Miriam and Ira D. Wallach Division of Art, Prints and Photographs: Print Collection, The New York Public Library.

proceedings of a State, to go unpunished?' the president cryptically asked a Maryland lawmaker. He continued, 'I ask these questions for your consideration. For myself, it is better that I should not interfere.' Jefferson clearly wanted something to be done regarding Chase, but stopped short of outright calling for the justice's removal (Boyd, 1950, XL: 372).

Based on the existing record, it appears Randolph introduced an impeachment resolution against Chase in January, though Jefferson's correspondence suggests that, at that point, he had yet to decide exactly what he wanted done about the associate justice. Afterward, the president reached the grim realization that Randolph had become more of a problem than the partisan associate justice. The Virginian Randolph had begun to oppose administration measures in Congress, and even had the audacity to criticize in public some of Jefferson's decisions. It appears Randolph intended the impeachment of Chase to aid his political career, which might end in a stay in the Executive Mansion. Randolph also wanted to bend the court to the will of the Democratic-Republican majority. Jefferson might be a Democratic-Republican himself, but he feared Randolph, already regarded as a radical by many in the party, might upset party harmony. If Randolph began impeaching and convicting judges, he might become so popular that other Republicans might turn to him as Jefferson's successor over the president's preference, Secretary of State James Madison.

Jefferson, still very popular with most members of his party, could have cut bait and run had he wanted. He also could have instructed his followers in Congress to let Samuel Chase off the hook. He did neither [*Doc 9*]. After two months of investigations and depositions, the House voted to impeach Chase by a vote of 73 to 32, with the adoption of articles coming afterward. Federalists, who had unanimously opposed the resolution impeaching the justice, did the same for all eight articles. Among the accusations, Chase's politically charged comments from the bench constituted criminal behavior, and he had committed procedural errors during trials. With the case on its way to the Senate, Democratic-Republicans faced a conundrum. If they voted to convict, they could choose as the grounds criminality or incompetence. Either option would open a can of worms and set new precedents that could be exploited by future members of Congress.

Lame-duck Vice President Aaron Burr, fresh off his duel with Alexander Hamilton—during which he had killed the former Treasury Secretary—gaveled Chase's trial into session on 3 February 1805. Several onlookers noted the irony because the murderer (Burr) arraigned the judge (Chase), whereas in a typical trial, the judge would be arraigning the murderer! Jefferson and his allies in Congress, usually worried about saving money, allowed Burr to spend lavishly. The vice president rearranged the Senate chamber to resemble the British House of Lords, which had concluded an impeachment trial for Lord Warren Hastings a few years earlier. Chairs and benches replaced the Senate tables, while brightly colored cloths covered just about everything.

Ostensibly, it seemed odd that Jefferson would give Burr such carte blanche. The president had largely ignored his immediate subordinate since Burr's attempt to steal the presidency from him back in 1801. Observers in Washington, though, realized the game Jefferson had begun to play. The president recognized that convicting Chase presented dangers to the Democratic-Republican Party. But, by allowing Burr to turn the trial into a spectacle—and combining that with accepting his vice president's requests for patronage—Jefferson could get what he wanted, which was Chase's acquittal.

On 4 February 1805, over 1000 spectators crammed into the Senate chamber to see the trial get underway. Chase had assembled a dream team of early nineteenth-century lawyers, who refuted many of the charges against him. Procedural mistakes were not impeachable, they argued. Nor were Chase's charges to juries, since the 1st Amendment protected his right to freedom of speech. Randolph, who had little experience presenting oral arguments before a jury, botched his presentations. When the Virginian made his summation on 27 February, he started by announcing that he had lost his notes, and then launched into a series of personal attacks on Chase and his other political opponents.

Two days later, on 1 March, the Senate voted on each of the eight articles. None received the two-thirds majority required for conviction and removal from office; indeed, only two garnered a slim 18–16 majority. On the single article impeaching Chase for procedural mistakes, Article 5, every senator voted not guilty. John Quincy Adams noted in his diary: 'I shall only remark that this was a party prosecution, and has issued in the unexpected and total disappointment of those by whom it was brought forward' (Adams, 1874, I: 370). One of Jefferson's best biographers, Merrill D. Peterson (1970: 796), echoed Adams when he wrote, 'Inevitably, the impeachment of Chase was a political act. Jefferson had no illusions on this point.' To this day, Samuel Chase remains the only member of the Supreme Court to be impeached.

Keeping the Process Intact

The day after Chase's acquittal, Vice President Burr delivered his farewell address. In it, he noted the role the Senate played in preserving democracy when it came to impeachment trials, calling it

> a sanctuary, a citadel of law, of order, and of liberty; and it is here—it is here, in this exalted refuge; here, if anywhere, will resistance be made to the storms of political phrensy, and the silent arts of corruption; and if the Constitution be destined ever to perish by the sacrilegious hands of the demagogue or the usurper, which God avert, its expiring agonies will be witnessed on this floor.
>
> (*Annals of Congress*, 8th Cong., 2nd sess., 1805: 71)

While Burr is remembered for killing Hamilton and for engaging in treason in the Southwest, his handling of Chase's trial and his eloquent statement afterward may yet redeem him. According to John Quincy Adams, some members of the Senate began to cry during Burr's farewell address (Adams, 1874, I: 367).

For his part, Randolph sought to make up for his embarrassment during Chase's trial by proposing an amendment to the Constitution that would allow the president to remove any judge or justice if the majority of both houses of Congress agreed to it. The proposal, which clearly lowered the bar for removal, elicited a lively discussion from the members of the House. John Smilie, a Democratic-Republican from Pennsylvania, supported the proposal, commenting, 'I do religiously believe that we cannot convict any man on an impeachment' (*Annals of Congress*, 9th Cong., 1st sess., 1806: 503). Others expressed reservations over replacing the two-thirds requirement for conviction with a simple majority. To this, Randolph responded by saying more important functions of Congress required a bare majority, including declaring war and raising taxes. Why could it not remove judges by the same threshold? The House decided to postpone further discussion, and Randolph's motion never came back up for consideration.

Several states submitted proposed amendments to Congress in the next five years related to impeachment and, like Randolph, got nowhere. These amendments demonstrated that the American people and their leaders desired alternatives to the method of impeachment as laid out by the delegates to the Constitutional Convention of 1787. But, since a consensus eluded members of Congress, the mechanism laid out by the Philadelphia Convention remained, and remains, intact (Ames, 1897: 150; *Annals of Congress*, 8th Cong., 2nd sess., 1805: 150).

3 Impeachment in the Antebellum Period

The issue of impeachment disappeared from the public mind after Samuel Chase's acquittal. With the dissolution of the Federalist Party in the wake of the War of 1812, the country entered into a period which historians often refer to as the Era of Good Feelings. Partisanship, for the most part, declined in the face of strong nationalist sentiment. The few discussions of impeachment related mostly to federal judges who presided over courts in territorial districts. Members of Congress introduced resolutions to examine the conduct of Judges Harry Innis (1808), Peter Bruin (1808), Harry Toulmin (1811), William P. Van Ness (1818), Mathias B. Tallmadge (1818), William Stevens (1818), Charles Tait (1822), Joseph L. Smith (1825), Buckner Thruston (1825), and Alfred Conkling (1830). In every case except for Stevens, who resigned, the House took no action, or absolved the judge of any wrongdoing or misconduct.

The Era of Good Feelings ended in 1828 with the election of ex-general and War of 1812 hero Andrew Jackson. Jackson's victory ushered in a new era of partisanship in America where his supporters, eventually dubbed the Democrats, battled his opponents, who at first called themselves the National-Republicans and then the Whigs. Naturally, because of increased partisanship, the doctrine of impeachment resurfaced during the so-called 'Age of Jackson'. Five judges—James Peck, Benjamin Johnson, Phillip Lawrence, John C. Watrous, and Thomas Irwin—became the target of impeachment inquiries. Of them, only Peck endured a lengthy impeachment process. With the other four judges, the House did not uncover enough evidence to warrant pursuing charges.

John Quincy Adams succeeded James Monroe as president of the United States in 1825, but not without controversy. In the election of 1824, Adams finished a distant second to Jackson in both the popular and electoral votes. But, since Jackson failed to receive a majority of the electoral votes, the House of Representatives had to determine who would be president. Working with Speaker of the House Henry Clay, who referred to Jackson as a modern-day Julius Caesar, Adams secured enough support among House members to win the presidency on the first ballot. When Jackson learned that Adams had won and that he had named Clay as his secretary of state, which

DOI: 10.4324/9781003565680-5

most deemed as the stepping-stone to the presidency, the former general exploded in rage. He charged that Adams had secured victory through 'bargain and corruption'—referring to Clay as the 'Judas of the West'—and predicted that Clay would hang himself just like the disciple who betrayed Christ. Following the midterm elections of 1826, Jackson's supporters seized control of Congress. Surprisingly, they did not institute any impeachment proceeding against Adams or Clay even though they had the votes in the House. In fact, it does not look like the topic was even broached. One can only speculate as to why Jackson's followers demurred. Perhaps they had simply forgotten about impeachment. Or maybe they did not want to make a martyr out of Adams or Clay. Instead, the next round of impeachments waited until after Jackson defeated Adams in the election of 1828.

A Hen-Pecked Judge

James Peck was the first target of impeachment during the Age of Jackson. Born in North Carolina in 1790, Peck became a federal judge in Missouri in 1822. Three years later, he held an attorney, appropriately named Luke Lawless, in contempt after Lawless had published an article in a newspaper criticizing Peck's actions. Peck's alleged overuse of judicial authority upset many in Missouri. It took five years, but on 24 April 1830, the House voted to impeach Peck by a vote of 123 to 49. After the tally had been completed, the House drafted articles of impeachment.

As he prepared for his Senate trial, Peck asked Vice President John C. Calhoun, who as president of the Senate would be the presiding officer, if Peck could be seated where he would have the sunlight at his back because he did not like looking into the sun. Furthermore, he pointed out that the events in question had taken place four years previous, and that he had 'not been careful to enquire or to reflect who might or might not be important to me as witnesses, in the apparently improbable event of an impeachment' (Meriwether, 1959, XI: 153, 156). Accordingly, he requested a delay so he could assemble counsel and gather evidence. The Senate agreed and postponed the start of Peck's trial until December.

James Buchanan, a Pennsylvania supporter of Jackson who later became president of the United States, acted as the lead manager for the House. Henry Storrs, George McDuffie, Ambrose Spencer, and Charles Wickliffe assisted Buchanan. The managers had a bipartisan composition since Buchanan, McDuffie, and Wickliffe all supported President Jackson, while Spencer and Storrs opposed the president. Former Attorney General William Wirt, who himself ran for president in 1832 as the Anti-Masonic Party's nominee, led Peck's defense. The proceedings came to a brief halt in January 1831 thanks to an unexpected snowstorm, prompting Massachusetts senator Daniel Webster to inform a friend, 'the impeachment goes on very slowly' (Wiltse, 1974, III: 92). The trial lingered until the end of January. Sadly, the speeches by Buchanan and Wirt went unrecorded, with the clerk simply summarizing their three-hour addresses before the Senate.

On 31 January, the Senate voted 21–22 not guilty on the single article. Two of Jackson's supporters, Thomas Hart Benton of Missouri and John Robinson of Illinois, abstained from voting. Why that was for Benton is not clear, while Robinson, who had won a special election to fill a vacant seat, joined the Upper Hose after Peck's trial began. Since Benton and Peck both hailed from Missouri, Benton perhaps had a personal relationship with the judge.

John Quincy Adams scribbled in his diary that Peck survived because Jackson 'did not wish to see an impeachment of a judge, commenced by Buchanan, successfully carried through' (Remini, 1981: 88). Jackson never trusted Buchanan and, as Adams suggested, perhaps did not want the Pennsylvanian to benefit from a conviction of Peck. Jackson's distrust of Buchanan went back to the election of 1824 when Buchanan approached Jackson with an offer of support from certain House members if Jackson appointed Clay to be secretary of state. Jackson strongly disapproved of political intrigues, and dismissed Buchanan and his overtures. After Peck's acquittal, Jackson, however, soon found himself in impeachment's crosshairs.

Targeting Old Hickory

Like President Donald Trump nearly 200 years later, Andrew Jackson evoked strong passion in the American people, who either loved or despised him. There was no middle ground. During the War of 1812, Jackson endured many hardships with his men, earning the nickname 'Old Hickory'. His political opponents soon found out that it took a lot to crack hickory, and looked to impeachment to rid the country of a president they viewed as a polarizing figure and a threat to the republic. But Jackson's main antagonist, Henry Clay of Kentucky, who regarded the nation's top political official as a tyrant, threw cold water on this idea. As early as 1831, Clay believed Jackson had committed impeachable offenses. 'But as present', he notified a friend and fellow National Republican Edward Everett of Massachusetts, 'from the present composition of the Senate, there is not the least prospect of such a prosecution being effectual' (Hopkins, 1959, XIII: 360).

Jackson's decision to remove the federal government's deposits from the Second Bank of the United States on 1 October 1833 drew the ire of his opponents. The first bank, which went into operation in 1791 under a twenty-year charter, had provided a place for the government to put its money, offered loans to businesses, and, by gathering paper currency issued by state banks, could regulate the country's banking system. Though the first bank disappeared in 1811, President James Madison, who as a U.S. representative had considered it unconstitutional, realized its usefulness to the country and chartered the Second Bank of the United States in 1816, again giving it a two-decade lifespan. Jackson, like then-Representative Madison, believed the federal government under the Constitution lacked the authority to create such an institution and determined to shut it down. As a first step, he began to withdraw federal deposits from the bank starting in October 1833. This spelled doom for the Second Bank, which disappeared in 1836.

By removing the deposits from the Second Bank, Jackson's detractors charged that he had overstepped his authority as president and had perhaps committed an impeachable offence. On New Year's Eve, Clay exclaimed, 'The premonitory symptoms of despotism are upon us; and if Congress does not apply an instantaneous and effective remedy, the fatal collapse will soon come on, and we shall die—ignobly die—base, mean, and subject slaves' (Hopkins, 1959, VIII: 685). The Kentuckian failed to elaborate on what he meant by 'an instantaneous and effective remedy', but impeachment must have been on his mind. Jackson privately mused about resigning if impeached [*Doc 10*], but that did not seem likely. It was true that the president's enemies held a majority in the Senate, but his friends still controlled the House. Andrew Stevenson, a Jackson supporter from Virginia who became Speaker of the House in 1827 and held that post for seven years, never allowed an impeachment resolution to come to the House floor.

Undeterred, Clay decided that if he could not impeach Jackson, he could at least embarrass him. He therefore introduced a censure resolution against the president in the Senate, charging Jackson with 'assuming upon himself authority and power not conferred by the Constitution and laws, but in derogation of both'. Had Clay had enough friends in the House, this could have easily been an article of impeachment. Senator Benton, who got into a barroom brawl with Jackson during the War of 1812 but who had since reconciled with Old Hickory, opposed the resolution. Responding to a Jackson critic, Benton announced, 'The Senator wishes to know what we are to do? I answer to leave this impeachment to the House of Representatives.' After months of debate, the Senate censured Jackson by a vote of 26 to 20. Never one to back down from a fight, the president delivered a protest to the Senate, accusing his opponents of seeking to impeach him while avoiding the accepted constitutional procedure. If the House had impeached the former general, a trial would ensue, and here Jackson could defend himself. A censure resolution, though, granted Jackson no such opportunity. And it would become an official part of the Senate record. For these reasons, Jackson declared the resolution 'assumes that a single branch of the legislative department may for the purposes of a public censure, and without any view to legislation or impeachment, take up, consider, and decide upon the official acts of the Executive' (Sollenberger, 2008: 52). In the end, the Senate ignored the president's protest.

Like the impeachments under President Jefferson, Jackson's battle with the Upper House elicited calls to amend the Constitution. Some favored having senators elected directly by the people instead of by state legislatures, as established under Article I, Section 3. Others wanted to shorten Senate terms from six to four years. But no serious calls emerged to modify the process of impeachment. In the end, Jackson got the last laugh. In the waning months of his presidency, his supporters secured a majority in the Senate, and used the power given to the majority to expunge the censure resolution in January 1837. That no other president since has been censured by Congress is strong evidence that lawmakers regard impeachment as the preferred, if not the only, course of action.

Nearly Impeached ... By His Own Party

That same year, 1837, a financial panic gripped the country. For the next four years, the Panic of 1837, as it came to be known, consumed much of the nation's attention. With an economy to repair and restore, few Americans wanted to devote any energy to impeachment. When talk of removing federal officials returned, it once again became partisan in nature. But there was a twist. Instead of one party trying to kick a member of the opposition out of office, it was that party going after its own. And again, it would be the president who would be the target.

The economic impact of the Panic of 1837 had played a major role in turning Americans against the incumbent president and Democrat, Martin Van Buren. Chanting 'Van, Van is a used-up man' and calling him 'Martin Van Ruin', the Whig candidate, William Henry Harrison, defeated the incumbent in a landslide in 1840. Harrison's inaugural address, which he delivered on 4 March 1841, remains the longest inaugural address in American history, clocking in at an hour and 40 minutes. Throughout, the 68-year-old refused to wear a coat or hat, despite a temperature in the low thirties (around freezing). The new president fell ill, probably from pneumonia, and breathed his last on 4 April, exactly one month after taking the oath of office. As a result, John Tyler became the first vice president to assume the presidency upon the death of the chief executive. Although both Tyler and Harrison belonged to the Whig Party, Tyler endorsed state rights, whereas Harrison embraced efforts to augment the powers of the national government. In an era when party conventions selected the party's standard bearers, no Whig bothered to ask Tyler where he stood on the issues about which Whig voters cared. Instead, the party's leaders placed Tyler on the ticket with Harrison to give it sectional balance since Harrison lived in Ohio while Tyler hailed from Virginia. The Whigs were to pay dearly for this oversight.

In the summer of 1841, the Whig majority in Congress passed a bill to create a third national bank. Considering the legislation federal overreach, Tyler vetoed it. The Whigs then modified the bill to conform to Tyler's objections, only to have the president reject it again. The next summer Tyler vetoed two tariff bills that the Whigs had passed. For his fellow party members in Congress, enough was enough. On 17 August 1842, former president and now Massachusetts Representative John Quincy Adams joined others in drafting a report outlining Tyler's objectionable actions. They favored impeaching the chief executive but realized they lacked support. The report declared:

> The majority of the committee believe that the case has occurred, in the annals of our Union, contemplated by the founders of the Constitution by the grant to the House of Representatives of the power to impeach

> the President of the United States; but they are aware that the resort to that expedient, might, in the present condition of public affairs, prove abortive.

The only option, therefore, was to leave it up to the voters. 'To them alone', wrote the report's authors, 'the final issue of the struggle must be left' (Bemis, 1956: 442).

The Whigs had a comfortable majority in the House and a slim one in the Senate. If the Democrats had wanted to aid them, the Whigs could easily have impeached and convicted Tyler. It was true that the Democrats did not embrace the president as one of their own, yet they refused to assist the Whigs because they enjoyed watching the White House's occupant give the Whigs headaches. Why remove a president who prevented one's opposition from implementing their agenda? It was once again a case of 'the enemy of my enemy is my friend'.

After learning of this report in the House, Tyler, like Jackson before him, replied with a lengthy protest. And, just like the Senate had done with Jackson after it censured him, the House refused to accept Tyler's objections. The president avoided being impeached because, in a great irony, his political opponents rescued him from his original friends. In an act befitting Tyler's stormy career, when he died in 1862, the Lincoln administration refused to acknowledge the ex-head of state's passing because Tyler had supported the Confederacy.

Third Time is the Charm?

For a few moments in the spring of 1850, President **Zachary Taylor** wondered if he would be the first president to be impeached. The scandal that had the potential to impeach Taylor stretched all the way back to the colonial era. A Georgia businessman named George Galphin had a monetary claim against the British, which the British refused to pay. Somehow, in 1835, the claim found its way into a federal treaty with Native Americans, thereby putting the national government on the hook for the money. After another decade of debate, Congress passed a bill authorizing Galphin's heirs to collect $43,518.97. The Treasury Department cut a check, and it looked like the matter had been resolved.

Or had it? One of the claimants' attorneys now suggested that interest should be applied to the agreed-upon debt. Secretary of the Treasury William Meredith consulted Reverdy Johnson, Taylor's attorney general. Johnson concurred and recommended giving an additional $191,352.89 to the claimants. This vast sum raised eyebrows in Washington and soon created a firestorm when it became apparent that George Crawford, the secretary of war, had quietly worked on the claim as an attorney and agreed to be compensated if his side won in court. Having achieved victory, Crawford could argue that he was entitled to half the original claim and half the interest! (Summers, 1987: 157–58).

The optics looked bad from every angle. The secretary of the treasury, after consulting with the attorney general, had agreed to pay the secretary of war over $100,000. It appears that nobody had broached this pending financial windfall at a cabinet meeting. The affair blindsided Taylor, the Whig Party candidate who had won the White House in 1848. An investigation quickly ensued, with Democrats insisting that the Whig cabinet members had fleeced the taxpayers out of an extravagant sum. Naturally, attention soon shifted to the president. Although nobody asked à la Senator Howard Baker during the **Watergate** hearings 125 years later what Zachary Taylor knew and when he knew it, curious congressmen probed around, hoping, but failing, to find a smoking gun. They also attempted to prove that Crawford had funneled some of his financial windfall to other cabinet secretaries, but again came away empty-handed. With that, talk of impeaching Taylor dissipated.

Yet these dead-ends in trying to impeach the nation's highest political officer did not deter partisan Democrats who wanted a scalp. Debates in Congress surrounding 'Galphinism' consumed much of the time needed to work out the various measures that became a part of the Compromise of 1850, the purpose of which was to find a way to settle a burgeoning national debate over slavery's potential expansion. Indeed, the 1850s became a decade marked by charges of government malfeasance.

James Buchanan

A New England editor ran a headline that included the phrase 'frauds astounding even for New York'. With so much rampant corruption, one would think that House committees would be busy with impeachment. Instead, crooked politicians escaped such an outcome until 1860, when the Covode Committee began to look into the alleged corruption of President James Buchanan's administration (Summers, 1987: 140).

On 5 March, John Covode submitted a resolution asking Congress to appoint a committee to investigate whether Buchanan had used patronage or money to influence congressional votes relating to territorial governments. A native of Pennsylvania, Covode was the member of a relatively new party, the Republican Party. Formed in 1854 and later earning the moniker Grand Old Party (GOP), Republicans drew support from former Democrats and Whigs, as well as, eventually, foes of immigration. Their members had strong reservations about slavery—though they disagreed on the best way to confront it—and the South's growing political influence in the country. Covode was the perfect man to introduce this resolution and lead the investigation because he had earned the nickname 'Honest John'. Conversely, Buchanan's supporters had received a nickname of their own—'the Buchaneers'—as a result of their alleged corruption.

Covode and his associates, who launched their investigation eight months before Buchanan left the presidency, did not plan to impeach the chief executive or any of his cabinet officials. Instead, they wanted to use the threat of impeachment to embarrass Buchanan and his fellow Democrats. In short, Covode sought to expose publicly the president's dirty laundry to score political points for his party. As chair, Covode barred any witness testimony that might incriminate his fellow Republicans. His investigation and grilling of witnesses, most of whom had been dismissed by Buchanan and thus had a grievance against the president, showed that the White House had overpaid for printing contracts, after which the recipients had funneled the excess funds to Democrats. One man, Cornelius Wendell, testified that he had given over $100,000 to Buchanan's party. Covode also showed that offices, patronage, and money were dangled before members of Congress in efforts to support administration measures. In June, after Buchanan sent two protests to the House professing his innocence, the House adopted five resolutions criticizing Buchanan and his secretary of the Navy, Isaac Toucey. Only one of the resolutions directly mentioned the president, but avoided the use of either the word 'censure' or 'impeachment'. Rather, it declared that 'they [Buchanan and Toucey] have set an example dangerous to the public safety, and deserving the reproof of this House'. This resolution passed by a vote of 106 to 61 (*Congressional Globe*, 36th Cong., 1st sess., 1860: 2951; Summers, 1987: 257–59).

Impeachment had clearly become a political tool that could be used to harass and embarrass political foes. The unending corruption had triggered impeachment talks, but this would change in the upcoming years. After all, the Republicans had nominated a candidate for president in 1860 with the nickname 'Honest Abe'.

4 Impeachment in the Era of Reconstruction

The Civil War brought a temporary hiatus to impeachment. With most of the country's attention directed to fighting, managing, and financing the conflict, few considered discussing that method of removing federal officers. Simply put, the national government had bigger fish to fry. As president, Abraham Lincoln perhaps committed impeachable offenses. He suspended the writ of habeas corpus, detained legislators, declared martial law, and defied court orders. Possibly apocryphal, Lincoln even contemplated arresting Chief Justice of the Supreme Court Roger Taney. But during Lincoln's presidency, few mentioned impeaching 'Father Abraham'.

During the Era of Reconstruction that followed Lincoln's presidency, impeachment resurfaced with a vengeance. In 1868 Andrew Johnson became the first president to be impeached. The 1870s saw eight judges investigated for malfeasance. Many of them resigned rather than face an impeachment inquiry. Then in 1876, the first cabinet secretary, William Belknap, was impeached. These impeachments of the post-Civil War era reaffirmed some old precedents and firmly established that quitting one's post was an alternative to an impeachment investigation.

Honing in on Humphreys

Although Lincoln faced no serious impeachment inquiries during his time as president, one other official was not as lucky. In 1862 the House quickly impeached, and the Senate speedily convicted, West H. Humphreys. Born in Tennessee in 1806, Humphreys' father had himself served on the state's supreme court. After attending Transylvania University and passing the state bar exam, Humphreys worked as an attorney. He then served briefly as a representative in the U.S. Congress and as his home state's attorney general before President Franklin Pierce nominated him in 1853 to serve simultaneously on several Tennessee district courts.

What got Humphreys into hot water was his failure to resign his federal judgeship after he announced his support for the Confederacy. He became the only federal officeholder in the South who refused to resign and give up his commission. Federal courts had ceased to operate in areas of rebellion,

DOI: 10.4324/9781003565680-6

so Humphreys' impeachment and conviction had more to do with setting an example than forcing him to give up a position that had no business coming before it. House managers drafted seven articles of impeachment, passed them without a recorded vote on 6 May 1862, and presented them to the Senate. These articles charged Humphreys with malfeasance while in office, judicial misconduct, and supporting the rebellion. The third article made it explicit why Humphreys had been impeached—his speeches and actions in support of the Confederacy constituted 'high treason'. Not wanting to take any chances, the managers assembled as much evidence as they could against the judge even though his guilt seemed all but certain since he had been impeached unanimously. In a great irony, they even tried to persuade Andrew Johnson, himself a future subject of impeachment who now served as military governor of Tennessee, to come to Washington and testify against Humphreys. Johnson declined. Before the trial commenced in the Senate, the Senate dispatched its sergeant-at-arms to Union-occupied Nashville to bring Humphreys back. Just like the William Blount Senate trial, the sergeant-at-arms returned to Washington empty-handed because Humphreys had gone into hiding (Hall, 1975).

In a one-day trial on 26 June, where nearly two dozen witnesses testified against Humphreys, the Senate voted for conviction on all seven articles. On the first and fifth articles the tally was unanimous. On the subsequent articles, respectively, 1 senator voted no, following by 4 senators, 10, 1, and 1 on the final article. Had Humphreys resigned, like almost every other officeholder who supported the Confederacy, he would have faded into obscurity.

The First Presidential Impeachment

Six years later, the nation experienced a far more divisive case of impeachment, one that would go down in the history books as the most famous of them all. This time, the target was not a judge but the president of the United States, Andrew Johnson.

Born in North Carolina in 1808, Johnson made his mark in the neighboring state of Tennessee. There, he earned a reputation as a formidable stump speaker, engaging both his political opponents and the audience in rancorous and profanity-laced debates. He began climbing up the political ranks in the 1840s and 1850s, and won a seat in the U.S. Senate in 1856. His egalitarian notions and love of democracy made him one of the last Jacksonian Democrats. He despised rich men and slaveholders alike. When Tennessee seceded in 1861, he became the only sitting senator from the South to remain loyal to the Union. When the Republican Party rebranded itself as the Union Party in 1864, the members of this coalition decided to replace Vice President Hannibal Hamlin with Johnson on the ticket with Lincoln. In the wake of Union General William T. Sherman's capture of Atlanta, Georgia, that September, the Lincoln–Johnson ticket cruised to victory. On 4 March 1865, a drunk Johnson took the oath of office, becoming vice president. A little more than a month later, Lincoln's assassination propelled Johnson into the Oval Office.

Johnson's love of democracy obscured two major flaws. For one, the new president did not believe that African Americans should enjoy the same rights as white Americans. 'This is a country for white men', he told Missouri Governor Thomas C. Fletcher in 1865, 'and by God, as long as I am President, it shall be a government for white men' (Trefousse, 1989: 326).

From the mountains of East Tennessee, Johnson had bested the state political machine in Nashville and then triumphed over secessionists. As Lincoln's successor, he sought to carry out the restoration of the country on his own. The Confederacy had surrendered in April 1865, and that summer and fall Johnson appointed friends who had remained loyal to the Union to governorships and offices in the seceded states. He granted pardons to ex-Confederates. He sought to settle Reconstruction—the process by which the seceded states of the South would be permitted to rejoin the United States—before Congress convened in December 1865. If he spared the South from a long and painful reconstruction, Johnson reasoned, its citizens would reward him with their votes when he ran for the presidency on his own in 1868.

When lawmakers returned in December 1865, they declared war against Johnson. Incumbents refused to sit those members of the House and Senate elected from the formerly seceded states. Johnson responded by vetoing a bill to extend the life of the Freedmen's Bureau, which aimed to provide assistance to former slaves. As the country commemorated George Washington's birthday, Johnson personally attacked many Republicans by name during an impromptu speech. Republicans in Congress offered an olive branch to Johnson in the form of the Civil Rights Act of 1866 that guaranteed legal protections to African Americans. If the chief executive signed it, party unity would be maintained. Instead, the president retaliated with the sword and vetoed the bill, calling it an example of the federal government overstepping its bounds, and in a way that discriminated against white Americans in favor of black citizens. Congress then overrode his veto. This pattern of vetoes and congressional overrides continued for the rest of 1866 and into 1867. In fact, lawmakers so honed the process of countermanding Johnson's vetoes that by the time he left the presidency, they could override him within an hour.

Johnson's vetoes, patronage decisions, and racist statements forced many Republicans to desert him. When the Tennessean first became president, the Republican Party found itself divided into two wings: the Radicals and the Moderates. The Radicals, led by Pennsylvania's Thaddeus Stevens and Charles Sumner of Massachusetts, believed in racial equality and wanted to punish the South. Moreover, they sought to extend the time frame of Reconstruction as long as possible, thereby allowing (they hoped) a Republican Party to develop in the South. The Moderates agreed with the Radicals on many issues, but were more pragmatic, fearful that the Radicals risked pushing their agenda so hard that they might cost the Republican Party seats in the North. In their minds, it was best to move more slowly. Johnson's actions, however, forced more and more Moderates into the arms of the Radicals.

As Republicans abandoned the president, talk of impeachment gained momentum. Some Republican members had broached the subject as early as

1866 in the wake of Johnson's veto of the Civil Rights Act, and, as 1867 got underway, their numbers grew. Yet they had not yet resolved to commence impeachment proceedings against Johnson. 'This great constitutional power should be exercised in the safest and most cautious manner—by no means lightly, or for a mere political end', the *Bangor Whig and Daily Courier* informed its readers in November 1866.

> We have been accustomed to regard it as a power to be used only in extreme cases—when 'popular rights' shall require clearly its exercise as a 'safeguard'—when the safety of the government and the country may *imperatively* demand its exercise—*when we cannot go on safely* without it.
>
> ('Proposed Impeachment of the President', 1866; Trefousse, 1989: 281–82)

Following a caucus, Republicans agreed that impeachment would have to come from the Judiciary Committee. This committee, with a balance of Radicals and Moderates, would give impeachment more legitimacy and political cover for some Republicans who had reservations about going after Johnson. In agreeing to allow the Judiciary Committee to handle impeachment, Republicans created a precedent whereby most future impeachments would originate in that body. Two days after the caucus, three Republicans introduced resolutions to remove the president from office. When James Ashley, an Ohio Radical who had shepherded the 13th Amendment through the House in 1865, introduced his resolution, he expressed his frustration with Johnson by referring to him as 'Acting President of the United States'. These resolutions were then referred to the Judiciary Committee (Trefousse, 1975: 54–56).

To try and get some dirt on the president, the committee launched a series of investigations. They attempted to link Johnson to Lincoln's assassination. They wondered why Confederate President Jefferson Davis had never been prosecuted, and suggested that it was because Johnson had accepted a bribe. The committee even examined the president's bank accounts in a futile attempt to find some sort of smoking gun. In early June, the Moderates on the committee prevailed by a vote of 5 to 4 against impeachment. 'So ends, we suppose, this pitiable and disgraceful passage in our legislative history', a Washington editor noted ('A Lame and Impotent Conclusion', 1867; Trefousse, 1989: 283–84).

The Radicals, though, refused to concede defeat. They believed that Johnson's occupation of the White House jeopardized their plans for racial justice. But impeaching the president necessitated him making a mistake, or possibly inducing him to commit one. Those who wanted Johnson gone appeared on their way to achieving their goal when, in the summer of 1867, he violated the Tenure of Office Act. Passed by Capitol Hill over another of the chief executive's vetoes, the bill declared that the president could only remove members of his cabinet with the approval of the Senate. Everyone recognized that the purpose of the law was to protect Secretary of War Edwin M. Stanton, the only Radical in Johnson's cabinet. Stanton's position was important to Radicals, for the military had begun to carry out in the South most of the Reconstruction policies enacted by lawmakers, including protections for African Americans. If Johnson could remove Stanton and replace him, even temporarily, with someone who thought like himself, he could unravel a lot of what the army had accomplished in the South.

Many Americans, including Stanton, viewed the Tenure of Office Act as unconstitutional. Even those who admitted that the law passed constitutional muster wondered if it applied to the secretary of war since he had received his appointment under Lincoln, not Johnson. Determined to resist what he regarded as unconstitutional legislation, on 5 August Johnson asked for Stanton's resignation. The secretary declined the next day. Following discussions with his cabinet, unofficial advisers, and friends, a week later Johnson 'suspended' Stanton and replaced him with the General of the Army of the United States, Ulysses S. Grant. Stanton first intended to fight to maintain his post, but quickly changed his mind and turned the War Department portfolio over to Grant.

Radical Republican newspapers howled in protest and demanded Johnson's impeachment. While these events unfolded, the Radicals suffered defeats in the fall elections, which the president took as evidence that voters supported him and his policies. When Congress returned in November, the Judiciary Committee, by a vote of 5 to 4, recommended that Johnson be impeached. On 7 December, the entire House defeated the impeachment resolution by a vote of 57 to 108. Although temporarily vindicated, the president faced a looming deadline—he had to notify the Senate of his reasoning for Stanton's removal. When he did so on 12 December, he argued that Stanton should have resigned once the secretary realized he did not agree with the policies of the president. By staying at his post, Stanton sought to embarrass the country's leader, Johnson argued. This justified the suspension. The Senate, however, balked and refused to accept the president's position. Stanton happily returned to the War Department and Grant stepped aside.

Still not prepared to back down, Johnson decided to fight. Perhaps if the Supreme Court declared the Tenure of Office Act unconstitutional, he could remove Stanton and then make a recess appointment. On 21 February, with an eye toward getting the Tenure of Office Act before the nation's highest tribunal, the president removed Stanton and replaced him with Lorenzo Thomas, an army officer. News quickly spread throughout Washington. For the president's political opponents, his firing of the secretary of war became the final straw. As soon as word reached the House, John Covode of Pennsylvania, the same man who had considered impeaching President James Buchanan, presented a motion to take that step vis-à-vis Johnson. On 25 February, after a lengthy debate, the House voted to impeach Johnson by a margin of 128 to 47. Observed House Speaker Schuyler Colfax in delivering his vote for the president's removal, 'the occupant of the chair cannot consent his constituents should be silent on so grave a question' (*Congressional Globe*, 40th Cong., 2nd sess., 1868: 1399; Castel, 1979: 171–75).

After drawing up a series of resolutions against Johnson, a special committee of the House reported ten articles of impeachment on 29 February, although two of them ended up consolidated into one. Almost all related to Johnson's firing of Stanton, which, according to the charges, violated the Tenure of Office Act. The House then adopted two additional articles, bringing the total to eleven. This last article summarized the previous ten. For Johnson's detractors, it could serve as a fallback if the Senate refused to convict on any of the others since it combined many of the grievances against the head of state.

In his looming trial, Johnson planned to defend himself personally before the Senate. Reminded by his friends of his drunken antics during his inauguration as vice president, and then his foul language while making campaign stops in the summer of 1866, Johnson changed his mind and assembled an all-star list of attorneys to defend him. They included former Associate Supreme Court Justice Benjamin Curtis, New York attorney William Evarts, Attorney General Henry Stanberry (who resigned his position to aid the president), former Tennessee Representative Thomas A. R. Nelson, and Ohio lawyer William Groesbeck. These men were all widely respected, and, unlike Johnson, they had not burned any bridges during their careers. They were also

Figure 4.1 The House managers who led the effort to convict President Andrew Johnson. From left to right, seated: Benjamin F. Butler, Thaddeus Stevens, Thomas Willams, John A. Bingham. Standing: James F. Wilson, George S. Boutwell, John A. Logan. Courtesy of the Miriam and Ira D. Wallach Division of Art, Prints and Photographs: Photography Collection, The New York Public Library.

politically diverse, with some having been Whigs, others Democrats, and still others Republicans. Johnson had made numerous political blunders during his years as chief executive, but his legal representation revealed his keen political instincts had not disappeared completely.

At one o'clock in the afternoon on 4 March, the seven House managers, led by Republican John A. Bingham of Ohio, entered the Senate chamber, upon which Bingham read the articles. It was the next day, however, that the first fireworks took place, when Supreme Court Chief Justice Salmon P. Chase began administering an oath to each of the senators, upon which they swore to act impartially. When Chase called the name of Benjamin Wade, an Ohio Republican and the president pro tempore of the Senate, Indiana Democrat Thomas A. Hendricks objected, asking how Wade could be impartial. Johnson's accession to the presidency had left the vice presidency vacant. Hence, if the Senate convicted Johnson, Hendricks reminded his colleagues, then Wade, as president pro tempore, would become the U.S. head of state under the Presidential Succession Act of 1792. Hendricks' observation triggered a debate that the Senate did not conclude until the next day. Wade said that the Constitution guaranteed the state of Ohio two votes in any impeachment proceeding. If the Senate did not allow him to participate, it would amount to discrimination against his entire state. He continued that his fellow senators had not objected when David T. Patterson, a Democrat from Tennessee, had taken the oath, even though he was Johnson's son-in-law. In the end, the Senate agreed to allow Wade to participate. Hendricks no doubt made his motion to embarrass Wade. He knew voters might not favor the idea of the Ohioan, who was one step from the presidency and whose name would be among the last in a roll call, casting the decisive vote (Trefousse, 1963: 297).

On 13 March, most of official Washington shut down. Not so the Senate, where Johnson answered a summons to appear. The galleries overflowed with observers whose anticipation turned to disappointment when the president's attorneys walked onto the Senate floor minus the president. They asked for a forty-day reprieve to prepare their case. They got ten, though the trial itself did not start until March 30.

No one disputed the facts. The House managers paraded dozens of witnesses into the Senate, who all confirmed that Andrew Johnson had fired Edwin Stanton. The defense began its arguments on 9 April. Former Supreme Court Associate Justice Benjamin Curtis reminded the Senate that Lincoln had appointed Stanton and, therefore, the Tenure of Office Act did not apply to Johnson. And, even if it did, Curtis maintained, a president had the right to test the legality of a law before the courts. Hence, Johnson had removed Stanton in an effort to get a federal tribunal to rule the legality of the Tenure of Office Act. Instead of waiting for a court of law to decide the matter, Curtis declared, Republicans rushed to remove the nation's leader. Attorney General Stanberry similarly criticized the managers. 'These alleged high crimes and misdemeanors', he stated, 'are all founded upon mere forms of executive administration' that had done no harm to the nation [*Doc 12*].

Johnson's critics and their allies outside of Congress had no qualms about discussing how a civil official could be impeached for political differences. After all, many Radical Republicans had concluded that they could not complete the work of Reconstruction with Johnson in the White House. In his only remarks before the Senate [*Doc 11*], Stevens said that, when the founders included impeachment in the Constitution, 'it was made to apply to political offenses—to persons holding political positions, either by appointment or election by the people' (U.S. Congress, Senate, 1868, II: 219–20). Senator Sumner, who had long called for Johnson's removal, echoed his Pennsylvania counterpart:

> Discerning the true character of impeachment under the National Constitution, we are constrained to confess that it is a political proceeding before a political body with political purposes; that it is founded on political offences, proper for the consideration of a political body, and subject to a political judgment only.
>
> (Sumner, 1873, XII: 323–24)

Johnson too grasped that his impeachment had more to do with politics than anything else. 'Their intent is clearly to gain control of the Union for political purposes', Johnson raged in private. While the Radicals believed they could convict the president on political grounds, they forgot about his skills as a politician. Throughout the trial, Johnson deferred to his counsel and heeded their advice even when he disagreed with some of their strategies. He refrained from giving any interviews, which could have cost him votes in the Senate if he said something inflammatory. He wrote a speech he wanted to deliver in the Upper House, only to change his mind after his lawyers advised against it (Trefousse, 1989: 318, 321).

Behind the scenes, however, Johnson took some steps to strengthen his chances of acquittal. He had his friends arrange a private dinner with Senator James W. Grimes. Grimes, a Republican from Iowa who had not yet made up his mind on how to vote, wanted assurances that Johnson would not meddle with Reconstruction and would appoint a competent individual to administer the War Department if the Senate failed to convict. The president agreed to those terms, and Grimes so informed other Senators. Johnson let it leak out that he would appoint John M. Schofield as the new secretary of war, a move that pleased Moderate Republicans. He then assured another wavering Republican, Edmund Ross of Kansas, that he would submit the newly drafted state constitutions of Arkansas and South Carolina to Congress for approval, moves Ross himself favored (Trefousse, 1989: 323–24).

As the trial neared its conclusion, people in Washington wondered what the final vote would be. An increasing number of Americans, including the president and his cabinet, began to feel that he would survive. Johnson and most of his cabinet felt good about their chances. Republican George W. Julian of Indiana wrote on 11 May, 'To the surprise and great consternation of everybody on our side the President is likely to be acquitted' (Trefousse, 1975: 163).

The capital shut down on 16 May, and observers crammed into the Senate's galleries to see what would happen. Several ill senators limped to their desks. The members of the Upper House elected to vote on the eleventh article first. This was the catch-all charge, and the House managers probably figured that if they convicted Johnson on the broadest article, they could then get him on the more specific articles since Johnson would be removed from office no matter what transpired next. A little after noon, Chief Justice Chase began his roll call. When completed, the tally was 35 in favor and 19 opposed, with seven Republicans, among them Ross, joining the 'nay' ranks. News that Johnson had avoided removal from office by a single vote—since the Constitution requires a two-thirds majority to convict in the Senate—elicited cheers and groans in the Senate. Stevens exclaimed that 'the country is going to the devil!' Wade, who had refrained from voting on most of the technical measures during the entire trial, endorsed Johnson's conviction, but he waited until after it became apparent that the president would be acquitted (Trefousse, 1997: 234).

Radicals still hoped they might succeed in booting Johnson from office on one of the other articles and began exerting pressure on the seven 'recusants', the term used for those Republicans who had supported acquittal. Ross himself faced both threats and offers of money. 'Tell the damned scoundrel, that if he wants money, there is a bushel of it here to be had', Massachusetts Benjamin Butler—who served as one of the House managers—said in reference to Ross. But when the subsequent votes took place on 26 May, the seven Republicans refused to budge. After senators rejected the second and third articles by the same 35–19 vote, George H. Williams, a Republican from Oregon, made a motion to end the entire proceeding. By a vote of 34 to 17, his colleagues seconded that request (Castel, 1979: 192).

Why did seven Republicans, who typically joined their Radical colleagues to override Johnson's vetoes, vote to retain the president? There are several reasons. First, the calendar worked in the chief executive's favor. By the time the Senate voted in May of 1868, Johnson only had ten more months to serve. Second, it appears Johnson had given assurances that he would act more pliantly towards congressional reconstruction if the Senate acquitted him. Third, Johnson met privately with or through intermediaries sent by some of the seven Republicans who voted not guilty. Fourth, a number of senators worried about the precedent they might set if they convicted Johnson. If they removed him on flimsy charges or for a political disagreement, succeeding Congresses might abuse the impeachment power. Finally, some favored acquittal because the devil they knew was better than the devil they did not. If the Senate convicted Johnson, Wade, who endorsed the entire Radical agenda, would enter the Oval Office. His fiscal views, however, included high tariffs and putting more money into circulation—policies that risked pushing up the rate of inflation, to the terror of bankers and financiers. Additionally, if Wade ascended to the presidency at this juncture, it might jeopardize the chances of Ulysses Grant obtaining the Republican nomination as the Radicals could now say that, since the party had a true Republican in the White House, it made sense to keep him there (Trefousse, 1989: 328–32).

Surprisingly, the final chapter in Andrew Johnson's impeachment had not yet been written. On 7 July, Thaddeus Stevens rose in the House to present five new articles of impeachment against the president. Like he had before, he stressed the political aspect of impeachment. He drew attention to the cases of Associate Justice Samuel Chase and Judge James Peck, asserting that everyone understood that their 'great offense was a political one'. Stevens followed by claiming that Johnson's acquittal had robbed the nation of an opportunity to establish a new precedent, one designed to prevent the use of violence to remove an autocratic leader. 'I have come to the fixed conclusion that neither in Europe nor America will the Chief Executive of a nation be removed by peaceful means', he proclaimed. 'If tyranny becomes intolerable, the only resource will be found in the dagger of Brutus' (Palmer and Ochoa, 1998: II: 460). As soon as Stevens finished, fellow Pennsylvanian Thomas Williams rose and submitted 14 more articles of impeachment. The House did not act on either of the Pennsylvanians' articles. Stevens died a month later, on 11 August.

Resignation as an Alternative to Impeachment

It was Ulysses Grant who ultimately ran as the Republican nominee in 1868, defeating the Democratic candidate, Horatio Seymour. The skills that made the former general a great military leader did not translate into his time as president. Even though Grant served two terms in office, scholars, until recently, have regarded his presidency as an absolute failure. The main reason for this stems from numerous acts of corruption during his tenure—involving members of Congress and the men with whom Grant surrounded himself, including members of his cabinet and both of his vice presidents, Schuyler Colfax and Henry Wilson. In fairness to the former general, it should be noted that he himself was never directly linked to any criminal malfeasance, but many of his close friends and confidants engaged in corrupt acts.

The desire to rid the country's leadership of such corruption no doubt explained a flurry of impeachment inquiries during the 1870s, when eight judges—Mark Delahay, Charles T. Sherman, Richard Busteed, Edward Durell, William F. Story, Andrew Wylie, D. C. Humphreys, and Henry W. Blodgett—faced impeachment inquiries. So did a member of Grant's cabinet, Secretary of War William Belknap. Of the judges, the House saw no reason to pursue impeachment of four of them, while the remainder resigned. Belknap too gave up his post prior to a House vote. Yet the cases of Delahay and Belknap deserve attention: Delahay because he became the only official impeached without any formal articles presented against him; and Belknap because he set a precedent—one that would come up during President Donald Trump's second impeachment—as to whether an official who had already left office should (or could) face impeachment by the House or a Senate conviction.

Born in 1817 in Maryland, Delahay had been a personal friend of Abraham Lincoln, who, in 1863, appointed him to a judgeship in Kansas. It appears that Delahay's love of intoxicating liquor got the better of him. On 28 February 1873, Benjamin Butler of Massachusetts, who had been one of the House managers during President Johnson's trial, informed the House that Delahay should be impeached because of his drunkenness. Suggesting that Delahay had acted in violation of the Constitution's 'good behavior' clause, Butler proclaimed, 'The most grievous charge, and that which is beyond all question, was that his personal habits unfitted him for the judicial office, that he was intoxicated off the bench as well as on the bench.' Butler reminded the House that Judge Pickering had been impeached and convicted for the same reason (*Congressional Globe*, 42nd Cong., 3rd sess., 1869: 1900).

Butler then produced depositions from witnesses in Kansas attesting to Delahay's inebriated behavior. One said that 'the cases of sobriety would be the exception and not the rule'. Another confirmed Delahay's drinking habits by adding, 'I have seen him frequently intoxicated in Topeka.' When asked if he saw Delahay imbibing only on the bench, the witness recalled, 'I have seen him fearfully drunk, so that he could not do anything.' That individual added that on many occasions Delahay had to be carried out of the courtroom to his home since he was so intoxicated. The testimony regarding Delahay's drunkenness was of such strength that Representative John P. Hale of New Hampshire, who had opposed impeaching Delahay ten minutes earlier, now proclaimed, 'I think from what I have heard read that Judge Delahay ought to be impeached.' The House then impeached Delahay via a voice vote. But, before lawmakers could draft articles of impeachment, Delahay resigned (*Congressional Globe*, 42nd Cong., 3rd sess., 1869: 1900).

If Delahay's resignation ended all talk of impeachment, such was not the case with William Belknap. Born in 1829 in New York, Belknap graduated from the College of New Jersey at Princeton, got his law degree, worked as an attorney and state official in Iowa, and fought with the Union Army during the Civil War. He returned to work for the Iowa state government after the South's surrender. On the suggestion of William T. Sherman, who had served as a general in the Union Army and then as General of the Army during Reconstruction, Grant appointed Belknap as his secretary of war.

Belknap came to Washington with a squeaky-clean reputation, making him one of the few Grant appointees who appeared beyond reproach. But that façade disappeared in 1876, largely because of his last name. His father, William G. Belknap, had spent almost his entire life serving in the army with distinction. His son had fought in a number of campaigns during the Civil War but never made much of a name for himself. It took Belknap junior two years to receive promotion from colonel to brigadier general, longer than many others at the same rank. Yet he had served in the Union Army under Grant and Sherman, and became friends with them both. His appointment to the Department of War thus amounted to an act of cronyism, something that defined Grant's presidency.

The scandal that got Belknap in trouble stretched back to 1870 when his second wife, Carita—Belknap's first wife had died in 1862—began receiving $6000 annually from John Evans so that Evans could keep his position as a sutler at Fort Sill in Oklahoma. Carita died shortly after the payments began, but they continued, with some of the money going to Belknap's third wife, Amanda, whom the secretary married in 1873 and who happened to be Carita's sister. By then, it appeared that the house of cards would collapse, as some traders at Fort Sill had begun grumbling about malfeasance.

At the end of February 1876, the Democrats, who had taken control of Congress after the 1874 midterm elections, began an investigation into the reports of Belknap's graft. They learned of Evans' payments and summoned Belknap to a committee hearing in secret. The secretary offered to throw himself on his sword and admit to his corruption if Congress agreed to keep his wife out of the sordid affair. To a tee, every member of the committee, Republicans included, refused. On 2 March, a teary-eyed Belknap tendered his resignation to Grant, who had only been partially briefed on the scandal. Grant accepted Belknap's resignation.

Figure 4.2 Political cartoon depicts Secretary of War William Belknap tearfully tendering his resignation to President Ulysses Grant. His impeachment trial raised the question as to whether a former federal official could be impeached and convicted. Courtesy of the U.S. Senate Collection.

News of the affair and Belknap's resignation lit up the telegraph wires. Many Americans howled in anger. It appeared to them that the secretary had escaped an embarrassing impeachment procedure by quitting. Nor did it appear that Belknap would face a court hearing, for the Justice Department seemed disinterested in prosecuting him.

The House of Representatives quickly removed any worries among Americans that Belknap was to get away scot-free. On the same day the secretary handed in his letter of resignation, Hiester Clymer, a Democrat from Pennsylvania and chairman of the House Committee on Expenditures, introduced an impeachment resolution. Upon presenting the evidence of Belknap's malfeasance, he said:

> The facts are so clear, so plain that everywhere throughout this broad land, and throughout Christendom wherever the English language is read or spoken, they will for long years constitute a record of official corruption and crimes such as has no parallel in our own history, or, so far as I know, that of any other country.
>
> (*Congressional Record*, 44th Cong., 1st sess., 1877: 1429)

Some eighty years earlier, Judge George Turner had resigned before facing an impeachment inquiry. The Senate in 1799 had forgone convicting Senator George Blount following his decision to quit Congress, and talk of removing Judge Delahay from office had ended after he vacated his post. The House thus faced the question as to whether it could impeach Belknap even though he no longer was in government. The secretary's foes lamented that they could find no precedent in America for such an action, but they found one in England. Both Warren Hastings and Francis Bacon became subject to impeachment after resigning their offices. 'Let us, if American precedents are not clear on this question, make a precedent which shall be clear to those who shall come after us', William R. Robbins (D-North Carolina) announced. John A. Kasson, an Iowa Republican who had earlier defended Belknap, rejoined and said that, since the impeachment provision in the Constitution contained the words 'removed', Belknap could not be impeached. If the House demurred from such thinking, he argued, then it could also impeach Jefferson Davis, who had served as secretary of war several years before assuming the presidency of the Confederacy, since he participated in a 'conspiracy to overthrow the government'. The Judiciary Committee rejected Kasson's line of thinking and reported five articles, which the House adopted without debate. It was the first time Congress had impeached a cabinet member (*Congressional Record*, 44th Cong., 1st sess., 1877: 1430, 1433, 2159–60).

All eyes turned to the Senate, which convened on 5 April. Joined by his lawyers, Belknap insisted that he could not be convicted, let alone impeached, as his resignation had made him a private citizen. As proof, one of his lawyers, Montgomery Blair, cited the Blount trial of 1798: 'From the day when Blount was tried until now no attempt has been made to impeach a private citizen.' He suggested that if the Senate convicted Belknap, it would turn the Upper House into a Star Chamber, which had been used by English kings to prosecute political opponents.

> If this court is to be opened to the persecution and prosecution of private men, and party passion and personal hate are to be invited to set themselves here upon private men because they may have been obnoxious officers, we have not yet passed by the days of tyranny.
>
> (U.S. Congress, Senate, 1976, 44th Cong., 1st sess, 94, 98; *Congressional Record*, 44th Cong., 1st sess., 1877: 2215, 2503).

Blair's appeal proved crucial. One of the first senators to vote on Belknap's guilt or innocence was Senator William B. Allison of Iowa. Shortly after the Upper House began its roll call on 1 August, Allison announced that, since Belknap no longer held a government office, the Upper House lacked jurisdiction to convict him. In turn, he intended to acquit on all counts. That argument appeared to have persuaded his colleagues, with twenty-five consequently voting not guilty—enough to prevent a conviction.

Reinforcing Precedents

The Era of Reconstruction ended in 1876 with Republican Rutherford B. Hayes' victory over his Democratic opponent, Samuel Tilden. Despite the fact that this period lasted barely more than a decade, it became important to the history of impeachment, for it reinforced three precedents. The first was that impeachment was primarily a political tool. The second was that judges could face impeachment if there was reason to believe that they had conducted themselves in ways regarded as immoral. Finally, these years firmly established resignation as an alternative to an impeachment inquiry. Indeed, Belknap's biographer, Edward S. Cooper, noted that, after the secretary's acquittal, seven judges, one customs collector, and President **Richard Nixon** all quit with impeachment probes pending (Cooper, 2003: 308–309). None of them faced an impeachment vote after giving up their positions. Not until 2021 would lawmakers consider violating that precedent.

With the end of Grant's scandal-laden presidency and, shortly thereafter, Reconstruction, the number of attempts to impeach federal officers declined substantially. The reason appears to be that the opposition party, despite its overwhelming majority in Congress, had come to realize that partisanship did not guarantee victory in the Senate, especially when the grounds for impeachment appeared at best questionable (Kyvig, 2008: 29). Only four judges faced impeachment inquiries. One of them, Samuel Axtell, resigned, and the House took no action against the remainder. Yet, just as the Era of Reconstruction had sparked a number of impeachments driven by efforts to reform the nation and root out corruption, so similar desires in the first two decades of the twentieth century would witness a new wave of attempts to remove federal officers from their posts.

5 New Rules, New Challenges

> Hear ye! Hear ye! Hear ye! All persons will keep silence, on pain of imprisonment, while the House of Representatives is exhibiting to the Senate of the United States articles of impeachment against Charles Swayne, district judge of the United States in and for the northern district of Florida.
>
> (U.S. Congress, Senate, 1905, 58th Cong., 6)

So began the trial in 1905 of Judge Swayne, the first federal official in two generations to have his case reach the Upper House of Congress. What made Swayne's trial unique was not that he came under criticism from political opponents or that he avoided removal from his post. Rather, it was a suggestion, largely ignored at the time, that a committee of the Senate, rather than the Senate as a whole, should hear the evidence against the accused.

Between the time Swayne came to the attention of the House of Representatives and a proposal in 1932 to make Herbert Hoover the second president of the United States to face an impeachment resolution, nearly two dozen federal officials were the targets of impeachment efforts, with three having their cases heard by the Senate. During that period, the House streamlined its impeachment procedures to make them more efficient. The outcomes of those three trials were different, with one defendant acquitted, another found guilty, and the third resigning. That only three of these cases reached the Upper House, and that only one was found guilty—though the one who quit almost certainly would have been—demonstrated that proving wrongdoing required meeting a high bar in the House and an even higher one in the Senate, where bipartisanship was all but required for conviction. Moreover, that eight of those whose cases did not reach the Senate resigned indicated that giving up one's job was an alternative to facing an impeachment hearing.

Swayne, Archbald, and the Criteria for Conviction

Born in Delaware in 1842, Judge Swayne had received his law degree from the University of Pennsylvania in 1871, working afterward as a lawyer in Philadelphia. He moved to Florida in 1885, where, running as a Republican,

DOI: 10.4324/9781003565680-7

he launched an unsuccessful bid for a seat on that state's supreme court. He made enough of a name for himself that, in 1889, he won a recess appointment to the District Court for the Northern District of Florida from President Benjamin Harrison, a fellow Republican.

Angered by the fact that they had no say in Swayne's appointment, congressional Democrats, whose party controlled Florida's legislature and governorship, found reason in 1904 to pass twelve articles of impeachment against him, accusing him of padding his expense accounts, using a private rail car owned by a railroad in his jurisdiction, not meeting a congressional requirement dating to 1789 that district judges live in the districts they served, and unfairly citing three persons for contempt. The Republican-led House found enough evidence to support the Democrats' claims that it voted to impeach Swayne that December, with Democrats making up the overwhelming majority of votes favoring his removal from office. Conviction seemed unlikely though, for Republicans controlled 58 of the Senate's 90 seats. Still, the Grand Old Party leadership gave the House managers 34 days to present their case, during which they heard from 29 witnesses. Swayne's lawyers disputed the charges against him. Citing the impeachment trials of Samuel Chase and James Peck, they said an impeachable offense required the intentional commitment of crimes 'in the accused's official capacity', a burden that the prosecution had not met (Bushnell, 1992: 208). The Upper House agreed, exonerating Swayne on every article. The vote was largely partisan, with Democrats favoring conviction more than Republicans; yet on no article were Democrats able to muster even a simple majority vote.

Swayne's case raised two matters. One was the time senators had to devote to impeachment trials while attempting to conduct their other constitutional duties. To free up his colleagues' schedules, in 1904 **George Hoar** (D-Massachusetts) of the Senate Judiciary Committee proposed that in an impeachment proceeding, members of the Upper House could establish a small committee to represent it and hear evidence. In one respect, this was not an unusual motion. The House of Lords in England had long used committees to conduct business. (Not until 1802 and 1816, respectively, did the U.S. House of Representatives and the Senate appoint their first standing committees.) Yet Hoar's proposal was unusual. While the House of Lords might have a select group consider 'sundry matters', the severity of impeachment deserved more than just a smattering of members present. Said a manager of the Lords in 1691, 'In the case of impeachments, which are the groans of the people ... and carry with them a greater supposition of guilt than any other accusation, there all the Lords must judge' (Berger, 1973: 170, 171). From its inception, the U.S. Senate had followed that precedent. Hoar's recommendation went to the Senate Rules Committee, where it died (Rae and Campbell, 2004). This, however, would not be last time such a proposal came up.

Addressed much sooner was a second question, which was whether a judge's impeachment rested on an indictable crime or the lesser charge of misbehavior. Swayne's trial had not offered a clear answer. Nor did the cases

Figure 5.1 Judge Robert Archbald. Courtesy of the Library of Congress, Prints and Photographs Division.

of the next two people who faced potential impeachment—Judge Lebbeus Wilfley of the U.S. Court for China and Judge Cornelius Hanford of the circuit court for the Western District of Washington. Wilfley had been criticized for requiring lawyers before his court to pass a bar exam, and for shutting down bordellos popular among Americans in Shanghai. Though the House Judiciary Committee recommended against his impeachment, he quit his job in 1908. Victor Berger, a Socialist Party representative from Wisconsin, had accused Hanford of revoking an immigrant's citizenship because of that individual's reported Socialist Party affiliations, for working while drunk, and for receiving benefits from a railroad company. In 1912, before Congress could begin its investigation of him, Hanford resigned.

Then came the case of Judge Robert Archbald, whom the House of Representatives impeached a month after Berger introduced his resolution. A Pennsylvania native, Archbald graduated from Yale University in 1871, passed the bar exam, and started working as an attorney in 1873. In 1901, he began serving as a judge for the U.S. District Court for the Middle District of Pennsylvania, followed by a brief stint as a circuit court judge before the Senate confirmed him to the Third Circuit's Court of Appeals in 1911. While holding that post, he also worked as an associate judge for the **U.S. Commerce Court**. Created in 1910, the Commerce Court heard appeals of decisions issued by the **Interstate Commerce Commission** (ICC). Established in 1887, the ICC's purpose was to regulate railroads, which had come under fire for engaging in unfair business practices that hurt small companies, farmers, and consumers.

The Commerce Court, which became pivotal to the Archbald case, had a short life span. It was born at the height of the Progressive Era that had started to take shape in the late 1800s and continued well into the second decade of the twentieth century. By the time of Archbald's hearing, **progressivism** was at its apex and had won powerful influence in both Democratic and Republican circles. The movement's adherents sought to reform the nation's political, economic, and social institutions by rooting out corruption and making these entities more efficient through the application of scientific principles. They targeted the Commerce Court as an example of government malfeasance because of its tendency to overturn ICC decisions upon appeal by the railroads. Theodore Roosevelt, a Republican running for the presidency in 1912 on an independent ticket, vowed to get rid of the Commerce Court, only to have Democrats, who held the majority on Capitol Hill, vote to do so that same year.

Arguably, the furor against the Commerce Court reflected broader antijudiciary sentiment in the nation. Predating the Progressive movement was The Grange, made up of farmers who had blasted rail and storage companies for charging unfair rates to house and ship their harvests, and which had played a leading role in convincing a number of states to enact laws favorable to themselves and consumers. Labor unions, which began appearing in greater numbers following the Civil War, had similarly taken action against big business, seeking the passage of bills at the state level aimed at reducing hours, increasing pay, improving working conditions, and ending child labor. Time and again, courts had overturned state legislation designed to meet farmers' and unions' demands. A good example was the Supreme Court which, in the 1905 decision *Lochner v. New York*, annulled a New York state law that protected bakers by limiting their daily and weekly work hours. Even though the Court two years later upheld an Oregon statute restricting daily work hours, other rulings made unions liable for violating antitrust laws, removed quotas on the number of foreigners an employer could hire, and overturned federal regulations on child labor rankled workers.

The bipartisan outcry against the nation's judicial system likely drew attention to Hanford, and certainly did so in the case of Archbald, who had been the subject of investigations by the Justice Department and then the House of Representatives. It was with Archbald's hearing that the House revised an element of its impeachment process. Previously, one committee conducted an investigation to decide whether the accused deserved impeachment, while another drafted the articles. What that meant was the full House could ask the Senate to convict someone even before it began detailing the specific charges. Deciding that that system was inefficient because it duplicated work, the House elected the Judiciary Committee to assume both functions. From then on, the Senate could expect to receive the resolution and the articles simultaneously.

The House Judiciary Committee discovered enough evidence to pass without dissent thirteen articles against Archbald. Among its claims, the judge had used his seat on the Commerce Court to get a railroad company then before that body to sell his associates coal waste at below-market prices, who then gave him a kickback, and had received similar benefits from other rail lines. In yet another instance, he had endorsed the appeal of a decision reached by his court after corresponding with one of the attorneys involved. With only one dissenting vote, the House in July 1912 sent Archbald's case to the Senate.

The Upper House decided to wait to try Archbald, as the nation was in the midst of the 1912 presidential election, which pitted the unpopular president and Republican candidate William Howard Taft against three opponents, including Roosevelt and the Democratic nominee, Woodrow Wilson. A month after Wilson secured the presidency, the Senate began its hearings. At issue was the question Swayne's case left unanswered, which was whether impeachment and conviction required a criminal act. Throughout the proceedings in the House and Senate, Archbald—who became the first judge in U.S. history to testify in his own defense before the Senate in an impeachment case—and his lawyers confessed that most of allegations against him were true. However, they contended there was evidence neither of wrongful intent nor of his business dealings bearing on his decision making on the Commerce Court. The English precedents that undergirded the Constitution's provisions on impeachment, the judge said, necessitated proof of criminality, and without it he deserved acquittal.

For the first time, Capitol Hill found itself devoting substantial attention to the impeachment powers granted it by the Constitution. According to the House managers, the Senate did not act as a criminal tribunal but, in the words of two legal scholars, 'as a political body ... exercising its political duty in a political manner and with a political end' (Firmage and Mangrum, 1974: 1052). It was on those grounds, rooted in the English precedents that influenced the Founding Fathers, that the Senate concluded misbehavior or misconduct, even if not criminal, was enough to convict. To do otherwise risked bringing the judiciary, which Americans expected to make decisions based on objective interpretation of the law, into disrepute. After a month of hearings, the Senate, in a strongly nonpartisan vote, found Archbald guilty of five of the counts against him, and voted as well to bar him from holding another federal office.

The *New York Times* implied that Archbald was simply the victim of bad luck, pointing out an association between the judge's case and the unlucky number thirteen: He was found guilty on 13 January after 13 roll-call votes on each of the 13 impeachment counts. Furthermore, the first four articles on which he was convicted—1, 3, 4, and 5—added up to 13, and the fifth article on which he was found guilty was number 13 ("Archbald Guilty on Five Counts', 1913: 1). On a more serious note, Progressive newspapers credited progressivism's sway in the country for Archbald's conviction and removal, with the *Pittsburgh Leader* arguing that the case could 'be traced directly to the popular protest against corruption in legislative, judicial, and executive circles'. The end result, it added, would 'frighten all corrupt judges and legislators from their iniquitous ways' ('Judge Archbald's Conviction, 1913: 170). Similarly, Representative **Henry Clayton** (D-Alabama), the chair of the House Judiciary Committee and one the managers who testified before the Senate during Archbald's trial, believed the outcome established 'a code of judiciary ethics for the first time in American history'—one that would ease the process of removing judges who acted unethically (Low, 1913: 9). Echoing the conclusion that criminality was not necessary to bring a judge to justice, *Nation* magazine opined, '[I]t will never be doubted that the Senate has power to impeach a judge against whom no indictable offence has been proved' ('The Week', 1913: 45).

Though it put judges on notice, Archbald's conviction left two important questions unanswered. First, because impeachment was a political rather than legal process, did Congress—or, more specifically, the Senate—have the right to decide the rules of that process once it began to consider the veracity of the charges brought before it by the House? George Hoar had suggested as much, but his proposal had been shelved. Second, as it was political and not criminal in nature, did impeachment permit or prohibit **judicial review** of a Senate conviction? Those two questions would reappear down the road.

Resignation as an Option

For a dozen years after Robert Archbald's hearing, no impeachment case reached the Senate, but the Progressives' demand for reform clearly played a part in the charges brought in the House against numerous officials: five district court judges; U.S. District Attorney H. Snowden Marshall of the Southern District of New York; five members of the **Federal Reserve Board** (FRB)—a body created in 1913 to oversee the nation's banking system; Attorney General Harry M. Daugherty; and U.S. Collector of Customs Clarence Chase. The House chose not to pursue the claims against four of the five judges, Marshall, and the members of the FRB, thus pointing to the height of the bar lawmakers had to meet in attempts to remove a federal official from office. Nor did the Judiciary Committee go after Daugherty, who served during the scandal-plagued presidency of Warren Harding (1921–1923). However, when Daugherty refused to grant a congressional committee investigating the Harding administration's misdeeds access to Justice Department files, the outrage on Capitol Hill forced him to resign in April 1924.

Had lawmakers decided they had reason to pursue any or all of these individuals, the accused would have faced a difficult choice. On the one hand, they could, like Swayne and Archbald, fight the charges. That was risky though. For one, the publicity surrounding impeachment proceedings stood to sully the reputation of the defendant, even if that person was ultimately acquitted. For another, conviction was always a possibility, bringing with it not just the taint on one's character but the loss of one's job. On the other hand, they could resign. Cornelius Hanford had chosen that option, and the fifth of the judges accused of malfeasance, Kenesaw Mountain Landis, followed suit. In 1920, Landis had accepted the position as the first commissioner of Major League Baseball (MLB) while serving as an Illinois district judge. Public indignation over his attempt to hold both positions in the face of an impeachment investigation convinced him in 1922 to give up his federal post for the better-paying job in baseball ($50,000 a year). Samuel Chase took that route as well. The collector of customs was the son-in-law of Albert Fall, President Harding's secretary of the interior who spent time in jail for accepting bribes from petroleum companies in return for leasing them government-owned property. Charged with conspiring with Fall, Chase quit his post shortly before Daugherty.

George English, the first judge whose impeachment case reached the Senate since Archbald's, initially chose to fight the charges against him but ultimately followed the lead of Hanford, Landis, and Chase. Born in Illinois a year after the Civil War ended, English received his law degree from Illinois Wesleyan University, worked in both private practice and for the Department of the Treasury, and won a position on the District Court for the Eastern District of Illinois in 1918 during President Wilson's second term in office. In January 1925, Representative Harry Hawes (D-Missouri) submitted a resolution calling for an investigation of English for misconduct. The evidence presented convinced the Judiciary Committee to file five impeachment articles against the judge. Articles 2 and 3 accused him of corruption involving bankruptcies, Article 4 charged him with putting the court's money into banks in which he had a financial interest, and the final article cited him with denying individuals their right to counsel. The most unique article, however, was the first one, which declared that English had 'abuse[d] the powers of his high office' by committing 'tyranny and oppression' on others (Lilienthal, 1926: 654). The last federal official to face such an accusation was Judge Peck a century earlier. Among the evidence brought forth was that English had disbarred two lawyers without granting them the chance to defend themselves in court. Then, when several newspapers published stories about those attorneys, English, using 'angry and abusive language', threatened to jail members of those media outlets 'to suppress the publication of the facts about [his own] official conduct' (Morgan et al., 1974: 706–07). In his defense, English claimed some of what he had done was justifiable, while some other of his actions were the result of ignorance. He admitted to what he characterized as 'mild profanity' and gave examples of it, but he denied having used the language cited by his accusers ('Judge English Defends Actions on Bench', 1925: 18). By a bipartisan vote of 306 to 62, the House impeached the judge.

In 1926, just before the Senate began its trial, English resigned, bringing the case to an end. There is good reason to believe that, he had not done so, the Upper House would have found him guilty. For one, Archbald's trial confirmed earlier precedents that established that a judge whose actions brought into question his own impartiality as well as that of the judiciary's good name could face removal from office. Stated the Judiciary Committee, 'A civil officer may have behaved in public so as to bring disgrace upon himself and shame upon the country.' While that individual 'might not be subject to indictment under any law of the United States ... he certainly could be impeached'. Yet English had also violated the Bill of Rights. His attacks on the media flouted the 1st Amendment's protection of a free press, and his disbarment of the lawyers stripped them of their 6th Amendment right to counsel (Turley, 1999: 74; Morgan et al., 1974).

It would not be until the early 1930s that the Senate would again consider a federal officer's removal. But the House remained busy, evaluating impeachment proposals brought against four more judges, District of Columbia Commissioner Frederick Fenning, Treasury Secretary Andrew Mellon, members of the Federal Reserve Board, and even President Herbert Hoover. Three of the judges ultimately had their cases dropped, while the fourth, Southern District of New York Court Judge Francis Winslow, resigned the same day the Judiciary Committee planned to commence hearings on his case. Fenning had impeachment charges brought against him by Representative Thomas Blanton (D-Texas) just a few weeks after the House impeached English. Among the claims were that Fenning had violated the law when it came to his fees, received preferential treatment insofar as representing clients suffering mental impairments, and gave false statements to lawmakers. Though the Judiciary Committee found some of what Fenning did deplorable, it concluded that the commissioner had not done anything illegal. Possibly out of fear of having his name dragged through the mud, Fenning resigned in August 1926.

Mellon was another matter. In January 1932, Representative Wright Patman (D-Texas) called for removing the Treasury secretary from office for a variety of transgressions, among them 'grant[ing] illegal tax refunds and rebates to companies in which he had a substantial interest' and not selling stock in a bank while he served on the FRB (Cannadine, 2007: 450). At the time, the nation was in the midst of the **Great Depression** that had begun three years earlier. Unemployment, at only 3 percent in 1929, had skyrocketed to about 20 percent by 1932, and thousands of banks had gone belly-up, taking citizens' life savings with them. Numerous Americans believed that Mellon was complicit in the nation's economic troubles. The Treasury secretary did not help himself when he admitted before the House of Representatives that he had sold bank stock to one of his siblings. It was an election year and the incumbent president, Herbert Hoover, did not need his lack of popularity to plummet any further. He therefore sought to get rid of his Mellon problem by offering him the ambassadorship to Britain. The Treasury secretary accepted and resigned his post. The Senate confirmed him to his new position the following February.

Hoover's decision vis-à-vis Mellon was one of several reasons that Representative Louis McFadden (R-Pennsylvania), a notorious anti-Semite and opponent of the FRB, called for impeaching the president himself in December 1932. It was the first time since Andrew Johnson that a member of Congress had proposed such a measure against a sitting chief executive. McFadden's resolution, submitted to force out of office a president who had just lost his bid for reelection a month earlier, infuriated not just his fellow Republicans but Democrats as well, who rejected it by a 361–8 vote. Just how great McFadden's mistake was became clear two years later, when he lost his congressional seat to a Democratic opponent.

Bars, Bipartisanship, and Resignation

The proposed or actual impeachments of the first three decades of the twentieth century lend themselves to four observations. The first, based on a precedent more than a century old, is that impeachment was a process limited to a federal officeholder whose post was in the judicial or executive branches (Kyvig, 2008). Second, forcing that individual from their job required meeting a high bar. More often than not, the House decided to forgo pursuing someone accused of an impeachable crime because of lack of evidence.

Third, the bipartisanship in impeachments that had taken hold by the end of the Reconstruction Era continued to predominate. In some cases, like that of George English, there was obvious support in both of the major parties for impeachment, and the seriousness of his offenses likely would have resulted in his removal from office. In others, such as with Charles Swayne and Robert Archbald, partisanship was clearly behind the accusations brought against them, but reaching the two-thirds vote necessary for conviction in the Senate required members of both parties to see eye to eye. And, even if the final vote was largely partisan, as was the case with Swayne, the controlling party retained the aura of bipartisanship by allowing its opponent ample time to make their case. Treasury Secretary Mellon, for his part, not only had Democrats against him, but Republicans—including the president—had also come to see him as a liability. Given the options of possible impeachment or reassignment, he chose the latter.

Finally, resignation remained an option. William Belknap's Senate trial had established that Congress had no jurisdiction over a former federal official. And anyway, pursuing such an individual risked squandering time better spent on other matters (Kyvig, 2008). Kenesaw Landis faced intense resistance to trying to maintain his judgeship while working as baseball's commissioner; English and Mellon could see the writing on the wall; and others, such as Samuel Chase, probably left their posts because their reputations had been, or might become, tarnished. Quitting offered a means of avoiding the publicity an impeachment hearing was likely to bring.

6 Rule XI and Judicial Review

It was, said Representative Hatton Sumners (D-Texas), 'the greatest farce ever presented'. His complaint was with the trial of Judge Harold Louderback, whom the House had impeached but the Senate had acquitted in 1933. Sumners, who had served as one of the House managers attempting to convince the Senate to find Louderback guilty, could not but note, 'At one time only three Senators were present and for ten days we presented evidence to what was practically an empty chamber' ('Judge on Trial', 1936: 16; 'Impeachment No. 13', 1936: 18). The reason for such poor attendance was simple: Senators did not have the time to sit days on end hearing testimony against Louderback and to consider and pass legislation to combat the Great Depression. It was that reality that persuaded the Upper House to revise the procedures involved in an impeachment trial.

Those changes did not come into question during the most heated impeachment effort of the 1930s, that of District Court Judge Halsted Ritter. But Ritter did offer a novel challenge to his Senate conviction by demanding that the judiciary review its legality. His bid, which ended unsuccessfully, helped further clarify, in the words of one historian, 'the framework of U.S. impeachment law' (Kyvig, 2008: 33). That clarification did not end impeachments, but, for the time being, made them less numerous.

Louderback and Rule XI

Five months after Representative Wright Patman brought charges against Treasury Secretary Andrew Mellon, Representative Fiorello La Guardia (R-New York) did the same for Harold Louderback. A native of California, Louderback had received a law degree from Harvard University before returning to his home state to practice. After serving with the U.S. Army in World War I, he resumed work as an attorney. In 1921, he received an appointment to a judgeship in San Francisco. In 1928, Republican President Calvin Coolidge nominated him to the U.S. District Court for the Northern District of California, and the Senate confirmed him later that year.

In 1932, a number of newspaper articles about Louderback brought him to the attention of the San Francisco Bar Association, which contacted President

DOI: 10.4324/9781003565680-8

Herbert Hoover. Hoover referred the case to his attorney general, who sent the matter to the House Judiciary Committee. That body formed a special committee to determine if Louderback deserved impeachment. Although a majority of the committee's members argued the evidence did not meet the standard required for impeachment and proposed a resolution of censure, a minority demurred, prompting the House to pass a different resolution calling for the judge's removal.

According to the first of the five articles brought against him, Louderback concocted a plan with an aide to establish a fake residence so he could move an expected lawsuit of which he was a party. Afterward, he tried to appoint a friend of the aide as an attorney to the defendant. Furthermore, he committed a felony by using that fake address to register to vote. The next three articles had to do with **receivers**, that is, persons appointed by a court to oversee the finances of an individual or company that had declared bankruptcy. Specifically, Louderback had shown favoritism by granting the son of a U.S. senator, who was one of his allies in Congress, the power to appoint many of the receivers, who turned out to be 'incompetent', and for permitting them to access 'excessive fees'. The last article summarized the first four, and then accused Louderback of 'unfair and arbitrary conduct' (Feerick, 1970: 45; Fenton, 1970: 744). By a 183–142 vote, the House in February 1933 sent the articles to the Senate.

Louderback's trial came at an exceptionally busy time for the Senate. New York Governor Franklin Roosevelt, the Democratic nominee for president in 1932, had defeated Hoover in a landslide, offering a '**New Deal**' to help Americans extricate themselves from the Depression. At the time of Roosevelt's inauguration in March 1933, unemployment had risen to 25 percent, some 4000 banks had gone belly-up, and Americans' faith in capitalism appeared to be wavering. Whereas Hoover had been reluctant to use the power of the federal government to ease the nation's ills, Roosevelt promised the opposite. He did just that five days after his swearing-in ceremony, calling Congress into emergency session and proposing over the next 100 days a slew of bills to address the banking crisis, help businesses stay on their feet, and aid farmers and the unemployed.

Despite its full calendar, senators devoted a fair amount of attention to Louderback's trial—at least at first. The judge told the Upper House that the claims made against him, even if valid, were not impeachable. He particularly berated Article 5 for its vague language, prompting the House to revise it at least three times. The fact the House managers had to make those alterations, as well as the fact that most members of the Judiciary Committee had argued against impeachment, made an impression on the senators. Additionally, unlike with Robert Archbald, there was no evidence that Louderback had received any kickbacks. Ultimately, as an annoyed Sumners explained, few senators attended the hearings. When the time came to vote, none of the first four articles received even a simple majority, and the fifth fell well below the two-thirds necessary to convict, with only forty-five voting guilty.

Once again, the results were largely bipartisan, with a significant number of Democrats voting with most Republicans in favor of acquittal.

Ritter, Rule XI ...

Louderback's trial reignited George Hoar's suggestion made three decades earlier to revise the Senate's impeachment procedures. Despite British and even U.S. precedents regarding turnout at impeachment hearings, the members of the Senate had concluded by the mid-1930s that their numerous responsibilities—made all the more pressing as a result of the need to combat the effects of the Great Depression—prohibited them from all sitting in attendance at an impeachment proceeding while conducting other affairs. Only one day into Louderback's trial, the *New York Times* took note that the Senate had heard from only three witnesses 'out of a possible forty from both sides'. During that day, senators had devoted ten hours to the Louderback case, which had turned their 'legislative program ... upside down' ('Louderback Trial Roils Democrats', 1933: 11). For that reason, it is likely many members of the Upper House breathed a sigh of relief when Judge James Lowell of the District of Massachusetts, against whom the House Judiciary Committee had adopted an impeachment resolution three weeks before Louderback's trial began, died.

They probably expressed similar sentiment again when, only a week after they began hearing evidence against Louderback, the Judiciary Committee quashed an attempt by Representative Louis McFadden (R-Pennsylvania)—the same man who had tried to impeach President Hoover—to impeach Treasury Secretary William Woodin, two of Woodin's predecessors, and a number of other current and former federal officers. Still, there was no way to know when or if other impeachment cases might make their way through the House. Indeed, in January 1934, Francis Shoemaker—a member of Minnesota's Farmer Laborite Party who served one term in Congress—attempted, but failed, to convince the Judiciary Committee to impeach Judge Joseph Molyneaux of Minnesota's district court on charges including corruption and senility.

Consequently, Senator **Henry Ashurst** (D-Arizona), who chaired the Judiciary Committee, suggested in May 1934 that it was time to amend their body's procedures for conducting an impeachment inquiry. His proposal was that, if it so desired, the Senate during an impeachment proceeding could name twelve of its members 'to receive evidence and take testimony' (*Congressional Record*, 73rd Cong., 2nd sess., 1934: 9016). Put another way, those dozen individuals were to conduct the trial as though the entire Senate was in attendance, unless the Upper House ordered otherwise. Once it had completed its work, the committee had to submit a report summarizing the evidence and testimony, as well as a full transcript of the same. A revised version of his motion included language making clear that, if it so chose, the

Senate could hear additional testimony. Afterward, the full Senate would vote. When it appeared that objections to Ashurst's proposal risked a lengthy debate, the Arizona senator withdrew it.

But Ashurst's recommendation was not dead. In 1935, the House Judiciary Committee considered, and killed, a motion by Representative Everett Dirksen (R-Illinois) to impeach Seventh Circuit Court Judge Samuel Alschuler on grounds of favoring a litigant before his court. In 1936, however, the Judiciary Committee, followed by the full House, voted to impeach Judge Halsted Ritter. Thus, for the second time in only three years, the Senate faced the prospect of a lengthy impeachment hearing, one that returned attention to Ashurst's motion.

Born in Indiana just three years after the Civil War ended, Ritter earned his law degree in 1892, worked briefly as an attorney in Indianapolis, and then moved to Denver, Colorado, where he continued his practice until 1925. That year, he relocated to Florida, believing the warmer climate would be beneficial to his ailing wife. In 1929, President Coolidge nominated him to the U.S. District Court for the Southern District of Florida and, despite the objections of both local Democrats and Republicans who accused him of being a 'carpetbagger' with no connections to the Sunshine State (Neumann, 2007: 246), the Senate confirmed Ritter later that year.

In March 1933, Democratic Representative Mark Wilcox of Florida submitted an impeachment resolution to the House accusing Ritter of charges similar to those brought against judges George English and Louderback: profiting from bankruptcy cases. Wilcox's motion came at the very same time that the Senate had before it not only Louderback's impeachment hearing but also numerous pieces of New Deal legislation. Facing once again the prospect of what could become a lengthy impeachment trial at the same time that they were busy conducting other business, senators adopted, with minor revisions, Ashurst's proposal, which became known as Rule XI [*Doc 13*].

Initially, it appeared Wilcox's resolution was dead in the water, as both a subcommittee of the Judiciary Committee and the full committee voted against pursuing Ritter. That changed in 1936 when Robert Green (D-Florida) delivered an impassioned speech on the House floor. Criticizing the Judiciary Committee's vote, he pointed out that he lived in the same part of the state where Ritter worked. Many of his constituents, Green continued, felt that, by trying to close Ritter's case, 'court justice has been miscarried, and they are now appealing through me to the Congress, as their only court of appeal, to relieve them of this deplorable situation' and remove from office a man who was 'ignorant, unjust, tyrannical, and corrupt' (*Congressional Record*, 74th Cong., 1st sess., 1936: 405). Among Green's accusations were that Ritter had allowed a former law partner, Albert Rankin, to serve as the receiver of a hotel and charge the excessive fee of $75,000, from which Rankin paid $4500 in cash to Ritter, and that Ritter had received payments from other receiverships. After listening to Green, the Judiciary Committee reversed itself and voted 10–8 for impeachment. The House, largely along partisan lines, followed suit, voting 181–146 to send the case to the Senate.

Partisanship and Judicial Review

The Senate chose not to invoke Rule XI in judging Ritter, whom the House had charged on seven counts. The first two had to do with the $4500 payment from Rankin and money the judge had obtained from other receiverships. Articles 3 and 4 said that Ritter had violated the Judicial Code by practicing law while working as a judge, while the next two accused him of tax evasion—specifically, of hiding the kickbacks he had received when he filed his tax returns. The final article repeated the crimes listed in the first six, adding that those alleged misdeeds had undermined the public's faith in him to render objective judgments, and brought 'his Court into scandal and disrepute' ('Article Seven', 1937: 8).

In defending Ritter, Rankin argued that he had paid an 'honest debt' in cash rather than with a check because, with so many banks failing or having runs on their deposits, he feared that Ritter would not be able to cash it ('Judge on Trial', 1936: 17). During his testimony, Ritter confessed that most of the prosecution's facts were accurate, but there was no intent to break the law. He denied the $75,000 receivership fee was exorbitant. On the $4500, he echoed Rankin, explaining it away as the money owed him for dissolving their legal partnership. As for the claim of tax evasion, he argued that losses he had incurred in an earlier year wiped out any money he received on his tax returns.

After hearing from Ritter and his defense, the Senate proceeded to acquit him on the first six articles, with most of those finding him guilty coming from the Democratic ranks and Republicans making up the majority of those favoring acquittal. But then came Article 7. By a 56–28 vote, exactly the two-thirds necessary to find guilt, the Senate convicted Ritter, making him the country's fourth federal judge to face conviction and removal from his seat. Once again, the Senate had found that tarnishing the judiciary's good name was enough to convict. Dumbfounded that Ritter could be found innocent of the first six charges but guilty on the seventh, Senator Warren Austin, a Republican from Texas, was prompted to challenge the outcome, only to find himself overruled.

Halsted Ritter's case raised two matters. One was the question of partisanship. In May 1935 and January 1936, the Supreme Court—most of whose members were political conservatives—declared unconstitutional the National Industrial Recovery Act (by a 9–0 vote) and the Agricultural Adjustment Act (in a 6–3 decision). Consequently, the Court had killed two of President Franklin Roosevelt's key 'First New Deal' programs. During 1935, Roosevelt had pushed through a series of 'Second New Deal' initiatives, among them the Works Progress Administration and Social Security.

He and Democrats, who held overwhelming majorities in both houses of Congress, could not but wonder if the Court might invalidate at least some of those programs as well. It was that possibility that, in 1937, led Roosevelt in an abortive attempt to 'pack' the Supreme Court by adding up to six new justices. According to the partisanship argument, Democrats took their anger out on the Republican Ritter and made sure he lost his judgeship (TenBroek, 1939; Bushnell, 1992).

The claim of partisanship, however, has little on which to stand. For one, Roosevelt's complaints were with the Supreme Court, not with the lower courts. Furthermore, the initial investigations of Ritter took place in 1933, four years before Roosevelt tried to 'pack' the country's highest court, and nearly a year after Ritter's conviction. Finally, given their power in both houses of Congress, Democrats could have restricted the number of witnesses and easily found Ritter guilty on every charge brought against him. Instead, the defense had eleven witnesses speak on the judge's behalf over a two-day period, and a good number of Democrats voted for acquitting him on every one of the first six articles. Even on the seventh article, ten Democrats defected to those favoring exoneration (Bushnell, 1992; Turley, 1999; Neumann, 2007).

The second issue was that of judicial review. Six weeks after the Senate delivered its judgment, Ritter appealed to the **U.S. Court of Claims**. Created in 1855, the purpose of that court, which Congress eliminated in 1982, was to hear claims for payment brought against the federal government. Ritter's argument was that he deserved his full April 1936 paycheck of $833, asserting that his removal from office was not constitutional. He based that conclusion on two rationales. One was that the Senate had had no right to consider the impeachment articles, as the accusations made against him were not impeachable offenses. The other was that the seventh article—the only one on which he was convicted—simply repeated the charges for which he had been acquitted in the first six.

Ritter's appeal raised a potentially explosive constitutional question: Were the results of an impeachment proceeding against a federal officer justiciable? In other words, could the judiciary review or even invalidate the results of an impeachment proceeding, which was inherently political in nature, against a federal officer? There was a precedent here. In the 1803 case *Marbury v. Madison* [*Doc 8*] the Supreme Court had first addressed what became known as 'the **political question doctrine**', arguing that political questions were not justiciable; only those cases where the rights of the individual were in question could come before a court of law. Keeping in mind that precedent and similar cases, as well as the work of legal scholars—and citing Article I, Section 3, which granted the Senate 'the sole Power to try all Impeachments'—the Court of Claims in *Halsted Ritter v. United States* (1936) concluded that the judiciary could not challenge the Upper House's decision [*Doc 14*]. Ritter was not done though. In the words of the popular magazine *Literary Digest*, he 'struck off a brand-new page of American judicial history' and took his case to the U.S. Supreme Court. Ritter commented:

> The Senate found that I was guilty of bringing the court into disrepute because of certain acts, but it found that I did not commit those acts ... This precedent, if permitted to stand, will make it simple for Congress to impeach a Federal Judge on any charge, real or imaginary.
> ('Article Seven', 1937: 7)

The Supreme Court found the judge's appeal without merit and refused to hear it.

An Infrequently Chosen Option

Though Louderback and Ritter faced impeachment trials in the Senate just a few years apart, the fact was that impeachment efforts had become less commonplace starting in the 1930s than in the previous two decades. In part, this can be attributed to the end of the reform-driven Progressive Era around 1920. But it was also probably because the first three decades had clarified the process of impeachment. Its use was only against incumbents in the judicial and legislative branches, not those who had resigned. It referenced an act that need not be criminal but that brought, or risked bringing, disrepute to one's office. Finally, conviction by the Senate, let alone impeachment by the House, necessitated reaching a high standard. But if these precedents remained the same, two aspects of the process had changed. The need to allow senators time to address other matters while considering impeachment had led them to adopt Rule XI. Additionally, the judiciary had made clear that it had no power to review a Senate conviction.

In the generation following Ritter's conviction, impeachment came up only four times. In 1938, J. Parnell Thomas (R-New Jersey), called for removing from office President Roosevelt's secretary of labor, Frances Perkins. A member of the recently established House Un-American Activities Committee (HUAC) that investigated claims of Americans with reported ties to **communism**, and a devout anticommunist himself, Thomas asserted that the New Deal had imperiled American capitalism. When Martin Dies, Jr. (D-Tennessee), HUAC's chair, demanded in August 1938 that Perkins deport a foreigner named Harry Bridges for attempting to undermine the U.S. government, she refused, contending that he was trying 'to usurp the functions of an executive department'. She added that to expel Bridges without due process would be tantamount to acting similar to Germany's Nazi Party, which was at that time forcing people to migrate from areas of Europe they controlled. An infuriated Thomas responded the following January by submitting a resolution demanding Perkins' impeachment for 'failing, neglecting, and refusing to enforce the immigration laws of the United States' (Kanstroom, 2007: 191, 192).

Perkins was the first woman both to sit in a presidential cabinet and to be the target of an impeachment resolution. Speaking before the House Judiciary Committee in February 1939, she stated the country's immigration statutes had 'peculiar significance to the future of our country', including making sure the nation was able to protect itself from foreign threats as well as helping foreigners become naturalized citizens. She urged that 'Congress and its committees … protect me and … my rights and my reputation if I have done no wrong' (Mohr, 1979: 255–56). The next month, lacking any evidence of malfeasance on Perkins' part, the Judiciary Committee voted to discontinue its hearings against her.

In 1945, judges Albert Johnson and Albert Watson, both of whom sat on the District Court for the Middle District of Pennsylvania, faced impeachment resolutions. Johnson quit after a House Judiciary subcommittee recommended he be tried for bribery. Watson, however, kept his job after lawmakers decided to terminate proceedings against him. President Harry Truman's decision in 1951, during the Korean War, to fire General Douglas MacArthur, followed by his order a year later to seize U.S. steel mills during a strike by steel workers, fomented cries for his removal from office, but nothing more happened. The 1960s, however, would witness a new round of determined impeachment efforts, with the highest court in the land in the crosshairs.

7 Partisanship and the Demand for Reform

Something was afoot in the Republican Party. Between 1933 and 1953, the Grand Old Party had failed to win the White House, and it had controlled Congress only for a single term (1947–1949). How to retake the Oval Office and restore the party's control over Capitol Hill split Republicans into conservative, liberal, and moderate ranks. Conservatives favored small government and berated the New Deal for moving the country down a path toward **socialism**. Liberals saw much in President Franklin Roosevelt's domestic program that they liked as well as Harry Truman's Fair Deal, which continued and expanded some of Roosevelt's New Deal initiatives. Moderates stood between the two, finding certain elements of the New Deal acceptable but believing the GOP could oversee those programs more effectively than Democrats.

Of these three wings, liberals were on the downswing, giving way to conservatives who had begun to flex their muscles. There was no better example of this than conservative Republicans' response to the two-term presidency of Dwight Eisenhower. The first member of the GOP to hold the Oval Office since Herbert Hoover, he came from the party's moderate wing. Eisenhower's preparedness to accept and expand Social Security and other New Deal initiatives infuriated the Republican right, including the John Birch Society (JBS). Founded in 1958 by **Robert Welch** to combat the international threat posed by Soviet- and Chinese-style communism, the JBS accused Eisenhower himself of being a communist sympathizer.

Although Welch never sought to impeach Eisenhower, he did attempt to do so when it came to Supreme Court Chief Justice Earl Warren. And while that effort failed, Welch suggested to others on the political right that impeachment offered a means of removing from office individuals whose liberal positions they found distasteful. Their record ended up mixed. More significantly, as the 1970s got underway, Republicans found themselves facing the impeachments of two of their own, President Richard Nixon and Vice President **Spiro Agnew**. Nixon and Agnew's misbehavior contributed to demands for reform, which played a role in a dramatic increase in the number of people cited for impeachable conduct during the second half of the 1970s as well as new legislation aimed at holding incumbents accountable for their actions.

DOI: 10.4324/9781003565680-9

Welch v. Warren

Earl Warren became a target of conservatives after World War II. During that conflict, he had served as California's attorney general, and had favored placing Japanese Americans in his state in internment camps because of questions regarding their loyalty to the country. After the war, though, Warren realized that what he had done constituted racial discrimination and, from that point on, sought to eliminate such hatred. In 1953, Eisenhower nominated Warren, then serving as California's governor, to the chief justiceship of the Supreme Court following the death of Chief Justice Fred Vinson. The Senate confirmed Warren shortly thereafter with no recorded opposition.

In 1954, the Warren-led Court, in the landmark decision *Brown v. Board of Education of Topeka*, unanimously struck down racial segregation of public schools as unconstitutional. Enforcement, however, encountered particularly strong resistance in the South, where segregation predominated, and where the decision was condemned as an attack on states' rights. As early as 1957, the Georgia state assembly endorsed a resolution demanding Warren's impeachment. It was Robert Welch, though, who assumed the mantle favoring the chief justice's ouster. To him, support for civil rights was simply part of a broader communist conspiracy to divide the country. Hence Warren, like Eisenhower, was little more than a dupe for the Soviets. Moreover, he echoed those in the South who contended that the chief justice had violated states' rights.

The JBS began its campaign against Warren in earnest in 1961, putting up billboards around the nation and sending letters to Capitol Hill demanding the chief justice's removal from office. That was as far as Welch and his supporters got. William Buckley, an increasingly influential conservative political commentator, regarded Welch as an extremist and dictatorial-minded individual who did not understand there was a difference 'between (1) an active pro-communist, and (2) an ineffectually anti-Communist liberal' (Bethune, 2022: 149). Quite simply, argued Buckley, Warren left much to be desired, but had done nothing that merited impeachment. Echoing Buckley was Barry Goldwater, an icon of the GOP's right wing who personified the burgeoning conservative movement, and who became the party's nominee for the presidency in 1964. (Goldwater ultimately lost his bid for the White House to the Democratic nominee, Lyndon Johnson.) His effort having run into a political wall, Welch declared defeat in 1967.

For all of its failures, the impeach Warren campaign had one important reverberation. For a generation, no federal official had had an impeachment case against them reach the Senate. If anything, many Americans may have forgotten it even existed as an option. However all the publicity surrounding Welch's crusade, as distasteful as it was for even fellow conservatives, did serve to raise the possibility of using impeachment as a means of removing from office persons considered ideologically unsuitable to hold a federal post. For Republicans, even those who came from the moderate wing, that was an appealing option.

Focus on Fortas

At the time Welch gave up his crusade against Warren, members of the House were considering whether to impeach three federal judges in Oklahoma: Alfred Murrah, Stephen Chandler, and Luther Bohanon. At the center was Chandler, who believed that Murrah and Bohanon were part of a conspiracy to destroy him professionally. An investigation by a subcommittee of the House Judiciary Committee concluded in 1968 that the judges had acted unacceptably but had not done anything to warrant impeachment.

If the judges in Oklahoma had not acted nefariously, liberalism had, or so argued conservatives. To them, the initiatives of the New Deal, the Fair Deal, and Lyndon Johnson's **Great Society** had moved the country down the path of big government, high taxes, wasteful spending, immorality, and criminality. Such liberal programs had encouraged people to live off of the government dole rather than earn a living, and had stifled economic growth. Moreover, liberalism had incentivized drug use, sexual promiscuity, and increasingly violent protests by civil rights and students' rights activists, as well as demands for the right to abortion. For those on the political right, 'activist' federal judges were at least partly to blame for all of these evils. The Constitution gave voters and their states means of redress: they could add amendments to it; or, though legally more problematic, Capitol Hill could restrict the types of cases on which the courts could decide.

But there was one other possibility, that of impeachment. In the spring of 1968, Warren announced his intention to retire. He was in his mid-70s, and he knew Johnson was more likely to replace him with a justice of a similar mind set than if he waited and the presumptive Republican nominee for president that year, Richard Nixon, won. The timing, however, was inauspicious: 1968 was one of the most, if not *the* most, troubled years of that decade. Johnson's approval numbers had fallen dramatically, both because of his inability to maintain order at home and to win an increasingly unpopular war in Vietnam, where U.S. troops had been in combat since 1965. The lack of support for the president convinced him in March 1968 not to seek another term in office.

Still unresolved was the matter of filling Warren's seat. To take the chief justice's place, Johnson in June 1965 selected Associate Justice Abe Fortas. A native of Tennessee, Fortas had received his law degree from Yale, served in the Roosevelt and Truman administrations, and developed a close personal relationship with then-Representative Johnson. He earned a reputation as a liberal-minded justice, supporting the rights of children and of student protestors, writing the Supreme Court's opinion that overturned an Arkansas state law that banned the teaching of evolution in schools, and upholding the 1965 Voting Rights Act that protected African American suffrage.

Johnson's desire to have Fortas take Warren's spot on the Court drew a strong rebuke from Senator Robert Griffin (R-Michigan). The president had made himself a lame duck by stepping out of the race for the White House,

Griffin said, so he should not have the right to select Warren's replacement. Everett Dirksen of Illinois, a fellow Republican who served as minority leader of the House, and who was a friend of Johnson, derided his Senate colleague, arguing not only that Johnson was still president, but that previous outgoing chief executives had named Supreme Court justices. Unmoved, Griffin did everything he could to extend the Judiciary Committee's confirmation hearings, charging that Fortas was too far to the political left to serve as chief justice. To save his nomination, Fortas became the first person recommended as the Supreme Court's top jurist to appear before the Judiciary Committee. He argued that he had never discussed with Johnson anything that came before the Court. But it quickly became clear that his nomination was in trouble, with Southern Democrats, who oftentimes voted in tandem with Republicans, joining Griffin's cause. Realizing Fortas had no chance of winning confirmation, Johnson withdrew the nomination. Later that year, Nixon won the presidency and convinced Warren to stay on the Court until he had selected a replacement.

But Fortas was not yet out of the woods. That fall, *Life* magazine reporter William Lambert discovered that the associate justice had worked as a consultant for a nonprofit run by a corporate financier named Louis Wolfson, who, along with some of Wolfson's associates, had come under investigation by the **Securities and Exchange Commission** (SEC) for not registering a planned company stock sale. Lambert published his piece in May 1969 and, while not charging Fortas with engaging in illegal acts, raised questions about the extent of the justice's relationship with Wolfson. Fortas did not help himself when he delivered a public response that failed to clarify matters. The ensuing public frustration gave ammunition to the justice's political foes, including Senator Griffin, who now called for Fortas' impeachment. Worse, the same day *Life* published Lambert's piece, the Internal Revenue Service (IRS) turned files over to the Justice Department that showed Fortas had not fully revealed his ties with Wolfson. John Mitchell, the attorney general for now-President Nixon, took those items to Earl Warren, who could not believe what he saw. The chief justice worried how the public might view the Supreme Court if an ethically challenged Fortas remained on it. Not wanting his beloved Court dragged through the mud, Warren had another associate justice, Hugo Black, encourage Fortas to resign. Meanwhile, in Congress, the number of voices urging Fortas to quit the Court grew, including among Democrats. Realizing he was in an untenable situation, Fortas stepped down. Not long thereafter, Warren did the same.

In two respects, Fortas' resignation followed precedents of other federal officers who had left their posts when facing the possibility of impeachment and conviction. First, while they may not have broken the law, the fact that they risked bringing their respective courts into disrepute was justification enough to urge them to leave their seats. Second, even if there were partisan motives in pushing for the removal of the individual in question, bipartisanship became an essential factor in leading to the targeted person's departure, whether willing to not.

But Abe Fortas' resignation added something new to the equation. Until Nixon's inauguration in 1969, Republicans had for over three decades largely been unable to move the country in directions they favored. With the exception of Eisenhower, every president had been a Democrat; and, aside from 1947 to 1949, the only other time the GOP had held both houses of Congress was 1953 to 1955. In turn, Democrats had been relatively free to nominate or confirm judges and justices they wanted, who then served until they retired or died. Impeachment, or the threat thereof, offered Republicans a way of removing members of the judicial branch they disfavored—a feat they achieved with Fortas' resignation.

Dumping on Douglas

The GOP now honed in on another associate justice, William O. Douglas. An appointee of President Roosevelt, Douglas, like Fortas, had earned a reputation as a liberal on the Supreme Court. In 1953, he had delayed the execution of Julius and Ethel Rosenberg, who had been found guilty of providing the Soviet Union with top-secret information on the atomic bomb, on the grounds that their sentencing had taken place without a jury trial. In the 1957 case *Roth v. United States*, Douglas had dissented from the majority of the Court, which had found that obscene material could be banned under the 1st Amendment. To Douglas, 'the arousing of sexual thoughts and desires happens every day in normal life in dozens of ways' (Duram, 1981: 120). Some twelve years later, he refused to recuse himself from a case involving magazine editor Ralph Ginzburg, even though Douglas himself had received payment for an article he had published in one of Ginzburg's magazines. Then, in 1970, he aroused the anger of conservatives by publishing *Points of Rebellion*. In that book, he asserted that violence had taken place at various points in American history; while he wrote the book as a warning that the unrest of the 1960s was a danger, conservatives contended that he wanted to incite lawlessness. Adding to the political right's fury was the fact that Douglas had portions of *Points of Rebellion* published in a magazine that included pornographic photos.

Seemingly unrelated events placed a target on Douglas. During his campaign for the presidency, Nixon had won support from the South, and, as a token of appreciation, he sought to replace Fortas with a southerner. His first choice was Clement Haynsworth, a South Carolina native who sat on the Fourth Circuit Court of Appeals. Haynsworth, however, became a lightning rod of controversy because of his history regarding unions and black rights, which led the Senate to reject his nomination. Nixon then turned to G. Harrold Carswell of the Fifth Circuit Court of Appeals. Carswell, who hailed from Georgia, was even more objectionable to the Senate because of comments and verdicts regarding minorities. Forced to go back to the drawing board, Nixon selected Harry Blackmun. Raised in Minnesota, Blackmun sat on the Eighth Circuit Court of Appeals and had a history of decisions that restricted the power of the federal government. To the president, Blackmun's record would sit well in the states' rights-minded South. Blackmun went on to win the Senate's unanimous approval in May of 1970.

Nixon, however, smarted from the response to his first two nominations and, according to some reports, encouraged House Minority Leader Gerald Ford (R-Michigan) to go after Douglas. Although Ford denied he came under pressure from the White House, he had begun to look into Douglas' history at around the same time as Haynsworth's nomination went to the Senate. Ford argued that federal judges had the right to serve as long as they engaged in 'good behavior'. But Douglas' past actions and decisions bothered Ford—indeed, it appears the excerpts of *Points of Rebellion* in the pornographic magazine especially offended him. Moreover, he discovered that Douglas had received payment from a private charity that, said Ford, had obtained 'some of its money from Las Vegas gambling interests' (Kaufman, 2017: 145).

In November 1969, the *Washington Post* had learned of Ford's plans to impeach Douglas, convincing observers that he was out to exact revenge against those who had opposed Haynsworth's appointment. The minority leader denied the charge, famously asserting that 'an impeachable offense is whatever a majority of the House of Representatives considers it to be at any given moment in history' (Van Tassel and Finkelman, 1999: 55). Representative Andrew Jacobs (D-Indiana) had no intention of allowing his colleague from Michigan to test that theory. A champion of the associate justice, Jacobs sought to undercut Ford and 'embarrass the White House' by submitting a resolution to impeach the justice, knowing it would fail. As he intended, the Judiciary Committee, headed by another Douglas ally, Emanuel Celler (D-New York), submitted a report finding Douglas had done no wrong. With Harry Blackmun having received the Senate's nod earlier that year, the White House gave up its pursuit of Douglas. Even Ford later admitted that his desire to remove Douglas from the bench 'was a mistake' (Kaufman, 2017: 146).

The abortive campaign to remove William Douglas from the Supreme Court proved significant for a couple of reasons. Maybe most important, it clarified for members of Congress and legal scholars what an impeachable offense was, as well as both the process and political ramifications of trying to kick someone out of federal office. Then and since, the overwhelming majority of scholars, even those who acknowledge Gerald Ford's definition has elements of truth, reject it (Lindberg, 2000; Gerhardt, 2019). Rather, they emphasize that the Founding Fathers established clear, limited standards as to what constituted an offense meriting impeachment. To adopt Ford's much broader definition would allow Capitol Hill to remove anyone from office at any time for any reason, and dismantle the Constitution's balance of powers (Thompson and Pollitt, 1970; Feerick, 1970; Morgan et al., 1974; Sunstein, 1998).

Moreover, unlike Fortas, Douglas refused to resign, despite the fact that, because of ill health, he had been thinking about it prior to Ford's challenge. Instead, he felt the need to prove he had done no wrong, and stayed on the

Court for another five years. In so doing, he denied Nixon an opportunity to move the Court in a more conservative direction. Up to that point, the president had chosen four of its justices, and if Douglas had resigned, Nixon could have taken credit for selecting the majority of those who sat on the Court's bench. Ironically, when Douglas called it quits in 1975, Ford, who had become president the year before, chose the justice's replacement.

Impeachment and an Unelected President

Gerald Ford's road to the White House came through a most unlikely series of events that included the certain impeachment and conviction of both of the president and the vice president. Those events began in June 1972 with the arrest of five men who had broken into the Democratic Party's national headquarters, located in the Watergate building in Washington, D.C. Although Nixon was a shoo-in to defeat the Democratic nominee, South Dakota senator George McGovern, the burglars hoped to gather information on the Democrats' strategy. The Federal Bureau of Investigation (FBI) took the lead probing the burglary, and discovered that two of the intruders had ties to Nixon's reelection committee.

Nixon's immediate response was to deny any involvement with the Watergate defendants. His problem was that he was a paranoid individual who saw enemies all around him, and feared the break-in could bring down his presidency. He therefore offered the burglars money to buy their silence and, claiming a need to defend the nation's security, ordered the Central Intelligence Agency (CIA) to stop the FBI's inquiry. In so doing, he committed the crime of obstructing justice, a felony that clearly was impeachable.

Slowly, the noose began to tighten around the Oval Office. Two reporters from the *Washington Post*, Carl Bernstein and Bob Woodward, undertook their own investigation, which began leading directly to the White House. Federal district court judge John Sirica, who tried the Watergate burglars, got one of them, James McCord, to admit that he and his four cohorts had come under pressure from administration officials to say nothing about the purpose of the break-in. The U.S. Senate, seeing clear indications of malfeasance within the executive branch, established a special committee headed by Sam Ervin (D-North Carolina), which commenced its own bipartisan inquest starting in May 1973. Nixon repeatedly and publicly denied any knowledge of events surrounding the brewing scandal; but maintaining that lie became problematic in July when White House aide Alexander Butterfield testified before the Ervin Committee that the president had an audiotape recording system in the White House. A battle ensued between the legislative and executive branches, the former demanding the tapes to see what Nixon knew and when he knew it, and the president refusing, citing executive privilege.

As Congress and the White House battled over the tapes, Vice President Spiro Agnew came under fire for different reasons. In August 1973, the

American people learned that he was at the center of a federal investigation on charges that included tax evasion and bribery. Under scrutiny himself, Nixon could not afford to try to protect his second-in-command. Agnew, for his part, claimed immunity from prosecution. He and his lawyers asserted that the language of Clause 7 of Article I, Section 3 and Section 4 of Article II of the Constitution made clear that the vice president—elected on the same ticket as the president by the American people, and serving as the chief executive's successor—was as important to the nation as the president himself. Consequently, just as it was for the president, the only way to remove a sitting vice president was through an impeachment process. As proof, they cited the case of Vice President John Calhoun, whom the House of Representatives in 1826 had absolved of charges that, as secretary of war, he had made money from U.S. Army contracts.

Agnew's defense drew rebukes from the Justice Department. In September 1973, its **Office of Legal Counsel** (OLC) concluded that there existed a clear delineation between the legal vulnerability of a sitting president and vice president [*Doc 17*]. The president was immune to 'criminal proceedings' while in the Oval Office, as, otherwise, it would be impossible for him to conduct 'his official duties'. Even indictment was out of the question, for to have charges 'hanging over [him] while he remains in office would damage the institution of the Presidency virtually to the same extent as an actual conviction'. The only constitutional way to remove a sitting president was through the impeachment and conviction of the American people's representatives in Congress. The vice president was another matter. Conviction, even indictment, of a vice president would not compromise the government's ability to function. If anything, said the OLC, the vice president's job was little different from that of a member of the cabinet. In early October, Solicitor General Robert Bork seconded the OLC. The 'whole executive power', penned Bork, rested in the hands of the nation's chief executive, making him 'indispensable to the operation of government'. The vice president, however, was 'clearly less crucial to the operations of the executive branch' (Coon, 2017–2018: 217).

If Spiro Agnew hoped for an impeachment hearing that might exonerate him, House Speaker Carl Albert (D-Oklahoma) proved uncooperative and refused to start the process. 'I knew instantly', he later wrote, 'that the House must not involve itself in a nearly completed criminal investigation before the federal courts'. Peter Rodino, the chair of the Judiciary Committee, seconded Albert, finding no foundation to support Agnew's claim that his case and John Calhoun's were the same (Albert and Goble, 1990: 359). Bork's boss, Attorney General Elliot Richardson, urged Agnew to resign. The alternative, the attorney general said, would be either a lengthy trial in court or on Capitol Hill. If Nixon had to vacate his office and the vice president's future was in doubt, Richardson continued, the nation would find itself paralyzed. After considering the options, Agnew in October 1973 resigned in return for a charge of one count of tax evasion, three years' probation, and a $10,000 fine. Agnew consequently became only the second vice president, the first being Calhoun in 1832, to resign while in office, though Calhoun did so for political rather than legal reasons. Using the recently adopted 25th Amendment that spelled out the process of presidential succession, Nixon nominated Ford to replace Agnew. The Senate confirmed the nomination in late November 1973, followed by the House early the next month.

The question now was whether Nixon would survive. The same month Agnew resigned, Nixon fired Archibald Cox. Appointed by Richardson as special prosecutor to investigate the Watergate scandal, Cox had decided to take Nixon to court for refusing to turn over his audiotapes. Afterward, Nixon's approval rating fell to below 20 percent, numerous media outlets and voters demanded the president's impeachment, and the House Judiciary Committee began hearings to do just that. Seeking to avoid the charges of partisanship that swirled around Andrew Johnson's impeachment, Committee chair Peter Rodino took great care to make sure his inquest avoided any stamp of political bias. Hoping to quell the furor, Nixon released edited transcripts of the tapes, but his obvious stonewalling began turning even some of his staunchest allies on Capitol Hill against him. Meanwhile, Cox's replacement, Leon Jaworski, decided to take the matter to the Supreme Court.

The nation's top tribunal now found itself addressing a question that had potential ramifications for the impeachment process. Previous presidents had asserted the right of executive privilege to withhold information from other branches of government. As early as 1795, George Washington refused to turn documents over to the House of Representatives related to treaty negotiations with Great Britain, arguing that, as the Senate confirmed treaties, only it deserved them. Other chief executives, including Thomas Jefferson, James Madison, Abraham Lincoln, Theodore Roosevelt, Calvin Coolidge, Dwight Eisenhower, and John F. Kennedy, likewise had cited privilege to retain or limit dissemination of documents or other materials. But was that right absolute? In July 1974, in the case of *United States v. Nixon*, the Supreme Court declared unanimously that it was not [*Doc 18*]. Rather, it was limited largely to matters relating to foreign or military affairs, and did not apply to cases involving 'the fair administration of justice'.

That same month, the Judiciary Committee, in a bipartisan vote, adopted three articles of impeachment against Nixon, accusing him of obstruction of justice, abuse of his power, and contempt of Congress for refusing to turn over the tapes. The Supreme Court having offered him no protection, Nixon gave lawmakers the evidence they had sought. One of tapes, later referred to as the 'smoking gun', proved that he had obstructed justice by telling the CIA to halt the FBI's investigation. Even the president's most ardent defenders turned against him. With that, Nixon realized it was a choice of certain impeachment and removal from office or resignation. He opted for the latter course on 9 August 1974. Later that day, Gerald Ford was sworn in, becoming the first and so far only unelected president in U.S. history.

Demands for Reform

The dubious claims of the Johnson administration that the United States was winning the war in Vietnam generated a '**credibility gap**', and Nixon's falsehoods heightened it. Adding to the furor were reports that Nixon and some of his predecessors had not just given U.S. support to repressive governments abroad but had also called upon the CIA to assassinate foreign leaders. Americans began to call for a government led by individuals who would promote honesty at home, and morality both in their country and abroad. As an example, during the first six years of the 1970s, the human rights organization Amnesty International had 10,000 Americans join its ranks annually (Schmidli, 2013: 91). Jimmy Carter, the Democratic nominee for the presidency in 1976, used that desire for truthfulness and virtue to defeat Ford that November.

As had taken place in the past, the yearning for reform—this time combined with a more aggressive, inquisitive media post-Watergate—contributed to an uptick in impeachment initiatives. Between the time the Ervin Committee began its inquiry into Nixon and the end of the decade, a span of just seven years, eight people faced possible removal from office. In the cases of Liam S. Coonan, the Special Crime Strike Force Prosecutor for the United States Department of Justice, and attorneys Jonathan Goldstein and Bruce Goldstein (no relation) of the District of New Jersey, the reason was not specified. Two others had obvious political overtones. In October 1977 and again in 1978, one of the most conservative Democrats in the House, Representative Lawrence McDonald of Georgia, set his sights on U.S. Ambassador to the United Nations, Andrew Young. McDonald, an ardent anticommunist and longtime member of the John Birch Society, charged that, in his public statements, Young had falsely accused the United States of holding political prisoners, wrongfully accused U.S. politicians and allies of endorsing racism, and encouraged the spread of communism. Both times, the House failed to pursue the charges. In 1978 as well, Representative John Ashbrook of Missouri, a member of the GOP's right wing who had long opposed federal desegregation of schools, called for ousting Judge Frank J. Battisti of the Northern District of Ohio for placing an undue financial burden on Cleveland's public schools by forcing them to integrate. His resolution did not make it out of the Judiciary Committee. (Ashbrook had a second go at Battisti in 1981, with the same result.)

In the remaining instances, though, the impetus for impeachment was that the accused had engaged in immoral or criminal behavior. In 1971, Otto Kerner of the United States Court of Appeals for the Seventh Circuit became the first sitting judge criminally indicted—in this particular instance, for bribery. Convicted in 1973, he resigned in July 1974 after it became clear Congress would impeach and convict him. In July 1975 Representative Robert Drinan (D-Massachusetts) sought to remove from office U.S. Ambassador to Iran and former CIA director Richard Helms for human rights and other violations in which the CIA had engaged on Helms' watch. Again, the motion died well before reaching the House floor. The same was true for Paul Rand Dixon of the Federal Trade Commission, whom Representative Edward Koch (D-New York) wanted impeached for calling consumer rights' advocate Ralph Nader a 'dirty Arab' (Charlton, 1977: 18).

That only one of the eight individuals cited for impeachable activities faced the likelihood of conviction continued to reflect the high bar one had to reach to remove a federal officer from their post. Still, there was an obvious desire for change, which led to the passage of two important pieces of legislation. The first was the Ethics in Government Act of 1978, which required public officials to provide information on their finances as well as their work history. More important, it required the attorney general to appoint an independent counsel to investigate any allegations of lawbreaking among members of the executive branch, including the president. If the evidence warranted, the counsel could recommend impeachment of their inquiry's target.

Two years later, lawmakers passed the Judicial Councils Reform and Judicial Conduct and Disability Act [*Doc 19*]. The story of this law began in 1939, when the Administrative Office Act established for each federal circuit a judicial council. That council had the power to oversee judicial assignments and to determine the ethical standards by which judges had to abide. A 1948 revision of the Act allowed the judicial councils to discipline judges who had done a poor job keeping up with their caseload, or who suffered from mental or physical impairment. When one of those councils in 1970 disqualified a district judge from continuing his job, he rejoined that deeming him unfit necessitated going through the impeachment process. It was the lack of clarity concerning the grounds for removing a judge that led to the Judicial Councils Act.

Under the Act's provisions, a person can submit in writing a complaint alleging a judge has committed misconduct, or has a mental or physical disability preventing them from performing their job. The chief judge of the district in which the accused presides reviews the complaint to determine if it is worthy of merit. If the chief judge concludes that the charges necessitate consideration, that person appoints a special committee made up of the chief judge as well as an equivalent number of district and circuit court judges. During this portion of the process, the committee can subpoena people or materials necessary for its investigation. If the committee decides the accused deserves some form of sanction, it will send such findings to the circuit's judicial council, which can choose from an array of punishments short of removal. If, however, it concludes that unseating the individual charged is justifiable, it can send the complaint to the **Judicial Conference of the United States.** Established in 1922 and headed by the chief justice of the Supreme Court, the Conference's primary job is to set guidelines for the federal courts. If called upon to investigate a judge, it can, if it chooses, conduct its own inquiry to see if impeachment and removal are warranted. If it reaches such a conclusion, it will send a recommendation to the House of Representatives to proceed with the impeachment process. Both this law and the Ethics in Government Act would end up at the center of future impeachment cases.

8 Judges, Justices, and Justiciability

In one respect, the last twenty years the twentieth century resembled those of previous ones, with more than a half-dozen members of the judiciary in the crosshairs of impeachment. Several features, however, set these impeachments, particularly of three judges that took place in the 1980s, apart from previous ones. First, despite their criminal convictions, two of the judges refused to retire from the bench. Meanwhile, the third jurist, though acquitted in criminal court, found himself facing impeachment in Congress. Second, these three cases were the first in fifty years to reach the Senate. Third, the judges' trials in the Upper House served to clarify further what constituted an impeachable offense. Finally, a Supreme Court decision that granted the Senate the right to determine how it conducted its impeachment trials created a debate over judicial review of impeachments that continues to the present.

Coming for Claiborne

The 1980s began as the 1970s ended, with abortive attempts to get rid of judges. In 1981, Congressman Lawrence McDonald (D-Georgia)—the same individual who twice had tried and failed to impeach U.S. Ambassador to the United Nations Andrew Young—attempted unsuccessfully to remove from office Nauman Scott, the chief judge of the District Court for the Western District of Louisiana. McDonald argued that Scott had undermined numerous rights, including those established by the 10th Amendment, by forcing the state to use bussing to integrate one of its public schools. Later that year, Representative Ron Paul (R-Texas) sought to do the same against Judge William Justice of the Eastern District of Texas, who had come under fire for desegregating schools in the state. Paul's resolution never made it beyond the Judiciary Committee.

But in 1983, a case brought against another jurist became the first to reach the Senate in a half century. Born in Arkansas in 1917, Harry Claiborne received his law degree from Cumberland University, served in the U.S. Army during World War II, and, after the war, worked as a defense attorney in Las Vegas. In 1978, President Jimmy Carter saw to it to appoint him as a District Court judge for the District of Nevada. A year before Claiborne received

DOI: 10.4324/9781003565680-10

his district court position, the authorities arrested one of his clients, brothel owner Joseph Conforte, on charges of tax evasion. Conforte appealed his conviction, lost, and fled the country in 1980, but not before claiming that he had given tens of thousands of dollars to Claiborne to pass out to other judges in the hopes of having his conviction overturned. Three years later, Conforte returned to the United States, where he testified against Claiborne. Charged with bribery, tax evasion, and obstruction of justice, Claiborne contended—along lines analogous to those used by Vice President Spiro Agnew a decade earlier—that the Constitution permitted only the impeachment of a sitting federal judge, not an indictment. Several courts, including the Supreme Court, rejected that argument, thereby allowing the trial to proceed. At first, it appeared Claiborne might retain his post, for evidence that Conforte had committed perjury while on the stand led to a mistrial. Deciding to focus only on tax evasion, prosecutors had Claiborne appear before another jury in 1984. Found guilty, he appealed on the grounds that he had not received the opportunity to correct errors on his tax returns, but lost. In March 1986, he became the first sitting federal judge in U.S. history to be sent to prison.

But Claiborne refused to resign, meaning not only that he continued to earn a salary but also that, once his sentence ended, he could resume sitting on the bench. Unwilling to allow a convicted felon to have such an opportunity, two members of the House Judiciary Committee, F. James Sensenbrenner (R-Wisconsin) and committee chair Peter Rodino (D-New Jersey), led the campaign to impeach Claiborne. In June 1986, a House Judiciary subcommittee adopted four articles. The first two accused him of purposely falsifying his tax records over a two-year period, while the third noted his conviction for tax evasion. The last one argued his deliberate attempt to defraud the government had embarrassed the judiciary. Later that month, the Judiciary Committee, followed in July by the full House, voted unanimously in favor of all of the articles.

With the case now in their hands, senators decided for the first time to use Rule XI, fearful that bringing the matter before the full Senate would divert their attention from other work. Though Republicans held a majority, they agreed to divide the twelve-person committee equally between themselves and Democrats. They then considered the evidence and took testimony. Claiborne argued that the errors on his tax returns were not intended to hide anything but were the result of mistakes committed by those who prepared them. He admitted having qualms about some of what he saw on the returns but did not make any effort to address them. When asked about his decision to cash large checks at Las Vegas casinos, some in the tens of thousands of dollars, Claiborne explained it away as something that was commonplace in the city and that he needed the money for home repairs. The judge also went on the attack, insisting that the Senate had to hear all testimony and require witnesses to testify, and that his conviction necessitated proof beyond a reasonable doubt. Taking the position that impeachment was a political process as opposed to a criminal one, members of the Senate paid Claiborne no heed.

When it came time to vote, the Senate in October 1986 approved three of the four articles by large, bipartisan margins. The only one that failed to meet the two-thirds requirement was the third charge. Here, senators worried that adopting it would set a dangerous precedent: If a person convicted of a crime in a court of law automatically was to suffer the same fate in the Senate, then, conversely, senators would have no choice but to acquit someone in an impeachment trial who had been found not guilty by a jury of their peers.

The entire process left Claiborne's lead attorney, Oscar Goodman, frustrated. He had made sure during the trial to provide the twelve-person committee all of the evidence proving his client's innocence; yet he questioned whether, when the full Senate voted, its members had taken the time to read the committee's report. '[S]ome senators', he later stated, 'who were not privy to the facts brought out before the committee, had not read the transcripts. (The bindings of their booklets were not even creased)' (*Report of the National Commission on Judicial Discipline and Removal*, 2003: 53).

Challenging Rule XI

Goodman had not tried to challenge Rule XI in the courts, but that was about to change. The same year the Senate voted on Claiborne's case, Judge Walter Nixon (no relation to former president Richard Nixon) was on his way to the hot seat. Born in 1928 in Mississippi, Walter Nixon received a law degree from Tulane University and worked as attorney in his home state beginning in 1952. In 1968, President Lyndon Johnson appointed him to the U.S. District Court for the Southern District of Mississippi. In 1982, he became that court's chief judge.

In 1980, Nixon had purchased leases on three properties owned by businessman Wiley Fairchild, a relative of one of Nixon's friends. That same year, Wiley's son faced drug-smuggling charges. The prosecuting lawyer, Paul Holmes, later argued that Nixon spoke with him about the case, which suggested to Fairchild that his son would receive a favorable resolution. In 1984, the judge found himself before a grand jury investigating a claim that he had taken a bribe from Fairchild in return for trying to protect his son from prosecution. Found guilty of perjury in 1986, Nixon received a five-year prison sentence. Like Claiborne, the judge refused to resign, even after exhausting his appeals.

Enter the Judicial Conference of the United States. Having become aware of Nixon's conviction and unwillingness to leave the bench, the Conference invoked the Judicial Councils Reform and Judicial Conduct and Disability Act, cited Nixon for misconduct, and recommended his impeachment. An impeachment resolution prompted a Judiciary Committee subcommittee in July 1988 to pass unanimously three articles of impeachment. Similar to those adopted in the Claiborne case, the first two cited Nixon's conviction in a court of law for lying under oath, while the last one declared that the judge had sullied the judiciary's reputation. And, as with Claiborne, the Judiciary Committee and a unanimous House adopted the articles.

Called upon to try another incumbent, the Senate again invoked Rule XI, with the committee made up of members of both parties. Nixon's attorney, David Stewart, blasted the process on two counts. The third article was so broadly worded that it was all but guaranteed to lead to the conviction of his client. Additionally, Rule XI was unconstitutional, for the language of Article I, Section 3 inferred that the full Senate was to hear an impeachment trial, as opposed to a committee thereof. The twelve-person committee rejected both assertions. After taking testimony, the case went to the full Senate, which convicted the judge on the first two articles by large bipartisan margins but acquitted him on the third. Infuriated, Nixon, represented by Stewart, challenged the Senate's finding in court, focusing on what they contended as the unconstitutionality of Rule XI.

As Nixon's case wound its way through the judicial branch, the Senate found itself having to contend with yet another impeachment trial. Judge Alcee Hastings was a Florida native who had received his law degree from Florida A&M in 1963, and began work as an attorney. In 1979, President Carter, who wanted to increase the number of minorities represented in the judiciary, appointed Hastings to the District Court for the Southern District of Florida, making him the first African American appointed to a federal bench in that state. Two years later, Hastings was arrested in a sting

Figure 8.1 Judge Alcee Hastings, who sought judicial review of his impeachment and conviction. U.S. government official portrait.

operation for supposedly taking money from William Dredge, a Florida antiquarian with a long criminal record. Dredge allegedly had passed his bribes to the judge via an attorney named William Borders. Hastings contested that charge and another accusing him of trying to evade the Federal Bureau of Investigation. With the evidence against him of a largely circumstantial nature, a jury acquitted him.

However, two members of the Eleventh Circuit Judicial Council invoked the Judicial Councils Reform and Judicial Conduct and Disability Act, and lodged a complaint against Hastings, believing that he indeed had conspired with Borders. Consequently, a five-person committee was set up, one member of which Hastings had previously accused of racism. After considering the evidence, the committee concluded that Hastings had perjured himself when he denied any connection with Borders. What made the Hastings case potentially problematic was that he, unlike Claiborne and Nixon, had been acquitted of any criminal wrongdoing. Maintaining that impeachment was a political process, the committee concluded that the outcome of the criminal trial had no bearing on whether Hastings deserved impeachment, and recommended his removal from office.

In March 1987, Representatives Sensenbrenner and Henry Hyde (R-Illinois) submitted an impeachment resolution in the House. Hastings replied that he was a victim of racial animus. To address simultaneously the questions of impeachment and racism, the House Judiciary Committee turned the case over to a subcommittee led by an African American, John Conyers (D-Michigan). Invited to defend himself before Conyers' group, Hastings refused. The length of the investigation and the Senate's other business—including the Nixon trial—delayed the subcommittee's report until July of the following year. It unanimously proposed 17 articles against the judge, including for having lied under oath and involvement in a conspiracy. The House, by a bipartisan 413–3 vote, endorsed the subcommittee's findings, thus making Hastings the first African American to be impeached.

Invoking again Rule XI, the Senate chose a committee to hear evidence. Hastings contended that he faced double jeopardy. The 5th Amendment to the Constitution precludes a person from facing trial twice for the same offense. Therefore, Hastings maintained, he could not be tried in the Senate on the same charges for which he had been acquitted in a criminal court. The House managers countered that the Constitution makes a distinction between criminal trials, which have the purpose of punishing an individual for violations of the law, and impeachment trials, which aim to defend the government from officials who might cause it harm. Moreover, they said, the Founding Fathers made clear that only Congress could impeach and convict. The members of the Senate found the managers' presentation persuasive, and rejected Hastings' claim of double jeopardy. After listening to Hastings' testimony, during which he claimed his innocence, and trying (and failing) to get Borders to appear, the Upper House, along a nonpartisan vote, acquitted the judge on nine of the articles but convicted him on eight that related to conspiracy.

Hastings did the same as Walter Nixon and challenged his Senate conviction in court, citing what he regarded as the unconstitutionality of Rule XI and insisting that he was a victim of double jeopardy. By this time, Nixon's case had reached the U.S. Supreme Court, but it had yet to issue its decision. The judge who heard Hastings' appeal, Stanley Sporkin of the U.S. District Court for the District of Columbia, ruled in Hastings' favor, but he stayed his decision pending the Supreme Court's verdict regarding Nixon's appeal.

Clarifying Justiciability

The Supreme Court had heard testimony in *Nixon v. United States* [*Doc 20*] in October 1993 and handed down its ruling three months later, one with tremendous consequences for the process of impeachment. Writing for a unanimous Court, Chief Justice **William Rehnquist**—who, ironically, had been appointed to the court by Richard Nixon and who six years earlier had written a history of the Supreme Court—did not cite the Court of Claims' rejection of Halsted Ritter's appeal. But he reached the same conclusion: Impeachment involved a political question that was not justiciable.

Rehnquist based his finding on two precedents. The first was the 1962 decision *Baker v. Carr* [*Doc 15*]. That case emerged from a challenge over redistricting—that is, the drawing of the boundaries of electoral districts—in the state of Tennessee. The plaintiff, Charles Baker, the former mayor of the town of Millington, sued the state's secretary of state, Joe Carr, on the grounds that Tennessee had failed to redraw its districts since 1901. The end result was to overrepresent rural voters in the state legislature and violate the 14th Amendment's requirement that all people receive 'equal protection of the laws'. At issue was whether redistricting was a legal matter reviewable by the courts or a political question that was not.

In a 6–2 decision, the Court concluded that redistricting was justiciable. To clarify matters, Justice William Brennan, writing for the majority, explained that there were six ways to determine whether a case was of a political nature and, hence, nonjusticiable. These included: if the matter at hand constitutionally fell under the umbrella of a 'political department'; if it 'lack[ed] ... judicially discoverable and manageable standards for resolving it'; and if, by taking on the case, a court risked 'expressing lack of the respect due coordinate branches of government'. Since the Founding Fathers expressly gave the Senate, not the judiciary, the power to try impeachment cases—including, by extension, *how* it would try them—no court had the right to question Rule XI (Smith, 1994: 866–67).

Rehnquist identified another possible precedent, though—the 1969 case *Powell v. McCormack* [*Doc 16*]. The plaintiff was Representative Adam Clayton Powell, a Democrat from New York. Members of the House, led by Speaker John McCormack (D-Massachusetts), had voted in favor of a resolution to exclude Powell from Capitol Hill because of a series of scandals in which the New Yorker had been involved. The same resolution declared

Powell's seat unoccupied. Powell sued McCormack, asserting that his exclusion amounted to expulsion.

In its 7–1 ruling, the Supreme Court determined that Powell's case was justiciable, for at its center was a question of constitutional interpretation rather than a political matter that risked having two branches of government at odds with each other. Examining the Constitution's Article 1, Section 5, the Court said that Congress did have the power to expel members. Powell's colleagues had not voted to expel him, though, and so his de facto expulsion amounted to the unconstitutional removal from Congress of a person who had legally won his seat. *Powell*, said Rehnquist, was not applicable to Nixon's case, for here too the Constitution was clear regarding the Senate's power to convict people whom the House had impeached. The Supreme Court having spoken, Nixon gave up any hope of returning to the bench, and returned instead to private practice as an attorney. Meanwhile, Sporkin changed his position, upholding Hastings' conviction and removal from office.

Hastings' career in government was not over, however. Only twice had the Senate barred a person who had been impeached and convicted from holding federal office. None of the judges removed in the 1980s were on that list. In 1990, Hastings tried, but failed to become Florida's secretary of state. In 1992, though, he won a seat in the U.S. House of Representatives, where he served until his death in 2021. His example demonstrated that impeachment did not mean an end to one's career, and that the public was prepared to forgive individuals who had been removed from office.

The Question of Justiciability

The same year the Supreme Court handed down its decision in *Nixon v. United States*, Representative Sensenbrenner sought to remove from office two judges: Robert Collins of the District Court for the Eastern District of Louisiana and Robert Aguilar of the District Court for the Northern District of Columbia. Unlike Nixon or Hastings, however, lawmakers did not begin impeachment proceedings against either. Why remains a matter of debate. Like the judges of the 1980s, Collins and Aguilar faced criminal charges, so it is possible Capitol Hill wanted to wait for the courts to issue their findings before proceeding (Van Tassel and Finkelman, 1999; Kyvig, 2008).

Both judges were Carter appointments designed to increase the number of minorities sitting on the federal bench. Collins, an African American, was charged with accepting a bribe in return for offering a drug smuggler a reduced sentence. Like Hastings, he argued racism was behind the accusation, despite the fact that investigators had found the money in his chambers. Sentenced to prison in 1991, he too refused to give up his job, prompting the Judicial Conference to recommend Congress impeach him. Realizing he stood little chance of winning an impeachment trial, Collins resigned in August 1993. Aguilar, the child of Mexican immigrants, faced indictments in 1989 that included obstructing justice by revealing the existence of a wiretap.

A jury found him guilty in August 1990, a circuit court of appeals court overturned the conviction, and the U.S. Supreme Court reimposed the initial sentence and sent the case back to the appeals court. Finally, in June 1996, the Justice Department offered, and Aguilar accepted, a deal by which he resigned and, in return, received his retirement benefits.

Because neither Collins nor Aguilar had their cases reach the Senate, there was no need for the Upper House to consider usage of Rule XI. But that rule, and the Supreme Court's *Nixon* decision upholding it, generated a debate that continues to the present. Though the justices were unanimous in their vote, two of them, Byron White and Harry Blackmun, argued that Rule XI was justiciable [*Doc 21*]. Although Article I, Section 3 gave the Senate 'the sole Power to try all Impeachments', White questioned if the word 'try' proscribed the judiciary from having any say in determining whether the process was fair to the accused.

Some legal scholars have seconded the claim of justiciability. First, they argue, there is no solid evidence that the Founding Fathers intended for the Senate to have an 'absolute' power to convict. Indeed, they find it intriguing that the Framers never explicitly discounted the judiciary having the right of reviewing the impeachment process. Second, anyone who feels it would be 'disrespectful' for the judiciary potentially to second-guess the Senate need not fear, for judicial review would be used on a case-by-case basis to make sure that the Upper House did not violate the rights of the accused (Fox, 1992; Smith, 1995). If anything, say those who favor justiciability, Rule XI violated Judge Nixon's individual rights (Kainec, 1993; Brown, 1993) and, by extension, the rights of anyone else against whom it has been used—including the 5th Amendment's protection of due process (Heflin, 1990; Isenbergh, 1998).

Others demur. The Framers decided to grant the Senate rather than the Supreme Court the ultimate right to determine an impeached individual's guilt or innocence because they wanted those making that decision to be fairly large in number and accountable to the voters. Additionally, it made no sense to grant judges or justices the power to try in criminal court and, potentially, impeach and remove from public office the same person (Gerhardt, 1994). With regard to the 5th Amendment, opponents of justiciability state that there is no proof that applying that provision of the Constitution to impeachment would affect in any way how Congress conducts impeachment hearings and trials (Gerhardt, 2019).

A final argument concerns the matter of political upheaval. In *Nixon v. United States*, the Supreme Court warned that allowing judicial review would 'expos[e] ... the country's political life—particularly if the President were impeached—to months, or perhaps years, of chaos during judicial review of Senate impeachment proceedings'. Justiciability's champions reject such thinking. The Senate, they argue, would act much more cautiously and make sure it addressed any 'constitutional defects' in its hearings to guarantee a quick decision by the judiciary (Kainec, 1993: 1524). One question is how daunting the interim would be for the judicial branch as a judge or justice waited for the outcome of their appeal. On the one hand, lower courts have had substitute judges take over the caseloads of jurists who have been unable to do their job, and the Supreme Court has historically operated with fewer than nine justices. On the other hand, a petitioner appearing, say, before the Supreme Court could find themselves on the losing end of a 4–4 ruling that might otherwise have been decided in their favor if the ninth justice was on the bench.

Another question is the president. Opponents of review consider it dangerous to believe that a chief executive seeking a review of their impeachment and conviction will have their case heard by a court in short order. In the meantime, the government would end up paralyzed as it waited to find out if the Senate needed to retry the nation's top political official. Could the vice president legitimately assume the president's duties as ascribed by the 25th Amendment pending the courts' rulings? Could any decisions the vice president made while serving as the acting president suddenly be overturned if the president won both their appeal and acquittal by the Senate? Which commander-in-chief would the military obey? The one impeached, convicted, and returned to office, or the one who, at least temporarily, took their place? Conversely, if in its initial trial the Senate acquitted the president, what would keep the House managers from asking the courts to step in (Black and Bobbitt, 2018; Sweeney, 1974; Firmage and Mangrum, 1974)? A final consideration is that of legitimacy. Could a president who had been impeached and convicted, but had held onto their office following appeal retain the legitimacy necessary to conduct effectively the affairs of state? While it appears the Supreme Court has put to rest the question of judicial review of impeachment procedures, the ongoing debate suggests the subject could come up again in the future.

9 Presidents and (Bi)Partisanship

At the time James Sensenbrenner submitted his resolution to impeach judges Robert Collins and Robert Aguilar, the historical record showed that most impeachments singled out members of the judiciary. This made sense, for the number of people sitting on federal benches had grown substantially since the founding of the country, commensurate with America's expanding geography and demography. In 1900, a total of 101 judges sat on district and circuit courts, in addition to the nine on the Supreme Court. In 1951, that number had increased to 233 (including the nine Supreme Court justices), and 752 by 1989 (Stephens, 1952). Similarly, the sum total of cases filed in federal court had swollen from 15,000 in 1915 to 120,000 in 1975 and 275,000 as of 1989 (Peterson, 1993). And, while the payroll of the executive branch had increased as well, there remained throughout only one president and one vice president.

Although presidents had faced talk of impeachment, only one, Andrew Johnson, had his case come before Congress—though Richard Nixon certainly would have, had he not resigned. This could be attributed to several factors, including the prestige surrounding the office, the potential political and economic instability that might accompany removing the country's leader, or the political ramifications a lawmaker might face for endorsing the impeachment of a president who is of the same party. Moreover, a president serves a certain number of years and answers directly to the voters. Dismissing a jurist, who holds lifetime tenure, was less likely to disrupt the nation because there were hundreds of others in the judiciary to take up their caseload.

The apparent immunity of the person serving in the Oval Office to impeachment began to dissipate as the twentieth century came to an end. Thanks to a deepening political divide, at least some opponents were certain to treat a president's actions as impeachable, even if arguably not so. Meanwhile, the chief executive's supporters were equally likely to label the accusers as partisan hacks. Such charges and counterclaims also increasingly surrounded those in the executive who served at the president's discretion or, conversely, posed a real or perceived threat to the Oval Office's occupant.

DOI: 10.4324/9781003565680-11

Reagan and Bush

The 1980 presidential election reflected the continued postwar backlash against liberalism. A crisis involving U.S. hostages held in Iran, a feeling that the United States had failed to stand up to the international communist threat, and a weak economy marked by high unemployment and inflation turned the electorate against the incumbent president and Democratic nominee, Jimmy Carter. His challenger, a former actor and governor of California named Ronald Reagan, came from the Republican Party's right wing. Reagan pledged to strengthen the U.S. military, take on communism abroad, solve the country's economic problems through tax and spending cuts, and promote 'family values'. He won in a landslide, securing votes not just from traditional Democratic constituencies such as labor unions but also from conservatives, including a burgeoning fundamentalist Christian movement upset with the Supreme Court's 1962 decision barring school-sponsored prayer, its 1973 judgment protecting the right to abortion, and other perceived threats to God's will.

In addition to displaying the growing power of conservatism, Reagan's election reflected the country's expanding political divide. Ideological differences, of course, were not new and had made themselves apparent in previous impeachment efforts, whether they be President Andrew Johnson after the Civil War, Judge Charles Swayne in the first decade of the 1900s, or Labor Secretary Frances Perkins in the 1930s. They appeared again in 1981, when Representative Henry González (D-Texas), who had long criticized the Federal Reserve Board (FRB) because he felt it had too much power, tried and failed to impeach FRB chairman Paul Volcker, a Carter appointee whom Reagan had kept on. González made at least two more attempts during the decade to remove Volcker, with the same result. What had changed, however, was the almost routine nature, beginning with Reagan, of accusing the president of impeachable crimes. And, whereas in Watergate members of the chief executive's party stood against him despite the political risks involved, deepening partisan discord made that increasingly less likely as the century came to an end.

What got Reagan in trouble was an arms-for-hostages deal that, unbeknownst to the American public at the time, the president himself had approved. In an attempt to free Americans being held against their will by terrorists with ties to Iran, members of the administration green-lighted arms sales to Teheran, which violated a law banning aid to that country. Money from those transactions went to the Contras, an anticommunist group in Nicaragua fighting the leftist Sandinista government there. That too was illegal, for Congress had outlawed such assistance in 1982. The so-called **Iran–Contra scandal** became public knowledge in 1986, when the Sandinistas shot down a plane and captured the pilot, who admitted bringing arms to the Contras. Afterward, a Lebanese national newspaper reported on the secret arms shipments to Iran.

To avoid charges of a cover-up similar to Watergate, in December 1986 Reagan created a special commission to examine what had happened. Headed by Senator John Tower (D-Texas), it took testimony from over 80 witnesses, including Reagan himself. Simultaneously, Attorney General Edwin Meese named a fellow Republican and former judge, Lawrence Walsh, to begin his own inquiry. The House and Senate, for their part, established their own investigative bodies that they merged into a single committee, headed by Representative Dick Cheney (R-Wyoming) and Senator Daniel Inouye (D-Hawaii).

In November 1987, González entered the fray when he submitted a resolution calling for Reagan's impeachment. While his was not the only voice favoring that measure, most lawmakers and Americans rejected it. One reason was lack of proof. The White House stymied Walsh by limiting cooperation with his inquiry. Two witnesses who appeared before the Tower Committee, National Security Adviser John Poindexter and a Marine Corps colonel named Oliver North, assumed the roles of mavericks who acted without Reagan's knowledge. Reagan himself claimed from the start that he was unaware of what Poindexter, North, and others were doing. He maintained that position when he appeared before the Tower Committee, and repeatedly declared his inability to recall specifics surrounding the scandal when questioned about them. In fact, in its report, published in February 1987, the committee blamed the president's '"lax" management style' as opposed to the president himself (Ling, 2021: 205). The lack of solid evidence of malfeasance set Inouye against pursuing Reagan.

Public opinion also gave lawmakers reason for pause. While a poll just prior to Reagan's congressional testimony found that just over half of Americans believed he had lied about his lack of knowledge of the Iran–Contra affair, his job approval remained high. In part, this was because of an improved economy. Additionally, the president had made progress with the Soviet Union's recently appointed leader, Mikhail Gorbachev, in negotiations to control the nuclear arms race, which not only pleased the U.S. public but also made Congress wary that pursuing impeachment could disrupt those talks. Finally, partisan politics had an impact. While most Americans doubted Reagan's veracity, they split ideologically over whether what he had done in any way compared to Watergate. Among them was Cheney, who was also a Reagan loyalist. Indeed, whereas two-thirds of Democrats viewed Watergate and Iran–Contra as of equal seriousness, only one-third of Republicans did.

Reagan's decision to sign a major arms agreement with Gorbachev in 1987 and, even more important, the strong U.S. economy allowed the vice president, **George H. W. Bush**, to run on his boss's coattails and win the presidency in 1988. Two years later, Iraq's president, Saddam Hussein, ordered the invasion and occupation of neighboring Kuwait, and raised the specter that he might try to take Saudi Arabia. If that happened, the Iraqi leader would have control over about one-quarter of the globe's oil reserves. To stop Hussein, Bush had the United States lead an international coalition that sent troops to protect Saudi Arabia in 1990. The following year, that same alliance launched a ground invasion of Iraq to free Kuwait, a goal it achieved in a matter of weeks. Shortly after that ground attack, Representative González submitted a resolution to the House Judiciary Committee calling for Bush's impeachment on the grounds that most of the U.S. troops came from minority backgrounds, that the president had violated the Constitution for not seeking congressional consent to go to war, and that the war would kill numerous innocent civilians. That was as far as his resolution got.

Clinton

Bush's successor, Bill Clinton, was not so lucky. The governor of Arkansas ran as the Democratic nominee for president in 1992, calling himself a 'New Democrat' who believed the country should rely more on the private sector than the government to solve its problems. Those problems included the economy, which had gone into recession into 1991, and, though improving by 1992, still seemed to many Americans as weak. His campaign also preached 'inclusiveness', which drew him the support of women, members of the LGBTQ community, and others.

Clinton's hero, President John F. Kennedy, had not been faithful to his wife, Jackie, and rumors had swirled around Clinton that he too had not abided by his vows to his spouse, Hillary. What turned those rumors into

Figure 9.1 Bill Clinton, the second president to be impeached. Official White House photo.

reality was what appeared to be an unrelated case involving a failed real estate venture in which the Clintons were parties. An investigation found no evidence of criminal conduct by either Bill or Hillary, but persistent public questions about their role prompted the president to have his attorney general, Janet Reno, appoint an independent counsel, Robert Fiske, to look into the matter. The fact that Clinton's attorney general had named the person to investigate the chief executive engendered claims of a conflict of interest. Fiske therefore stepped down, and an independent panel of three judges appointed Kenneth Starr as his replacement.

During his investigation, Starr learned of a separate matter involving Paula Jones. A state employee in Arkansas, she accused then-Governor Clinton of sexual harassment, and in 1994 filed suit in federal court. Now-President Clinton's lawyers adopted the stand taken by the Justice Department's Office of Legal Counsel in its 1973 memo, insisting that trying to defend himself would take up time the president needed for more pressing national and international matters. In May 1997, the Supreme Court unanimously demurred in *Clinton v. Jones* [*Doc 22*]. Fifteen years earlier, the Court had determined in the case *Nixon v. Fitzgerald* that a sitting president was immune from civil lawsuits that arose from their official acts, and it repeated that finding in *Clinton*. But Jones had sued for wrongdoings of an unofficial nature committed by Clinton before the entered office, and for those, wrote the justices, he was not free from liability.

With the case allowed to go forward, Jones' lawyers continued their preparations. While doing so, they and Starr learned of a sexual relationship Clinton had had with a White House intern named Monica Lewinsky. During his deposition before Jones' lawyers, Clinton denied under oath Jones' charges. When asked if he had had 'sexual relations' with Lewinsky, which Jones' attorneys defined as vaginal sex, the president said no (as his meetings with the intern had involved oral acts). Starr concluded that Clinton had perjured himself and, with Reno's approval, expanded his investigation to include Lewinsky.

The salacious story garnered the attention of the U.S. media and public starting in early 1998. Clinton publicly denied the accusations of infidelity or lying, but he found himself on the defensive when one of Lewinsky's friends turned over to Starr a dress the intern had worn during one of her trysts. On it was a sample of the president's semen. The special counsel therefore had Clinton appear before a grand jury. There, the president admitted to an 'inappropriate' relationship with Lewinsky, but again refused to admit to anything sexual in nature. Simultaneously, he told the American people that he had lied to them when he said he had not had an affair with Lewinsky, but refused to admit to any legal malfeasance.

Republicans saw an opportunity. Their candidate, George H. W. Bush, had lost to Clinton in 1992. In 1994, they had regained control of Congress and used their power to try to force the president to cut spending on various federal programs. When he said no, they refused to fund the government and forced a shutdown of nonessential federal agencies during the winter of 1995–1996. The angry public reaction to the Grand Old Party's (GOP's) heavy-handed measures, Clinton's success in claiming for himself issues that conservatives had long championed—such as relying more heavily on the private sector and preaching 'family values'—and an improved economy helped him win a second term in 1996 (though Republicans maintained control on Capitol Hill). In a comment reflective of the capital's deepening political polarization, Republican Tom DeLay of Texas, the House majority whip, said in 1997 that he favored impeaching judges whose beliefs did not align with his own. Now, he and many of his colleagues saw a chance to remove Clinton. Republicans in the House had Starr release his report in September 1998, and followed that by calling for the Judiciary Committee to pass a resolution to impeach the president.

While Clinton's infidelity and the pornographic details in the Starr Report appalled many Americans, they shared the opinion of Democrats who adopted an argument akin to that used by President Andrew Johnson's defenders: There was a difference between a president's personal conduct (including lying to hide an affair) and his professional conduct as the nation's chief executive. Most important, the president had high approval ratings, with the economy humming along, and inflation and unemployment both low. In language that President Donald Trump's defenders would use two decades later, some Clinton supporters accused the chief executive's opponents of attempting a 'coup' (Whittington, 2020b: 670). They were willing to see Clinton censured but not impeached. Even so, House Republicans pressed forward.

Hoping to prove his objectivity, House Judiciary Committee chairman Henry Hyde (R-Illinois) offered to run his hearings akin to those of Peter Rodino during Watergate. Democrats, though, cited Hyde as being part of a broader GOP 'fishing expedition' (Baker, 2018: 174). Along a strict party-line vote, the Judiciary Committee in October submitted four articles of impeachment, including perjury and obstruction of justice, with only Republican Representative Lindsey Graham of South Carolina voting nay on one of the charges. Democrats rallied around the president. Alcee Hastings, the same individual who as a judge had been impeached and who now served in the House, called for doing the same to Starr, but received the cold shoulder, including from Democrats. Voters also expressed their displeasure, giving Democrats on Election Day five more House seats (though they were still in the minority); it was just the third time since the Civil War that the president's party had gained seats in a midterm election. Even with the electorate's obvious sentiment, Republicans took their effort to the full House in December. There, two of the four articles passed along largely partisan lines, with only five Democrats voting to impeach. It was the first time an elected president had been impeached.

Observers knew the GOP's pursuit of Clinton would die in the Senate, where Republicans held 55 seats—well short of the two-thirds threshold to convict. During the trial, Clinton's lawyers argued that, while what the president had done was immoral, he had not committed any impeachable acts. Senators also heard from Monica Lewinsky, White House aide Sidney Blumenthal, and Vernon Jordan, a friend of the president who had tried to help Lewinsky find a job in New York City. Both Lewinsky and Jordan denied doing anything wrong, while Blumenthal offered nothing new in his testimony. After 36 days of hearings, the Senate voted, with all Democrats proclaiming Clinton not guilty on both counts; ten Republicans joined them on the first article (perjury) and five on the second (obstruction of justice). The partisan nature of the effort to remove Clinton actually led his approval rating to rise to 73 percent, the highest ever during his two terms in office.

In two respects, the effort to impeach Clinton resembled the case of Andrew Johnson more than Richard Nixon. Talk of removing Nixon from office quickly developed a bipartisan tone; partisan politics drove the desire to remove Clinton, as had they had Johnson (Baker, 2001; Rae and Campbell, 2004; Baker, 2018). Moreover, there were serious questions one could ask regarding whether either Johnson or Clinton had committed impeachable offenses. The constitutionality of the Tenure of Office Act was in doubt, as presidents have the right to remove members of their cabinet. As for Clinton, most legal experts contend that his wrongdoing was of a personal nature that, unlike President Nixon, involved no abuse of his office. While Clinton may have lied under oath, a president could not be impeached if, say, he perjured himself regarding a traffic ticket or a friend who accidentally broke a neighbor's window. Nor have presidents been impeached for lying about the rationale for going to war (Sunstein, 1998; Bloch, 2000; Neumann, 2007; Phillips and Yoo, 2021).

Some, however, contend that Clinton indeed lied under oath—an impeachable offense (Cooper, 1999; Posner, 1999)—but the partisan politics that Alexander Hamilton feared saved him from removal from office (Turley, 1999; McNulty, 2019). It was that partisanship that worried the legal scholar Cass R. Sunstein. 'The 1998 impeachment of President Clinton', he wrote that same year, 'may signal more frequent resort to the impeachment mechanism, especially in a world in which recent events are highly salient, and in which political opponents like to play "tit for tat".' He continued that, 'in an era in which the opposing party and the mass media are likely to be aligned in accusing political opponents of criminality or severe misconduct, there is a continuing risk that impeachment proceedings will become decreasingly exceptional' (Sunstein, 1998: 280, 281).

The Judiciary a Target

In one respect, Sunstein was incorrect. Judges continued to be targets of impeachment for violating the Constitution's provision on good behavior or engaging in lawbreaking, as opposed to their political leanings. In 2006, Judge

Manuel L. Real of the Central District Court of California became a subject of controversy for allegedly aiding a debtor whom he had placed on probation following that person's criminal conviction. Representative Sensenbrenner, who now chaired the Judiciary Committee, introduced a resolution to impeach Real, but it went no further than that. In 2009, the House of Representatives impeached Judge Samuel Kent of the Southern District of Texas for the sexual assault of two coworkers and obstruction of justice. Before the Senate could begin its trial, however, he resigned. Five years later, Representative Terri Sewell (D-Alabama) asked the Judiciary Committee to consider impeaching Mark Fuller of the Middle District Court of Alabama after his arrest for domestic abuse. Rather than face possible dismissal from his judgeship, Fuller quit.

One judge, however, became the first (and, so far, only) of the twenty-first century to have his case reach the Senate. In 2008, the House began an inquiry into Judge G. Thomas Porteous, Jr., of the Eastern District Court of Louisiana on charges of perjury and corruption. Two years later, the House of Representatives unanimously passed four articles against him for those same crimes. Porteous argued that the behavior cited took place before he became a federal judge, and therefore he could not be impeached for it. The House managers replied that such a defense was not constitutionally valid. The Senate agreed. Citing in part Porteous' violations of the Ethics in Government Act, it passed the first article unanimously and the other three by large majorities, and prohibited him from ever holding federal office again.

In another respect, though, Sunstein was prescient, for even if ideology was not the reason for efforts to impeach the aforementioned judges, it increasingly became justification for doing so. Many of those who sought to remove people from federal office came from the political right. Georgia's Republican Newt Gingrich, who served as speaker of the House from 1995 to 1999, said in 2005 that he favored impeaching a number of circuit court judges who declared unconstitutional the maxim 'one nation under God'. That same year, members of the GOP on Capitol Hill demanded the courts force the insertion of a feeding tube into Terri Schiavo, a Florida woman who had entered a permanent vegetative state in 1990 following a heart attack that left her brain severely damaged. Doctors kept her alive using a feeding tube, but her husband stated she would not have wanted to remain in such a condition. When he petitioned a court in 1998 to remove the tube, Schiavo's parents took him to court, believing both her husband's claim and the doctors' diagnosis were wrong. Some in the GOP said that they would seek the impeachment of any judge who took the husband's side. Not until 2005 was Schiavo's feeding tube removed, after which she passed away. In 2005 as well, some leading conservatives—among them a key opponent of the Equal Rights Amendment for women, Phyllis Schlafly—demanded the impeachment of Supreme Court Justice Anthony Kennedy. A Reagan appointee, Schlafly and others asserted that Kennedy had become too moderate in his views to stay on the Court.

Cass Sunstein's comment regarding the media also had merit. The effort to impeach Clinton was the first that took place in the era of 24-hour news networks and the internet. Starting in 1980, Americans could turn to the first of those day-long news channels, Cable News Network (CNN), but conservatives charged that it and the big three U.S. TV commercial broadcasting networks—the National Broadcasting Company (NBC), the Columbia Broadcasting System (CBS), and the American Broadcasting Company (ABC)—were too liberal. To combat the so-called 'mainstream media', Australian media mogul Rupert Murdoch in 1996 founded Fox News, which appealed to conservative voters. That same year, NBC spun off MSNBC (Microsoft NBC), which was more liberal in orientation. The internet, founded in the early 1980s, became a global phenomenon with the development of the World Wide Web in 1990. By the middle of that decade, there were more than 10,000 servers on the web and over 10 million users. On the one hand, these new information outlets meant it was possible at any time to learn the latest news (be it based on fact or innuendo), including that surrounding Clinton's impeachment. On the other hand, it became easier for Americans to find press reporting and web sites that validated their own views and to ignore those that did not.

Bush and Obama

While most of the attacks against federal incumbents came from the political right, some came from the left. In 2000, the Republican nominee for the presidency, **George W. Bush**, defeated his Democratic opponent and Clinton's vice president, Al Gore. A son of former president George H. W. Bush, the GOP candidate called himself a 'compassionate conservative', and his deep religious commitment, support for small government, and desire for tax cuts garnered him enough support to win one of closest and most controversial elections in U.S. history. In September of the following year, terrorists affiliated with the group al-Qaeda hijacked four commercial jets, crashing them into the World Trade Center in New York City and the Pentagon in Washington, and killing 3000 people. To prevent another attack, Bush ordered U.S. troops to invade Afghanistan, where al-Qaeda had training bases; got Congress to pass legislation to make it easier to conduct searches and wiretaps; and established a new Department of Homeland Security. Claiming that Iraqi leader Saddam Hussein sought to obtain weapons of mass destruction and was an al-Qaeda ally, the president, with widespread congressional support, had U.S. forces invade Iraq in 2003 and oust Hussein. Bush and his top aides anticipated a quick victory in Iraq that would replace Hussein's dictatorship with a democracy and allow the United States in short order to leave. Instead, it became a drawn-out, deadly fight that took a toll on the president's popularity.

As early as March 2003, just prior to the invasion of Iraq, Representative John Conyers (D-Michigan) of the House Judiciary Committee held hearings to consider impeaching Bush, Vice President Dick Cheney, and Attorney General John Ashcroft for violating international law by encouraging the assault on Iraq. Three years later, former Congresswoman Elizabeth Holtzman, journalist Cynthia Cooper, reporter Dave Lindorff, and constitutionalist Barbara Olshansky made their own case for impeachment, citing not only the war against Iraq but also illegal wiretaps, the use of torture on enemy combatants, and the president's handling of the damage caused in 2005 to the U.S. Gulf Coast by Hurricane Katrina. In 2008, Representative Dennis Kucinich (D-Ohio) joined the fray. Among his 35 articles of impeachment, the president had lied to the American public to justify the Iraq war. In all of these instances, the Judiciary Committee decided not to pursue the charges.

Nor did cases against Donald Rumsfeld or Jay Bybee get as far as their opponents wanted. In 2003, Congressman Charles Rangel (D-New York) sought and failed to impeach Rumsfeld, Bush's secretary of defense, for his role in getting the United States mired in the Iraq conflict. The campaign against Bybee had its origins in 2002, when, as the president's assistant attorney general, he signed a memorandum justifying coercive interrogation techniques on captured terrorists, including waterboarding. The next year, Bush appointed him to the Ninth Circuit Court of Appeals. In 2009, Bybee came to the attention of Professor Bruce Ackerman of Yale University, who sought his impeachment for endorsing torture. Others joined the call, including Congressman Jerrold Nadler (D-New York), but their campaign never reached the floor of the House.

The combination of an unpopular war in Iraq and a serious economic downturn in 2008 swung opinion against Republicans and in favor of the Democratic nominee for the presidency, **Barack Obama**. The nation's first (and so far only) African American president, Obama had worked as a state senator in Illinois and won a seat to the U.S. Senate from that state in 2004 before he sought the Oval Office. More liberal in his views than Bush, he supported a stimulus program to help the United States out of its economic troubles, signed the Affordable Care Act (ACA) that provided federal subsidies so all Americans could have health insurance, and began the process of withdrawing U.S. troops from Iraq. As with Bush, Obama and his aides became the target of opposition calls for his impeachment. Among the claims: Obama had offered patronage to a Pennsylvania representative, Joe Sestak, so that Sestak would not run against one of the state's incumbent senators, Arlen Specter; he participated in covering up a terrorist attack on the U.S. embassy in Libya in 2012; he released criminals from U.S. prisons who were in the country illegally; and he backed the ACA, which infringed the 10th Amendment's protection of states' rights. None of these proposals made it to the article-writing phase, largely because the Republican speaker of the House, John Boehner of Ohio, knew that, in light of public opposition to such a move, his party would suffer at the polls.

The (In)Credibility of Impeachment?

Five years after Bill Clinton's impeachment, the historian Lewis Gould wrote in a book on the presidency,

> To be a viable part of the constitutional process, presidential impeachment should not be used lightly, nor, once begun, is it good for an effort to fail ... If impeachment is seen merely as a potential annoyance, acted upon out of partisanship, then it loses much of its credibility and deterrent capacity.
>
> (Gould, 2003: 230)

In an age of deep political divisions, however, impeachment by the end of the century had become a weapon to threaten or, if it worked, to remove from office those regarded as having distasteful viewpoints. What was once regarded as a 'nuclear' option, particularly when directed against the country's most powerful political leader, had become, if anything, more routine.

10 Flexing the Impeachment 'Muscle'

In 2016, the Republican chair of the House Oversight and Government Reform Committee, Jason Chaffetz of Utah, called impeachment 'a muscle that has atrophied over time'. He continued, 'Get that muscle working again—this should be a common occurrence, this shouldn't be once in a century' (Wegmann, 2016). Arguably, that 'muscle' had begun to flex itself far more commonly than in the past, with conservatives leading the effort against their political opponents. In September 2014, Senator Ted Cruz (R-Texas), threatened to impeach President Barack Obama's attorney general, Eric Holder, if Holder did not investigate the Internal Revenue Service (IRS) for politically motivated targeting of conservative organizations, despite a lack of evidence to substantiate the charge. In September of the following year, Representative Paul Gosar (R-Arizona), who had long complained about what he regarded as excessive government regulations, tried to impeach Obama's head of the Environmental Protection Agency, Regina McCarthy, asserting she had perjured herself during congressional testimony. Then, in 2016, Chaffetz went after the head of the IRS, John Koskinen. He and the members of the right-wing Freedom Caucus, made up of conservative Republicans, reiterated Cruz's charges, and declared that Koskinen had abused his agency's power and misled lawmakers about his intentions. Their proposed resolutions all died in the Judiciary Committee.

For Democrats, Republicans wanted to use impeachment (or the threat thereof) for nothing more than political gain. Matthew Miller, who had worked for Holder, said of the threat against the attorney general, 'The more time [Republicans] spend on this, the crazier and more out of touch they would look' (Bresnahan, 2013). Elijah Cummings (D-Maryland) blasted the threat against Koskinen—and, by extension, others the Grand Old Party (GOP) politically disfavored—calling it a 'Republican obsession with diving into investigative rabbit holes that waste tens of millions of taxpayer dollars while having absolutely no positive impact on a single American' (Schleifer and LoBianco, 2015).

Republicans leveled similar charges just a few years later at Democrats. This time, the target was one of their own, President Donald Trump. Not only did Trump become the first president to be impeached twice by the

DOI: 10.4324/9781003565680-12

House, but those impeachments also raised serious questions about the ability to hold accountable elected officials in an age of deeply divided public opinion and partisan politics.

Trump—Round One

With President Obama unable to seek a third term in office, Democrats selected as their nominee Hillary Clinton. Following her tenure in the White House as first lady, she had served as both a New York State senator and as Obama's secretary of state. Republicans chose a billionaire real estate mogul, Donald Trump. Although Clinton won the popular vote, Trump's anti-globalist, anti-immigrant, America-first platform amassed him enough support to capture the all-important Electoral College. It marked the first time in U.S. history that a person without governmental or military experience had secured the presidency.

The political polarization by this time had become so deep that even the concept of a 'fact' came into question. Two days after his inauguration, Trump's counselor, Kellyanne Conway, argued that there were 'alternative facts', thereby suggesting that 'truth' was a misnomer. Media outlets such as Fox News allowed conservatives who accused the 'mainstream media' of bending the truth to fit a liberal agenda to hear opinions more in line with their own. Social media helped deepen this political divide. At the time of

Figure 10.1 Donald Trump, the only president impeached twice. Official White House photo by Shealah Craighead.

Fox News' founding, the internet was in its infancy, and social media outlets like Facebook (now Meta) and Twitter (now X) did not exist. By 2010, though, Facebook and Twitter had both been established, and the internet had more than 200 million domain names globally and over 266 million users in North America alone. With a few clicks of a mouse, it became even easier to select from any number of web sites that, like 24-hour news stations, validated one's own opinions, even if the factual basis of their presentations was, at best, questionable. The ability to 'spin' the truth reached the point that Trump during the 2016 campaign bragged he could murder someone in cold blood, and get away with it by asserting that it was committed in self-defense. Even the Senate, which the Founding Fathers had hoped would avoid the political pitfalls of the House during impeachment, was not immune. A study in 2019 found that the Upper House was more polarized than at any time in U.S. history for which there were statistics—that is, since about 1880 (Hollis-Brusky, 2020: 507).

Almost immediately upon taking office, Trump faced calls for his impeachment. One argument was that he had violated the Constitution's Article I, Section 9, Clause 8, also known as the 'Emoluments Clause'. This provision prohibits any federal officer from receiving, 'without the Consent of the Congress ... any present, Emolument, Office, or Title, of any kind whatever, from any King, Prince, or foreign State'. The purpose of that clause was to prevent any U.S. government official, particularly the president, from falling under the influence of foreign interests. According to his critics, Trump had failed to divest himself of his business ventures, including some in other countries. Additionally, he had permitted foreign officials to use his real estate, including leasing property in New York City's Trump Tower.

Another argument had to do with the 2016 presidential campaign. Less than a month after Trump's inauguration, his national security adviser, Michael Flynn, had to resign. The reason was that he had lied to Vice President Mike Pence concerning discussions Flynn had had with the Russian ambassador to the United States, Sergey Kislyak. Those conversations had to do with sanctions the United States had imposed on Moscow after Russia launched a military campaign against its neighbor, Ukraine, in 2014. News of the Flynn–Kislyak talks and Flynn's resignation moved the Federal Bureau of Investigation (FBI) to look into possible collusion between the White House and Russia. Matters grew more heated after Trump fired the FBI's director, James Comey, and admitted that he did so because of the inquiry. The aura of malfeasance prompted the acting FBI director, Rod Rosenstein, to appoint **Robert Mueller** (himself a former head of the FBI) as special counsel, and authorized him to continue probing the Trump–Russia relationship. At issue for Mueller was whether Trump, by trying to stop the FBI inquest and firing Comey, had knowingly obstructed justice. That Trump cashiered his attorney general, Jeff Sessions, after Sessions recused himself from Mueller's investigation only added to the sense that the president had something to hide.

The questions swirling around Trump encouraged Harvard University law professor Laurence Tribe in May 2017 to call for impeaching the president. Two months later, Democratic Representative Brad Sherman of California submitted articles to do just that, accusing Trump of obstructing justice and abusing his power. The bill, however, got nowhere, in large part because Republicans controlled the House. Meanwhile, seconding Trump's claims that the Mueller probe was 'rigged' and a 'witch hunt', some GOP lawmakers took the unprecedented step of demanding an investigation of those investigating the president, starting with Rod Rosenstein. When Rosenstein rebuffed demands from Republicans on Capitol Hill for documents related to Mueller's work (as well as other inquests), two members of the Freedom Caucus, Congressmen Mark Meadows (R-North Carolina) and Jim Jordan (R-Ohio), championed an effort in July 2018 to file articles to impeach the FBI director. Trump's opponents saw the maneuver as an effort to deter Mueller's investigation and protect the president. Concern that pressing forward would divide the GOP—not of all whose members favored trying to remove Rosenstein—convinced Meadows and Jordan to back down.

Further intensifying the debate was Mueller's investigation and report. The special counsel found evidence to bring charges against Trump's 2016 campaign chairman, Paul Manafort, co-chair Rick Gates, and a lawyer who worked with Manafort, Alex van der Zwaan. Mueller also reached a plea agreement with Flynn. (Trump later pardoned all of them except Gates, who served 45 days in jail and 3 years' probation.) While Mueller raised the possibility that Trump himself had obstructed justice, he took into account the Office of Legal Counsel's (OLC) 1973 memo—which the OLC had reconfirmed in 2000—that a sitting president could not face indictment. As such, Mueller (2019) concluded that holding the president accountable for any violations of the law 'requires a process other than the criminal justice system'. As an indication of how politically polarized the country had become, numerous Republicans in Washington rushed to Trump's defense, as did 75 percent of Republican voters. Conversely, 86 percent of Democrats concluded the special counsel had conducted an objective, fair inquiry.

Then, in August 2019, a whistleblower in the U.S. intelligence community alleged that, the month previous, Trump had phoned Ukraine's president, Volodymyr Zelensky. In the call, Trump reportedly demanded a quid pro quo: Zelensky was to investigate President Obama's vice president (and possible Democratic presidential nominee), Joe Biden, and Biden's son Hunter with regard to Hunter's activities as a board member of a Ukrainian natural gas company. If Zelensky refused, Trump would not provide Ukraine with recently approved military aid to defend itself against Russia. News of the complaint reached the media and piqued the interest of Democrats, who had regained control of the House in the 2018 midterm elections. The chair of the House Intelligence Committee, Adam Schiff (D-California), demanded a copy of the whistleblower's report, only to have Trump's acting director of national intelligence, Joseph Maguire, refuse. Angered with the administration's stonewalling, House Speaker Nancy Pelosi (D-California) asked a half-dozen House committees to see if there was enough evidence to impeach the president. Though the White House stated it would not cooperate with the inquiry, three House committees gathered enough proof through documents and witness testimony to determine that Trump had indeed demanded the deal spelled out by the whistleblower. Both the president's counsel, Pat Cipollone, and the president himself received invitations to appear before the Judiciary Committee. In so doing, they could have presented evidence to explain the White House's actions. Not only did they refuse, but Cipollone sent a letter accusing Democrats of trying to undermine the outcome of the 2016 election and democracy itself. Rebuffed, the Judiciary Committee authored two articles of impeachment. The first charged Trump with abusing his power as president by trying to influence the 2020 election. The second cited him with obstructing the House's investigation by refusing to cooperate with its inquiry. Along near-perfect party-line votes, both passed the full House. Only two Democrats and one independent (who caucused with the GOP) broke ranks on the first article, while three Democrats voted 'no' on the second.

In the Senate, Trump's lawyers, among them Harvard professor Alan Dershowitz, contended that the president could only be impeached if he broke existing criminal law, which they said he did not. Dershowitz then relied on Supreme Court Justice Benjamin Curtis' defense of President Andrew Johnson, asserting the Founding Fathers considered phrases like 'obstruction of Congress' and 'abuse of power' so vague and broad that they could not be impeachable; otherwise, the president would find himself at the mercy of the legislature (Sumrall, 2020: 953). The House managers countered that Trump's attorneys wrongly tried to make impeachment a criminal process, when it is in fact political in nature.

Republicans held a 53-seat majority in the Senate, so there was no chance of it convicting the president. Even before the case was handed over to them, some Senate Republicans said they did not believe that what Trump had done constituted an impeachable offense. Two of them, Lindsey Graham of South Carolina and majority leader Mitch McConnell of Kentucky, announced that they had already decided to acquit. Moreover, Republicans refused to permit witness testimony or to allow new evidence, even though Trump's former national security adviser, John Bolton, said he could offer proof supporting the claims of a quid pro quo with Ukraine. In February 2020, every Democrat and the Senate's two independents voted for both articles. Republicans unanimously acquitted Trump on the second count; on the first, only Mitt Romney of Utah broke ranks and joined Democrats in favoring conviction.

James Madison had expected senators to set aside their political predilections and allow the evidence to determine their vote. But the outcome suggested, as had been the case with Ronald Reagan and Bill Clinton, that a president's popularity, particularly with the party base, could affect the outcome. Trump's approval rating at the time of the Senate trial stood at about

40 percent—higher than Nixon's at the height of Watergate; but his base, which was unswervingly loyal, was particularly strong in smaller red states from which most of the GOP's senators came. To many of those red-state voters, Democrats had proven nothing. If anything, they averred, the phone call with President Zelensky might have been nothing more than an innocent effort to improve ties with Ukraine. In their minds, Democrats had conspired to stage a coup and overthrow Trump, and maybe even his vice president, Mike Pence. If that happened, then one of their own, Speaker Nancy Pelosi, would assume the presidency. Simply put, to vote for conviction was for many Republicans a political death sentence.

Contributing to the debate over Trump's guilt or innocence were 'bots', or 'automated social media accounts'. The internet and the ease of accessing it allowed bots to manipulate what appeared on widely used social media sites, emphasizing certain news stories and spreading misinformation. According to one study of Trump's impeachment, bots made up less than 1 percent of all accounts that addressed impeachment, but constituted almost one-third of all impeachment-related content. They were also '66 times more active than normal human users' (Rossetti and Zaman, 2023: 2), allowing them quickly to spread their message.

Trump—Round Two

Nine months after the 2020 Senate vote, Americans went to the polls and elected the Democratic nominee, Joe Biden. Trump, however, refused to concede. Claiming for months that his opponents intended to 'rig' the election, he and a significant proportion of his supporters inculpated Biden and his allies of having engaged in voter fraud. Encouraged by Trump, thousands of his followers gathered outside the Capitol Building two months later. On 6 January 2021, the outgoing president spoke before the mob, warning, 'If you don't fight like hell, you're not going to have a country anymore.' Shortly thereafter, hundreds of Trump's backers broke into the Capitol, with the intent of preventing lawmakers from certifying the Electoral College results and keeping Trump in the White House. It took several hours before the authorities restored order, and only after Trump told his supporters to go home. Later that day, lawmakers completed their certification of the election results.

Trump drew condemnation not just from Democrats but also from a significant number of Republicans, including McConnell, for trying to subvert democracy. Less than a week after the unrest at the Capitol, the House passed a single article of impeachment that, citing the 14th Amendment, accused Trump of inciting an insurrection. Despite the anger among members of his own party, fealty and the power of Trump's base remained powerful considerations when it came time to vote. Of the 207 Republicans present, only 10 joined all 222 Democrats in sending the article to the Senate.

There were two aspects of this second impeachment of the president that were unique. First, it was the only time in the history of the nation that the House had endorsed impeachment based on a single article. Second, no effort to remove the president had ever made reference to the 14th Amendment. Article three of that amendment states that no one who had 'engaged in insurrection or rebellion against' the United States could hold a federal office. Given that that amendment had been added to the Constitution three years after the Civil War ended, the question was whether it was directed strictly at those who had supported the Confederacy or if its intent was to bar anyone at any time who had partaken in the transgressions cited—including Trump—from holding a U.S. government post (Gerhardt, 2024).

The Senate began its trial in early February 2021. Its makeup had changed, with Democrats gaining three seats the previous November, thereby dividing the Upper House evenly between the two parties. (Two of the senators were independents, but they caucused with the Democrats.) Who was to preside over the hearings became an issue of contention. Under the Constitution, the chief justice of the Supreme Court assumes that role when the Senate deliberates; but, because Trump was no longer president, Chief Justice John Roberts announced he was under no obligation to take part. Next in line was the incoming vice president, Kamala Harris, but she had no desire to assume such a responsibility after having just assumed her post. Therefore, it fell upon the president pro tempore of the Senate, Democrat Patrick Leahy of Vermont, to act as the presiding officer. To try to assuage Republicans, he affirmed he would assume a nonpartisan role.

The question senators faced was one they had confronted in the cases of Senator William Blount and Secretary of War William Belknap: whether they could or even should convict a federal official who no longer held office. The House managers said they should. The majority of senators agreed, deciding 56–44 in the affirmative—with all Democrats voting yes. Afterward, both sides presented their case. The House managers maintained there was a direct correlation between Trump's statements and actions and the Capitol insurrection. Trump's lawyers, for their part, denied any connection between the former president and the mob, and cited Democrats for leading all along a political hit job against him. Moreover, they averred that it was unconstitutional to convict a former federal officer. Otherwise, any private citizen, even one who did not previously hold a federal office, could become a target of lawmakers. By a 57–43 vote, with seven Republicans joining the Democrats and two independents, the Senate acquitted Trump.

The Scholarly Debate

Trump's second impeachment has left scholars debating two matters. One is whether Congress has the right to impeach federal officials after their tenure has ended. Those who argue in the negative point out that James Madison's notes from the constitutional debates offer no indication that he envisioned a former officeholder facing impeachment (Byas, 2021). If Congress did have the power to engage in 'continuous impeachment', then lawmakers could for any reason, including partisan political ones, disqualify from a federal post—and, in the process, eliminate the pension of—any individual, including a former president, whose incumbency ended years or even decades earlier (Krent, 2020). Should an individual commit an 'indictable crime', then it makes sense for the criminal justice system to take the lead. And in that case, Congress has means other than impeachment to punish the offender, such as voiding their retirement benefits or censuring them (Firmage and Mangrum, 1974).

Those contending yes point out that in Great Britain, as well as during the colonial era, there were instances of individuals who were impeached despite giving up their offices. Madison, they argue, suggested impeachment post-resignation was an option, and the Constitution's impeachment provisions offer no time limit as to when that process can take place. Furthermore, it might be necessary for lawmakers to impeach and convict an ex-officeholder to prevent a corrupt individual from returning to a position of power or allowing them to maintain their retirement benefits (Firmage and Mangrum, 1974; Gerhardt, 2019; Krent, 2020). Falling in between these two lines of thought is a third, which argues that the Senate can try an officeholder who no longer holds office under the condition that the House of Representatives had finished its impeachment proceedings prior to the officeholder leaving their post. By that definition, the Senate constitutionally had the right to proceed with its trial against Trump, even if it took place after Biden's inauguration (Gerhardt, 2022a, 2022b; McConnell, 2022).

The second debate is whether the contemporary impeachment process is broken. In one corner are those who say that, although the process has its faults, it remains viable. For one, there are only three options to deal with a president who 'is deemed out of control': doing nothing, invoking the 25th Amendment (which relates to presidential succession), and impeachment. Doing nothing is dangerous, and no one has invoked the 25th Amendment. This leaves impeachment. The process, however, must not only provide the public with the evidence but must also grant the president and their opponents the chance, via hearings, to present their cases (Harrington and Waddan, 2024: 257). Turning specifically to the Upper House, more than 67 senators—the two-thirds necessary for conviction—denounced Trump for his role in the January 6 insurrection. The 57 votes in favor of his conviction (including seven from the former president's own party) was the largest number reached in any presidential impeachment trial (Gerhardt, 2024)—though Andrew Johnson came far closer to conviction. And, even if Trump held onto the Oval Office, the effort to remove him was worth it. For one, 'certain irreducible minimum standards of behavior must be upheld'. For another, Trump's impeachment brought 'public attention on presidential wrongdoing that might otherwise escape serious scrutiny' (Bowman, 2024: 383).

Others demur. What Trump did, they state, was arguably worse than what Nixon or Clinton did, yet Republicans were less willing to get on board than they were five decades earlier (Healey, 2022; Katyal, 2019; Rakove, 2024). Furthermore, to assert that 7 out of 50 Republicans voting for conviction points to a properly functioning bipartisan process sets a very low bar (Rattey, 2021). Still others blame both parties, saying that, while Republicans indeed did everything they could to protect Trump, Democrats' ineptitude made a mess of holding the president accountable for his malfeasance. The end result was to leave Capitol Hill weaker than before and, in turn, less capable of holding chief executives accountable for their actions (Bade and Demirjian, 2022). For these doubters in the impeachment process, the hope for the future lies not in Congress but in state officials and the federal judiciary. Despite charges of a rigged election, state officers kept the electoral process honest. Simultaneously, federal judges rejected all but one of the 62 cases brought by Trump's supporters who had said the election was fraudulent (Gerhardt, 2023). The one victory was a minor one in Pennsylvania that had to do with mail-in ballots in which voters failed to provide identification. (In 2021, the Pennsylvania Supreme Court overturned that decision.)

One thing was clear, however—partisanship, though not new, had split the nation like never before and, warned political commentator Lee Drutman a month before the 2020 election, posed a threat to democracy itself. Such 'hyper-partisanship', to use Drutman's phrase (2020), made it increasingly likely that Jason Chaffetz's desire to make impeachment more commonplace would come to fruition. At the same time, the very questioning of what constituted facts and truth, wrote presidential historian Jeffrey Engel (2018), made it less likely for presidents in particular to face the possibility of a Senate conviction.

11 Assessment

'We currently live in an age of impeachment', proclaimed political scientist Keith Whittington in 2020. 'If actual use of the impeachment power has not yet become commonplace, the power lies ominously on the political stage waiting to be used liked Chekov's gun' (Whittington, 2020a: 383). Just three years later, two reporters for the Associated Press suggested that in fact the U.S. had crossed Whittington's threshold. The 'threats of impeachment', they said was 'becoming routine'. Even if those threats had little chance of moving forward in the House or the Senate, just making them gave those lawmakers a means of garnering media attention and raising money (Groves and Amiri, 2023).

The evidence points to impeachment as indeed having become part of the new normal. In 2021, Representative Lauren Boebert of Colorado, a member of the Grand Old Party's right wing, sought but failed to win support for a resolution to impeach Vice President Kamala Harris for supporting President Joe Biden's decision to withdraw U.S. troops from Afghanistan. The next year, another conservative Republican, Representative Marjorie Taylor Greene of Georgia, called for removing from office Biden's attorney general, Merrick Garland, for 'persecuting' former President Donald Trump by seeking a search warrant for one of his homes (U.S. Congress, House of Representatives. 2022). With that warrant, authorities found Trump had illegally taken boxes of classified documents to his home in Mar-a-Lago, Florida. Greene's impeachment resolution, for its part, made it no further than the House Judiciary Committee.

In April 2023, Representative Alexandria Ocasio-Cortez of New York, who came from the Democratic Party's 'progressive' wing, demanded the impeachment of Clarence Thomas, one of the Supreme Court's most conservative justices, for breaching the Ethics in Government Act by not reporting numerous luxury vacations funded by a Republican Party donor. Two months later, Boebert forced a vote to impeach President Biden for failing to stop large numbers of immigrants from crossing the border from Mexico into the United States. Republican leaders in the House were able to prevent her initiative from moving forward, in part because they said they needed time to gather evidence. In June of that year, another Freedom Caucus member,

DOI: 10.4324/9781003565680-13

Andy Ogles (R-Tennessee), made his own attempt to oust Harris, saying that she had not done enough to stop illegal immigration from Mexico. The following June, Biden performed poorly in his only presidential debate against the Republican nominee, former president Donald Trump. Facing calls to drop out of the race, Biden did so on 21 July and urged Democrats to rally around Harris. Two days later, Ogles submitted another resolution to remove Harris, asserting not only that she had continued to do a poor job securing the border but also that she had been derelict in her duties by failing to invoke the 25th Amendment and relieving Biden of his office.

Five months after Ogles made his first bid against Harris, Representative Greene led another impeachment drive, this one aimed at Homeland Security chief Alejandro Mayorkas. Greene argued that he, like Harris, had failed to protect the U.S.–Mexican border. Her proposal died when eight Republicans joined all Democrats in rejecting the measure. Undeterred, Republicans made a second go at Mayorkas in February 2024, which failed as well. A week later, they tried for a third time, succeeding by a single vote and making Mayorkas the first cabinet member impeached in 150 years. The Senate, where Democrats held a 51-seat majority, voted along party lines—with one Republican declaring himself 'present'—to throw out the articles and end the trial. Three months later, Representative Cory Mills (R-Florida) renewed calls for impeaching President Biden, this time because Biden had talked of withholding aid from Israel to protest the deaths of Palestinian civilians during an ongoing war between Israel and the Palestinian terrorist organization Hamas.

A Political Process

Though these charges brought against federal officials involve some form of criminality, they are at their base political in nature, which is exactly what the Founding Fathers intended. James Wilson, one of the nation's Founders who later served on the Supreme Court, wrote in 1791, 'In the United States … impeachments are confined to political characters, to political crimes and misdemeanors, and to political punishments' (Sunstein, 1998: 289–90). Likewise, Supreme Court Associate Justice Joseph Story commented in 1805 that impeachment is 'a proceeding purely of a political nature. It is not so much designed to punish an offender as to secure the state against gross official misconduct' (Firmage, 1973: 689–90).

While it is true that the Constitution makes reference to impeaching a federal officer for 'Treason, Bribery, or other high Crimes and Misdemeanors'—all of them criminal acts—the phrase 'high Crimes and Misdemeanors' refers to more than criminal deeds. It must be borne in mind that when the country's Founders wrote the Constitution, there were few criminal laws in the United States. In that respect, the word 'other' provides a catch-all for future legislation. At the same time, that word and the word 'high' make it clear that the offense in question must be of a severity comparable to treason and bribery for it to be impeachable. The act of malfeasance in question need not be criminal. A president who rebuffs appeals to lead the defense of the country places the nation in danger. One who fires all of his cabinet members and refuses to nominate replacements risks bringing the government to a halt. A judge might commit acts that threaten to bring the judiciary into disrepute. All are not necessarily criminal, but of such consequence as to justify impeachment and removal.

The Framers, though, had intended for impeachment to be treated as the method of last resort. In some ways, it has been. While dozens of judges and justices have faced the threat of impeachment, only eight ended up convicted by the Senate and lost their jobs. Given that members of the federal judiciary serve for life—and considering that several who served jail time refused to give up their positions—impeachment may be the only option for removing them. Those who serve in the executive branch are another story. Lawmakers have means other than impeachment to punish the president or those around him. They can refuse to support legislation submitted to them by the White House or reject the president's nominees for federal posts. They also know that voters can express their disapproval every four years at the ballot box.

Because of the duties and functions of the office they hold, and the methods of recourse for their wrongdoings, Congress historically adopted a different standard for impeaching judicial and executive branch officials. Unlike executive branch officers, judges must abide by the Constitution's 'good Behavior' clause, and act both apolitically and impartially; indeed, most jurists were impeached not for a criminal act but for violating that behavior provision. If judges cannot prove that they remain in good standing, the perception will be that they cannot objectively preside over the cases brought before them. Moreover, as there are hundreds of judges, it is not necessarily burdensome to find someone to take over the caseload of a jurist who has lost their job. There is only one president, though. While that individual might engage in legal malfeasance—such as not paying taxes, punching a foreign official in the face, or lying under oath about an affair—removing them threatens not only to void the votes of millions of voters but also to cause significant disruption to the country. Additionally, as presidents are not bound by the 'good Behavior' clause, their legal infractions could be regarded as private matters that do not affect their ability to do their job.

Because of the particularly serious implications of removing a president from power, most scholars argue that members of Congress, and especially the senators who ultimately decide whether to convict, should give very careful thought to voting in favor of doing so (Amar, 1999; Sunstein, 2017; Hirsch, 2018; Tribe and Matz, 2018). As such, lawmakers should interpret the phrase 'high crimes and misdemeanors' narrowly when targeting the Oval Office and limit impeachment to those cases where the president has placed the state's welfare in jeopardy. Some go a step further, maintaining that Capitol Hill needs to be even more wary when the president is in their second term. Because the 22nd Amendment restricts the same individual to two full terms in the Oval Office, any president who gets another four years automatically becomes a lame duck, making it even harder for them to engage in 'long-term abuse of office' (Peck, 2000: 788). A minority of legal theorists, however, reject these arguments and the differential adopted for jurists and presidents. In their mind, it makes no sense to hold that a judge who lies under oath to hide a personal matter should be impeached but a president, like Clinton, who does the same should not. Both are high crimes, contend these scholars, and if a judge can be removed from office for committing acts unrelated to their official capacity, the same should hold true for the president (Cooper, 1999).

Whether or not the president is immune from indictment while serving in office is also a subject of disagreement. The Office of Legal Counsel (OLC) has argued in the affirmative, and most experts second that conclusion on the grounds that a chief executive who has to face lengthy trials will be unable to do their prime job, which is to effectively lead the nation (Isenbergh, 1998; Amar, 1999). There are others, though, who contend that such a position allows presidents to abuse their power (Firmage and Mangrum, 1974; Finkelstein and Painter, 2022).

In July 2024 the Supreme Court weighed in. By then, former President Trump had become the target of two federal investigations related to his role in the January 2021 Capitol insurrection and for taking classified documents to Mar-a-Lago. Using the OLC's conclusions, Trump asserted that, because these cases involved actions he took in his official capacity as president, he was immune from prosecution. In *Trump v. United States* [*Doc 23*], the Court largely agreed. In a split 6–3 decision, it ruled that the country's chief executive had complete immunity 'for actions relating to the core powers of their office' over which Congress has no say, which include their authority to issue pardons or their role as military commander-in-chief, and broad protection from prosecution for acts they commit in their official capacity as the country's leader. Only in the case of unofficial acts—that is, acts that 'are based on his private conduct'—did immunity not apply (Howe, 2024).

The Court's findings received a warm response from Trump, many Republicans, and some legal experts, who said that it necessarily shielded the leader of the executive branch from suits that could stymie the effective functioning of the government. But a large number of Democrats and scholars blasted the justices, warning that the Court had jeopardized the Constitution's system of checks and balances by making it exceedingly difficult to hold the president accountable for violations of the law (Holmes and Reid, 2024; Mannweiller et al., 2024; Parlatore, 2024; Tarinelli, 2024; Gerhardt, 2024). Angered by the decision, Representative Ocasio-Cortez two weeks later submitted articles of impeachment against two of the justices who had found in Trump's favor, Samuel Alito and Clarence Thomas. As with her first attempt to remove Thomas, she alleged both men had illegally accepted gifts. Her bid made no headway in the face of opposition from the Republican-dominated House.

The Partisanship Problem

Adding to the 'when or if' debate over impeachment is the matter of partisanship. When they wrote the Constitution, the Founding Fathers did not foresee the development of a two-party system. Rather, they assumed the establishment of multiple parties, which would have to collaborate with one another to enact legislation. Presupposing that the House of Representatives was more likely than the Senate to fall into the trap of the ideological hatreds that would endanger the nation's welfare, they limited the House only to drawing up the charges against the accused, with ultimate guilt or innocence determined by those in the Senate. There have been periods in U.S. history of intense political disagreement, but it arguably has reached new levels in the twenty-first century. In 2022, for instance, as many as 70 percent of both Democrats and Republicans viewed their political opponents as 'serious threat[s] to the United States and its people', and 42 percent considered their political rivals as 'downright evil' (Healy, 2022: 778–79). Trust in Congress has plummeted. Whereas 42 percent of Americans in 1973 had high confidence in their elected officials on Capitol Hill, that number had fallen to only 11 percent in 2018 (Bowman, 2019). In 2024, it was at about that same level.

Simultaneously, trust in the press has fallen. A Gallup poll taken in 1997 found that 53 percent of Americans believed that the mass media reported the news 'fully, accurately and fairly'. By mid-2016, only 20 percent of respondents felt that way. Even more telling was that then-President Trump's attacks on journalists led Democrats' trust in the news to rise 20 points, to 72 percent, between his election and the fall of 2017. Throughout that same period, Republicans' faith in an unbiased press held firm at 14 percent (Tribe and Matz, 2018: 210). The internet and social media have made their own contribution to the political divide, for, in the words of one law professor, they have 'largely served as an echo chamber rather than the means for educating the public on matters of civic importance' (Gerhardt, 2022a: 746).

Such polarization has implications for impeachment, particularly when it comes to the president. While far more judges have been impeached than presidents, if one examines the matter on a per capita basis, presidents are more likely to face impeachment than judges: 15 federal judges had their cases reach the Senate; of them 11 left office, be it because of a Senate conviction or resignation; and 3 presidents were impeached, with another, Richard Nixon, resigning. Yet, while more than 3700 people have served as federal judges, only 45 have sat in the Oval Office. Indeed, of the last five presidents, two have been impeached, and members of Congress submitted impeachment resolutions against the other three. In light of the many responsibilities of the country's chief executive, there are numerous opportunities for abuses of power. At the same time, the impeachment weapon offers opponents numerous opportunities to accuse the White House's most important resident of abuse.

Conversely, there is the matter of conviction. The Founding Fathers made at least two assumptions. The first, most clearly espoused by James Madison, was that Americans would want to learn more about the Constitution and its system of checks and balances. The second was that the Senate would give far more serious thought to the implications of ousting a federal official than the House. Therefore, they gave senators the power to decide whether an impeached officer should be removed, and that in itself necessitated a two-thirds majority vote. Only rarely in U.S. history has a single party held two-thirds of the seats in the Upper House, the last time being the 89th Congress (1965–1967). Thus, reaching the requisite threshold requires dialogue among senators from the two major parties.

Much has changed, however, since the writing and ratification of the Constitution. By establishing the direct election of senators, the 17th Amendment, ratified in 1913, forced those in the Upper House to be even more attuned to their constituents' sentiments than before when casting their votes. As much as a senator may feel conviction is warranted, they may decide in today's polarized environment that their own political survival necessitates voting 'nay', particularly if the person in question is the president. Furthermore, there are those who in recent years contend that Article II grants the president full authority over the executive branch. Accordingly, he has no obligation to abide by legislative subpoenas during an impeachment investigation. Despite the demands from Capitol Hill and the Supreme Court, Nixon could have refused to turn over any incriminating material, but he felt obligated to do so. More recent presidents, most notably Trump, have shown less reverence for constitutional norms, and could depend on Republicans in and out of Congress to stand behind his stonewalling.

For some legal experts, impeachment was a means for Congress to defend itself 'against a contumacious Executive' (Broughton, 2021: 310), but partisanship has made it 'ineffectual' (Healy, 2022: 774). Senators, they note, take an oath during an impeachment hearing to 'do impartial justice according to the Constitution and laws'; yet the willingness of individuals such as Mitch McConnell and Lindsey Graham to decide their vote even before hearing the evidence proves otherwise. Indeed, at least one expert has warned that such hyper-partisanship has so undermined the process of holding presidents liable for acts of malfeasance that it has placed the nation's welfare in jeopardy (Gerhardt, 2024). Maybe, says another observer, the answer is to make oath-breaking by senators a crime on a par with perjury (Rattey, 2021). It is doubtful, however, that members of Congress would accept such a solution.

Prosecution and Self-Pardons

The extent to which bipartisanship remains part of the impeachment process is one matter in debate among scholars. Others, previously addressed as well in this book, include whether the judiciary should have the power to review

Senate convictions of individuals impeached by the House, or whether a public official who no longer holds office should be subject to impeachment. But there are two others. Although the Constitution specifies impeachment as the means of removing a sitting president, is it the only one? What about indictment and conviction in court for criminal acts? The Justice Department Office of Legal Counsel's 1973 and 2000 memos replied that impeachment is the only option. During oral arguments over whether President Trump deserved as least some measure of immunity from prosecution for his role in efforts to overturn the 2020 election results, Supreme Court Justice Sonia Sotomayor asked Trump's lawyer, John Sauer, whether the president merited immunity if he ordered the assassination of a political rival. Sauer's response was to differentiate between what were 'official' and 'private' acts; if the assassination was 'official', then the only means of recourse was for Congress to impeach and convict the president. Once removed from office, then criminal charges could be brought against him (Fritze et al., 2024). That argument drew a rebuke from former attorney general Alberto Gonzales (2019: 910), who declared that 'no one can credibly argue that murdering a political rival or assaulting a media critic would constitute an official duty'.

Others have criticized the OLC memos themselves, especially that of 2000. The OLC, say critics, is made up of government lawyers who advise the attorney general, and who cannot be guaranteed to give unbiased counsel. Nor are they impressed by the claim that sitting presidents would face 'public stigma and ... mental and physical burdens' if confronted with civil or criminal litigation. In fact, in the 2020 case *Trump v. Vance*, the Supreme Court declared that the president is not above the law. As such, Trump could not reject a subpoena issued by a New York State grand jury for his financial records. For these various reasons, critics argue that it is time to stop viewing the OLC's memos as 'legally definitive' and to treat the country's leader 'like any other citizen' (Wehle, 2020: 1, 56; Finkelstein and Painter, 2022: 149). It is also important to point out that a president who commits crimes while in office, even if he is not impeached, can still face prosecution after leaving the White House.

Another, and as yet untested, challenge to impeachment is the president's power to pardon individuals for federal crimes. That power is considered absolute. But could a chief executive apply it to himself, even prior to facing indictment? A half-dozen of Trump's allies in Congress requested pardons from him before he left office for the part they played in trying to overturn the 2020 election results. If the president commits what he knows is a crime, could he issue a self-pardon to protect himself from punishment?

This remains an unanswered but important question. During the height of the Watergate scandal, President Richard Nixon's lead attorney, Fred Buzhardt, argued that Nixon could pardon himself, and Trump contended that his power to do as much was 'absolute' (Eisen, 2018). Just before Nixon left office, though, the Justice Department rejected such an assertion, declaring, 'Under the fundamental rule that no one may be a judge in his own case, the President cannot pardon himself' (Gerhardt, 2024: 88). It is important to remember that pardons are only for federal crimes, not state ones, but even there, most experts assert that abuse of the pardon power is a justifiable cause for impeachment. A president has never tried to pardon himself, and it is likely the Founding Fathers would have rejected such a suggestion on the grounds cited by the Justice Department (Finkelstein and Painter, 2022; Gonzales, 2019; Alschuler, 2021). Furthermore, it would open the door to a president committing any federal crime of his choice, knowing that while in the Oval Office he could not be prosecuted, and then pardoning himself on his last day in office. The chief executive could also potentially offer pardons to prevent witnesses from testifying against him or to get his supporters to commit crimes on his behalf. In the last of these situations, the president could be charged as an accomplice in the crime committed, while offering pardons to witnesses could justify indictment for bribery.

The 25th Amendment could also come into play, for it too has provisions relating to the president's removal from office (Sunstein, 2017; Bowman, 2024). That amendment, which became part of the Constitution in 1967, explains what occurs if the president dies, resigns, is impeached and convicted, or is determined by the vice president and a majority of the cabinet (or a body chosen by Congress) mentally or physically unable to perform their duties. But it also permits the president temporarily to transfer their powers to the vice president when the chief executive is otherwise indisposed. Numerous presidents have invoked this latter provision, among them Ronald Reagan while recovering from an assassination attempt against him, and both George W. Bush and Joe Biden while undergoing colonoscopies. There were individuals, including Speaker of the House Nancy Pelosi, who, prior to Trump's second impeachment, had suggested that Trump's vice president, Mike Pence, invoke that provision of the Constitution. Pence refused.

The 25th Amendment, in the words of one scholar, 'is not impeachment-lite' and was not intended to confront situations such as that seen on 6 January 2021 (Gerhardt, 2024: 157). But it does raise some potentially disturbing questions. Could a president facing legal trouble invoke the 25th Amendment and, while serving as acting president, the vice president provide the president with a pardon? While that too would be abuse of the pardon power, whom would Congress seek to punish? In such a situation, would lawmakers be willing to consider impeaching and removing both the president and the vice president? These are important questions that remain unanswered.

Part II

Documents

Documents

Document 1

Massachusetts State Constitution: Part 2, Chapter 2, Section I, Article 8 (1780)

The power of pardoning offences, except such as persons may be convicted of before the senate by an impeachment of the house, shall be in the governor, by and with the advice of council; but no charter of pardon, granted by the governor, with advice of the council before conviction, shall avail the party pleading the same, notwithstanding any general or particular expressions contained therein, descriptive of the offence or offences intended to be pardoned.

Source: Massachusetts House of Representatives, *Rules and Orders to be Observed in the House of Representatives in the Commonwealth of Massachusetts for the Year 1831* (Boston: Dutton and Wentworth, 1831), 74.

Document 2

Gouverneur Morris at the Constitutional Convention on the Senate Trying Impeachments (1787)

No other tribunal than the Senate could be trusted. The Supreme Court were too few in number and might be warped and corrupted. [James Madison] was ag[ain]st a dependence of the Executive on the Legislature, considering the Legislative tyranny the great danger to be apprehended; but there could be no danger that the senate would say untruly on their oaths that the President was guilty of crimes or facts, especially as in four years he can be turned out.

Source: Max Farrand, ed., *The Records of the Federal Convention of 1787*, vol. 2 (New Haven, Conn.: Yale University Press, 1911), 551.

DOI: 10.4324/9781003565680-15

Document 3

The Powers of the Senate

Alexander Hamilton, Federalist *No. 65 (1788)*

We will ... conclude this head with a view of the judicial character of the Senate.

A well-constituted court for the trial of impeachments is an object not more to be desired than difficult to be obtained in a government wholly elective. The subjects of its jurisdiction are those offenses which proceed from the misconduct of public men, or, in other words, from the abuse or violation of some public trust. They are of a nature which may with peculiar propriety be denominated POLITICAL, as they relate chiefly to injuries done immediately to the society itself. The prosecution of them, for this reason, will seldom fail to agitate the passions of the whole community, and to divide it into parties more or less friendly or inimical to the accused. In many cases it will connect itself with the pre-existing factions, and will enlist all their animosities, partialities, influence, and interest on one side or on the other; and in such cases there will always be the greatest danger that the decision will be regulated more by the comparative strength of parties, than by the real demonstrations of innocence or guilt.

The delicacy and magnitude of a trust which so deeply concerns the political reputation and existence of every man engaged in the administration of public affairs, speak for themselves. The difficulty of placing it rightly, in a government resting entirely on the basis of periodical elections, will as readily be perceived, when it is considered that the most conspicuous characters in it will, from that circumstance, be too often the leaders or the tools of the most cunning or the most numerous faction, and on this account, can hardly be expected to possess the requisite neutrality towards those whose conduct may be the subject of scrutiny.

The convention, it appears, thought the Senate the most fit depositary of this important trust ...

Where else than in the Senate could have been found a tribunal sufficiently dignified, or sufficiently independent? What other body would be likely to feel CONFIDENCE ENOUGH IN ITS OWN SITUATION, to preserve, unawed and uninfluenced, the necessary impartiality between an INDIVIDUAL accused, and the REPRESENTATIVES OF THE PEOPLE, HIS ACCUSERS?

Could the Supreme Court have been relied upon as answering this description? It is much to be doubted, whether the members of that tribunal would at all times be endowed with so eminent a portion of fortitude, as would be called for in the execution of so difficult a task; and it is still more to be doubted, whether they would possess the degree of credit and authority, which might, on certain occasions, be indispensable towards reconciling the people to a decision that should happen to clash with an accusation brought by their immediate representatives. A deficiency in the first, would be fatal to the accused; in the last, dangerous to the public tranquillity. The hazard in both these respects, could only be avoided, if at all, by rendering that tribunal more numerous than would consist with a reasonable attention to economy. The necessity of a numerous court for the trial of impeachments, is equally dictated by the nature of the proceeding. This can never be tied down by such strict rules, either in the delineation of the offense by the prosecutors, or in the construction of it by the judges, as in common cases serve to limit the discretion of courts in favor of personal security. There will be no jury to stand between the judges who are to pronounce the sentence of the law, and the party who is to receive or suffer it. The awful discretion which a court of impeachments must necessarily have, to doom to honor or to infamy the most confidential and the most distinguished characters of the community, forbids the commitment of the trust to a small number of persons.

These considerations seem alone sufficient to authorize a conclusion, that the Supreme Court would have been an improper substitute for the Senate, as a court of impeachments. There remains a further consideration, which will not a little strengthen this conclusion. It is this: The punishment which may be the consequence of conviction upon impeachment, is not to terminate the chastisement of the offender. After having been sentenced to a prepetual [*sic*] ostracism from the esteem and confidence, and honors and emoluments of his country, he will still be liable to prosecution and punishment in the ordinary course of law …

Source: Avalon Project, https://avalon.law.yale.edu/18th_century/fed65.asp.

Document 4

Objections to the Power of the Senate to Set [sic] as a Court for Impeachments Further Considered

Alexander Hamilton, Federalist *No. 66 (1788)*

A REVIEW of the principal objections that have appeared against the proposed court for the trial of impeachments, will not improbably eradicate the remains of any unfavorable impressions which may still exist in regard to this matter.

The FIRST of these objections is, that the provision in question confounds legislative and judiciary authorities in the same body, in violation of that important and well established maxim which requires a separation between the different departments of power. The true meaning of this maxim has been discussed and ascertained in another place, and has been shown to be entirely compatible with a partial intermixture of those departments for special purposes, preserving them, in the main, distinct and unconnected. This partial intermixture is even, in some cases, not only proper but necessary to the mutual defense of the several members of the government against each other. An absolute or qualified negative in the executive upon the acts of the legislative body, is admitted, by the ablest adepts in political science, to be an indispensable barrier against the encroachments of the latter upon the former. And it may, perhaps, with no less reason be contended, that the powers relating to impeachments are, as before intimated, an essential check in the hands of that body upon the encroachments of the executive. The division of them between the two branches of the legislature, assigning to one the right of accusing, to the other the right of judging, avoids the inconvenience of making the same persons both accusers and judges; and guards against the danger of persecution, from the prevalency of a factious spirit in either of those branches. As the concurrence of two thirds of the Senate will be requisite to a condemnation, the security to innocence, from this additional circumstance, will be as complete as itself can desire.

[...]

A SECOND objection to the Senate, as a court of impeachments, is, that it contributes to an undue accumulation of power in that body ...

[...]

If we take this course, it will lead to a more intelligible, if not to a more certain result. The disposition of the power of making treaties, which has obtained in the plan of the convention, will, then, if I mistake not, appear to be fully justified by the considerations stated in a former number, and by others which will occur under the next head of our inquiries. The expediency of the junction of the Senate with the Executive, in the power of appointing to offices, will, I trust, be placed in a light not less satisfactory, in the disquisitions under the same head. And I flatter myself the observations in my last paper must have gone no inconsiderable way towards proving that it was not easy, if practicable, to find a more fit receptacle for the power of determining impeachments, than that which has been chosen. If this be truly the case, the hypothetical dread of the too great weight of the Senate ought to be discarded from our reasonings.

[...]

But independent of this most active and operative principle, to secure the equilibrium of the national House of Representatives, the plan of the convention has provided in its favor several important counterpoises to the additional authorities to be conferred upon the Senate. The exclusive privilege of originating money bills will belong to the House of Representatives. The same house will possess the sole right of instituting impeachments: is not this a complete counterbalance to that of determining them? The same house will be the umpire in all elections of the President, which do not unite the suffrages of a majority of the whole number of electors; a case which it cannot be doubted will sometimes, if not frequently, happen. The constant possibility of the thing must be a fruitful source of influence to that body. The more it is contemplated, the more important will appear this ultimate though contingent power, of deciding the competitions of the most illustrious citizens of the Union, for the first office in it. It would not perhaps be rash to predict, that as a mean of influence it will be found to outweigh all the peculiar attributes of the Senate.

A THIRD objection to the Senate as a court of impeachments, is drawn from the agency they are to have in the appointments to office. It is imagined that they would be too indulgent judges of the conduct of men, in whose official creation they had participated. The principle of this objection would condemn a practice, which is to be seen in all the State governments, if not in all the governments with which we are acquainted: I mean that of rendering those who hold offices during pleasure, dependent on the pleasure of those who appoint them. With equal plausibility might it be alleged in this case, that the favoritism of the latter would always be an asylum for the misbehavior of the former. But that practice, in contradiction to this principle, proceeds upon the presumption, that the responsibility of those who appoint, for the fitness and competency of the persons on whom they bestow their choice, and the interest they will have in the respectable and prosperous administration of affairs, will inspire a sufficient disposition to dismiss from a share in it all such who, by their conduct, shall have proved themselves unworthy of the confidence reposed in them. Though facts may not always correspond with this presumption, yet if it be, in the main, just, it must destroy the supposition that the Senate, who will merely sanction the choice of the Executive, should feel a bias, towards the objects of that choice, strong enough to blind them to the evidences of guilt so extraordinary, as to have induced the representatives of the nation to become its accusers.

[...]

A FOURTH objection to the Senate in the capacity of a court of impeachments, is derived from its union with the Executive in the power of making treaties.

[...]

This objection has been circulated with more earnestness and with greater show of reason than any other which has appeared against this part of the plan; and yet I am deceived if it does not rest upon an erroneous foundation.

The security essentially intended by the Constitution against corruption and treachery in the formation of treaties, is to be sought for in the numbers and characters of those who are to make them. The JOINT AGENCY of the Chief Magistrate of the Union, and of two thirds of the members of a body selected by the collective wisdom of the legislatures of the several States, is designed to be the pledge for the fidelity of the national councils in this particular. The convention might with propriety have meditated the punishment of the Executive, for a deviation from the instructions of the Senate, or a want of integrity in the conduct of the negotiations committed to him; they might also have had in view the punishment of a few leading individuals in the Senate, who should have prostituted their influence in that body as the mercenary instruments of foreign corruption: but they could not, with more or with equal propriety, have contemplated the impeachment and punishment of two thirds of the Senate, consenting to an improper treaty, than of a majority of that or of the other branch of the national legislature, consenting to a pernicious or unconstitutional law, a principle which, I believe, has never been admitted into any government. How, in fact, could a majority in the House of Representatives impeach themselves? Not better, it is evident, than two thirds of the Senate might try themselves. And yet what reason is there, that a majority of the House of Representatives, sacrificing the interests of the society by an unjust and tyrannical act of legislation, should escape with impunity, more than two thirds of the Senate, sacrificing the same interests in an injurious treaty with a foreign power? The truth is, that in all such cases it is essential to the freedom and to the necessary independence of the deliberations of the body, that the members of it should be exempt from punishment for acts done in a collective capacity; and the security to the society must depend on the care which is taken to confide the trust to proper hands, to make it their interest to execute it with fidelity, and to make it as difficult as possible for them to combine in any interest opposite to that of the public good.

Source: Avalon Project, https://avalon.law.yale.edu/18th_century/fed66.asp.

Document 5

The Judiciary Department

Alexander Hamilton, Federalist *No. 78 (1787)*

[...]

According to the plan of the convention, all judges who may be appointed by the United States are to hold their offices DURING GOOD BEHAVIOR; which is conformable to the most approved of the State constitutions and among the rest, to that of this State. Its propriety having been drawn into question by the adversaries of that plan, is no light symptom of the rage for objection, which disorders their imaginations and judgments. The standard of good behavior for the continuance in office of the judicial magistracy, is certainly one of the most valuable of the modern improvements in the practice of government. In a monarchy it is an excellent barrier to the despotism of the prince; in a republic it is a no less excellent barrier to the encroachments and oppressions of the representative body. And it is the best expedient which can be devised in any government, to secure a steady, upright, and impartial administration of the laws.

Source: Avalon Project, https://avalon.law.yale.edu/18th_century/fed78.asp.

Document 6

Impeachment and Trial of William Blount (1799)

Congressman James Bayard on impeachment after resignation

[...]

If the impeachment were regular and maintainable when preferred, I apprehend no subsequent event, grounded on the willful act, or caused by the delinquency of the party, can vitiate or obstruct the proceeding. Otherwise the party, by resignation or the commission of some offense which merited and occasioned his expulsion, might secure his impunity. This is against one of the sagest maxims of the law, which does not allow a man to derive a benefit from his own wrong.

Source: Hinds' Precedents, vol. 3, chap. 70, U.S. Government Publishing Office, https://www.govinfo.gov/content/pkg/GPO-HPREC-HINDS-V3/html/GPO-HPREC-HINDS-V3-19.htm.

Document 7

Impeachment and Trial of William Blount: Effect of Resignation of Respondent

Alexander Dallas, lawyer to Senator William Blount

[...]

It is among the less objections of the cause that the defendant is now out of office, not by resignation. I certainly shall never contend that an officer may first commit an offense and afterwards avoid punishment by resigning his office; but the defendant has been expelled. Can he be removed at one trial and disqualified at another for the same offense? Is it not the form rather than the substance of a trial? Do the Senate come, as Lord Mansfield says a jury ought, like blank paper, without a previous impression upon their minds? Would not error in the first sentence naturally be productive of error in the second instance? Is there not reason to apprehend the strong bias of a former decision would be apt to prevent the influence of any new lights brought forward upon a second trial?

Source: *Hinds' Precedents*, vol. 3, chap. 70, U.S. Government Publishing Office, https://www.govinfo.gov/content/pkg/GPO-HPREC-HINDS-V3/html/GPO-HPREC-HINDS-V3-19.htm.

Document 8

Marbury v. Madison (1803)

When the heads of the departments of the Government are the political or confidential officers of the Executive, merely to execute the will of the President, or rather to act in cases in which the Executive possesses a constitutional or legal discretion, nothing can be more perfectly clear than that their acts are only politically examinable. But where a specific duty is assigned by law, and individual rights depend upon the performance of that duty, it seems equally clear that the individual who considers himself injured has a right to resort to the laws of his country for a remedy.

[...]

The province of the Court is solely to decide on the rights of individuals, not to inquire how the Executive or Executive officers perform duties in which they have a discretion. Questions, in their nature political or which are, by the Constitution and laws, submitted to the Executive, can never be made in this court.

Source: *Marbury v. Madison*, 5 U.S. 137 (1803), https://supreme.justia.com/cases/federal/us/5/137/#tab-opinion-1958607.

Document 9

Letter, Thomas Jefferson to Joseph Nicholson (1803)

[Y]ou must have heard of the extraordinary charge of Chace to the grand jury at Baltimore. ought this seditious & official attack on the principles of our constitution, and on the proceedings of a state, to go unpunished? and to whom so pointedly as yourself will the public look for the necessary measures? I ask these questions for your consideration. for myself, it is better that I should not interfere.

Source: Barbara B. Oberg, ed., *The Papers of Thomas Jefferson*, vol. 40 (Princeton, N.J.: Princeton University Press, 2013), 372.

Document 10

Andrew Jackson Talks with Adviser William Berkeley Lewis re the Bank of the United States (1833)

> I then inquired of him [Jackson] what he would do if Congress, when it met, should pass a joint resolution, directing the Secretary to restore the deposits to the bank?

'Why,' said he, 'I would veto it.'

[...]

[S]uppose they should be able to carry the resolution over your veto? What then would you do? If you refuse to permit the secretary to do it, the next step, on the part of the House, would be to move an impeachment, and if Congress have the power to carry this resolution through in defiance of the veto power, they would be able to prosecute it to a successful termination.

'Under such circumstances', he replied ... 'then, sir, I would resign the presidency and return to the Hermitage!'

Source: James Parton, *Life of Andrew Jackson*, vol. 3 (New York: Mason Brothers, 1860), 506.

Document 11

Representative Thaddeus Stevens Calls for Removing President Andrew Johnson from Office (1868)

When Andrew Johnson took upon himself the duties of his high office he swore to obey the Constitution and take care that the laws be faithfully executed. That, indeed, is and has always been the chief duty of the President of the United States. The duties of legislation and adjudicating the laws of his country fall in no way to his lot. To obey the commands of the sovereign power of the nation, and to see that others should obey them, was his whole duty—a duty which he could not escape, and any attempt to do so would be in direct violation of his official oath; in other words, a misprision of perjury.

I accuse him, in the name of the House of Representatives, of having perpetrated that foul offense against the laws and interests of his country.

[...]

We charge that, in defiance of frequent warnings, he has since repeatedly attempted to carry those orders into execution, and to prevent Edwin M. Stanton from executing the laws appertaining to the Department of War and from discharging the duties of the office.

[...]

The respondent, in violation of this law, appointed General Thomas to office, whereby, according to the express terms of the act, he was guilty of a high misdemeanor. But whatever may have been his views with regard to the tenure-of-office act he knew it was a law, and so recorded upon the statutes. I disclaim all necessity in a trial of impeachment to prove the wicked or unlawful intention of the respondent, and it is unwise ever to aver it.

Source: C. M. Whitman, *American Orators and Oratory: Comprising Biographical Sketches of the Representative Men of America* (Chicago: Fairbanks, Palmer, 1884), 391–93.

Document 12

Andrew Johnson's Impeachment Trial (1868)

Taken from the closing argument of Attorney General Henry Stanbery, defending President Johnson

We see, them [*sic*] that, according to the case made in these eight articles, the President did not succeed in getting Mr. Stanton our [*sic*] of office or of putting General Thomas in, either in law or in fact. We see, according to these articles, that the President did not succeed, either by force or otherwise, in preventing Mr. Stanton from holding his office or in getting possession of the public property in that Department. There has been, according to the very case made in these articles, no public mischief. The lawful officer has not been disturbed; the lawful custody of the public property and public money of the Department has not been changed. No injury has been done either to the public service or the public officer. There has been no removal of Mr. Stanton—only an abortive attempt at removal. There has been no acting Secretary put in an office vacant by death resignation, or disability—put there during the time of such actual vacancy or temporary absence. All the time of such actual vacant or temporary absence. All the time the Secretary himself has been there in the actual performance of his duties. No ad interim officer has, in law or fact, been constituted, for in law or fact there has been no interim as to the Secretary himself. There has been no moment of time in which there could be an acting Secretary or an ad interim Secretary, either in law or in fact, for it is impossible to conceive of an ad interim Secretary of War when there is no interim, that is, when the lawful Secretary is in his place and in the actual discharge of his duties.

Mark it, then, Senators, that the acts charged are high crimes and misdemeanors in these eight articles, in respect to putting Mr. Stanton out and General Thomas in, are things attempted and not things accomplished. It is in the attempt, and the unlawful interest with which it was formed, that the president is to be held responsible for. So that it comes to be a question of vital consequence in reference to this part of the case whether the high crimes and misdemeanors provided for in the tenure-of-office act and in the second section of the military appropriation act purport to punish not only the commission of the acts, but to punish as well the abortive attempt to commit them ....

And here, Senators, before I proceed to consider these articles in detail, seems to me the proper time to bring your attention to another consideration, which I deem of very great moment. What is the subject-matter which constitutes these high crimes and misdemeanors? Under what legislation does it happen that the President of the United States is brought under all this penal liability? What are these high crimes and misdemeanors? Has he committed treason or bribery? Has he appropriated the public funds or the public property unlawfully to his own use? Has he committed any crime of violence against any person, public officer or private individual? Is he charged with any act which amounts to the *crimen falsi* or was done *causa lucri*? Nothing of the sort. These alleged high crimes and misdemeanors are all founded upon mere forms of executive administration. For the violation, they say, of the rules laid down by the legislative department to regulate the conduct of the executive department in the manner of administration of executive functions belonging to that department.

Source: Douglas O. Linder, 'Famous Trials: Accounts and Materials for 100 of History's Most Important Trials', https://www.famous-trials.com/johnson/473-closingargument.

Document 13

Rule XI (1936)

Procedure and guidelines for impeachment trials in the United States Senate

[I]n the trial of any impeachment the Presiding Officer of the Senate, if the Senate so orders, shall appoint a committee of Senators to receive evidence and take testimony at such times and places as the committee may determine, and for such purpose the committee so appointed and the chairman thereof, to be elected by the committee, shall (unless otherwise ordered by the Senate) exercise all the powers and functions conferred upon the Senate and the Presiding Officer of the Senate, respectively, under the rules of procedure and practice in the Senate when sitting on impeachment trials.

Unless otherwise ordered by the Senate, the rules of procedure and practice in the Senate when sitting on impeachment trials shall govern the procedure and practice of the committee so appointed. The committee so appointed shall report to the Senate in writing a certified copy of the transcript of the proceedings and testimony had and given before such committee, and such report shall be received by the Senate and the evidence so received and the testimony so taken shall be considered to all intents and purposes, subject to the right of the Senate to determine competency, relevancy, and materiality, as having been received and taken before the Senate.

Source: U.S. Government Publishing Office, *Procedure and Guidelines for Impeachment Trials in the United States Senate*, Senate Document 99-33, rev. ed. https://www.govinfo.gov/content/pkg/CDOC-99sdoc33/html/CDOC-99sdoc33.htm.

Document 14

Halsted Ritter v. the United States (1936)

Our conclusion is that we have no authority to review the impeachment proceedings held in the Senate and decide whether the accusations made against the plaintiff were such that he could properly be impeached thereon, nor can we pass upon the question of whether his acquittal on the first six articles was a bar to prosecution under the seventh. In our opinion, the Senate was the solo tribunal that could take jurisdiction of the articles of impeachment presented to that body against the plaintiff and its decision is final.

Source: Cases Decided in the Court of Claims of the United States, vol. 84 (Washington, DC: GPO, 1937), 300.

Document 15

Baker v. Carr (1962)

[...] Prominent on the surface of any case held to involve a political question is found a textually demonstrable constitutional commitment of the issue to a coordinate political department; or a lack of judicially discoverable and manageable standards for resolving it; or the impossibility of deciding without an initial policy determination of a kind clearly for nonjudicial discretion; or the impossibility of a court's undertaking independent resolution without expressing lack of the respect due coordinate branches of government; or an unusual need for unquestioning adherence to a political decision already made; or the potentiality of embarrassment from multifarious pronouncements by various departments on one question.

Source: *Baker v. Carr*, 369 U.S. 186 (1962), https://supreme.justia.com/cases/federal/us/369/186/#tab-opinion-1943625.

Document 16

Powell v.McCormack (1969)

As we pointed out in *Baker v. Carr* ..., there is a significant difference between determining whether a federal court has 'jurisdiction of the subject matter' and determining whether a cause over which a court has subject matter jurisdiction is 'justiciable'.

[...]

In deciding generally whether a claim is justiciable, a court must determine whether 'the duty asserted can be judicially identified and its breach judicially determined, and whether protection for the right asserted can be judicially molded'.

[...]

Unquestionably, Congress has an interest in preserving its institutional integrity, but in most cases that interest can be sufficiently safeguarded by the exercise of its power to punish its members for disorderly behavior and, in extreme cases, to expel a member with the concurrence of two-thirds. In short, both the intention of the Framers, to the extent it can be determined, and an examination of the basic principles of our democratic system persuade us that the Constitution does not vest in the Congress a discretionary power to deny membership by a majority vote.

Source: *Powell v. McCormack*, 395 U.S. 486 (1969), https://supreme.justia.com/cases/federal/us/395/486/#tab-opinion-1948095.

Document 17

Office of Legal Counsel (OLC) Memorandum (1973)

Memo regarding the amenability of the president, the vice president, and other civil officers to federal criminal prosecution while in office.

A necessity to defend a criminal trial and to attend court in connection with it ... would interfere with the President's unique official duties, most of which cannot be performed by anyone else. It might be suggested that the same is true with the defense of impeachment proceedings; but this is a risk expressly contemplated by the Constitution, and is a necessary incident of the impeachment process. The Constitutional Convention was aware of this problem but rejected a proposal that the President should be suspended upon impeachment by the House until acquitted by the Senate.

During the past century the duties of the Presidency, however, have become so onerous that a President may not be able fully to discharge the powers and duties of his office if he had to defend a criminal prosecution.

[...]

A possibility not yet mentioned is to indict a sitting President but defer further proceedings until he is no longer in office. From the standpoint of minimizing direction interruption of official duties—and setting aside the question of the power to govern—this procedure might be a course to be considered. ... [But] it would overlook the political realities [as] an indictment hanging over the President while he remains in office would damage the institution of the Presidency virtually to the same extent as an actual conviction. To be sure, there could also be damage flowing from unrefuted charges. It also may be noted that the possibility that a President may escape all prosecution by the running of the statute of limitations is not a constitutional matter. The policy regarding statutes of limitation is within legislative control.

[...]

We resort then to an analysis similar to that made with respect to the amenability of the President to criminal proceedings. We based the President's immunity from criminal proceedings essentially on two grounds. First, that the person who controls criminal prosecutions as the head of the Executive branch, controls part of the evidence as holder of the power of Executive privilege, and is vested with the pardoning power under Article II, section 2, clause 1 of the Constitution, cannot at the same time be a defendant in a criminal case. This set of considerations obviously is not applicable to the Vice President.

The second reason was the effect of a criminal prosecution on the President's office.

[...]

[W]e must note the highly contingent nature of the possibility that the Vice President would be called to assume the office of President or Acting President. Moreover, it has not been the custom to sequester the Vice President to make certain that he is always available to assume his potential Presidential duties at a moment's notice. The Vice President is frequently absent from the capital, possibly in remote and inaccessible parts of the country, or even abroad on ceremonial functions. Nothing, of course, can prevent him from being sick or otherwise temporarily incapacitated.

Under such a practical interpretation of the extent of the Vice President's immediate availability, it appears as a general proposition that his duty to stand and wait does not necessarily require his total immunity from criminal prosecution. If the Office of the Presidency was vacated while a criminal proceeding was being conducted against the Vice President, the process could be halted at once. Whether or not impeachment proceedings would then ensue against the former Vice President, now President, would depend on the will of Congress. The situation then would be exactly the same as if the Vice President had been President when the allegations of criminality first surfaced—no better, no worse. Thus, a criminal indictment against a Vice President need not abrogate in any way his constitutional duty to stand and wait. This duty, therefore, does not afford a basis for granting to a Vice President immunity from criminal prosecution.

As a further practical observation, it may be noted that if a trial of the Vice President proceeded to a sentence of imprisonment, and were sustained in what might be expected to be an expeditious appeal, the Vice President might well resign. He could be replaced under the Twenty-fifth Amendment's procedure for filling a 'vacancy' in the office of Vice President. Thus, the uninterruptibility of the Presidency would be preserved. There is, of course, no provision in the Constitution (other than impeachment and removal) for determining that a Vice President is incapacitated. The Constitution contains such incapacity-determination process only for the Presidency.

Source: 'Legal Memos about Whether a Sitting President May Be Indicted', https://www.documentcloud.org/documents/3896903-Legal-Memos-About-Whether-a-Sitting-President/.

Document 18

United States v. Nixon (1974)

Certiorari to the United States Court of Appeals for the District Of Columbia Circuit.

Although the courts will afford the utmost deference to Presidential acts in the performance of an Art. II function, ... when a claim of Presidential privilege as to materials subpoenaed for use in a criminal trial is based, as it is here, not on the ground that military or diplomatic secrets are implicated, but merely on the ground of a generalized interest in confidentiality, the President's generalized assertion of privilege must yield to the demonstrated, specific need for evidence in a pending criminal trial and the fundamental demands of due process of law in the fair administration of criminal justice.

[...]

[N]either the doctrine of separation of powers nor the need for confidentiality of high-level communications, without more, can sustain an absolute, unqualified Presidential privilege of immunity from judicial process under all circumstances. The President's need for complete candor and objectivity from advisers calls for great deference from the courts. However, when the privilege depends solely on the broad, undifferentiated claim of public interest in the confidentiality of such conversations, a confrontation with other values arises. Absent a claim of need to protect military, diplomatic, or sensitive national security secrets, we find it difficult to accept the argument that even the very important interest in confidentiality of Presidential communications is significantly diminished by production of such material for *in camera* inspection with all the protection that a district court will be obliged to provide.

The impediment that an absolute, unqualified privilege would place in the way of the primary constitutional duty of the Judicial Branch to do justice in criminal prosecutions would plainly conflict with the function of the courts under Art. III.

[...]

We conclude that, when the ground for asserting privilege as to subpoenaed materials sought for use in a criminal trial is based only on the generalized interest in confidentiality, it cannot prevail over the fundamental demands of due process of law in the fair administration of criminal justice. The generalized assertion of privilege must yield to the demonstrated, specific need for evidence in a pending criminal trial.

Source: *United States v. Nixon*, 418 U.S. 683 (1974), https://supreme.justia.com/cases/federal/us/418/683/#tab-opinion-1950929.

Document 19

Judicial Councils Reform and Judicial Conduct and Disability Act (1980)

§ 351. Complaints; Judge Defined

(a) Filing of complaint by any person. Any person alleging that a judge has engaged in conduct prejudicial to the effective and expeditious administration of the business of the courts, or alleging that such judge is unable to discharge all the duties of office by reason of mental or physical disability, may file with the clerk of the court of appeals for the circuit a written complaint containing a brief statement of the facts constituting such conduct.

(b) Identifying complaint by chief judge. In the interests of the effective and expeditious administration of the business of the courts and on the basis of information available to the chief judge of the circuit, the chief judge may, by written order stating reasons therefor, identify a complaint for purposes of this chapter and thereby dispense with filing of a written complaint.

(c) Transmittal of complaint. Upon receipt of a complaint filed under subsection (a), the clerk shall promptly transmit the complaint to the chief judge of the circuit, or, if the conduct complained of is that of the chief judge, to that circuit judge in regular active service next senior in date of commission. ... The clerk shall simultaneously transmit a copy of the complaint to the judge whose conduct is the subject of the complaint. The clerk shall also transmit a copy of any complaint identified under subsection (b) to the judge whose conduct is the subject of the complaint.

§ 352. Review of Complaint by Chief Judge.

(a) ... The chief judge shall expeditiously review any complaint received under section 351(a) or identified under section 351(b). In determining what action to take, the chief judge may conduct a limited inquiry for the purpose of determining

(1) whether appropriate corrective action has been or can be taken without the necessity for a formal investigation; and
(2) whether the facts stated in the complaint are either plainly untrue or are incapable of being established through investigation. [...]

After expeditiously reviewing a complaint under subsection (a), the chief judge by written order stating his or her reasons, may –

(1) dismiss the complaint ...
(2) conclude the proceeding if the chief judge finds that appropriate corrective action has been taken or that action on the complaint is no longer necessary because of intervening events. [...]

§ 353. ... If the chief judge does not enter an order under section 352(b), the chief judge shall promptly

(1) appoint himself or herself and equal numbers of circuit and district judges of the circuit to a special committee to investigate the facts and allegations contained in the complaint;
(2) certify the complaint and any other documents pertaining thereto to each member of such committee;

and (3) provide written notice to the complainant and the judge whose conduct is the subject of the complaint of the action taken under this subsection. [...]

§ 354. Action by Judicial Council.

(a) Actions upon receipt of report.

(1) Actions. The judicial council of a circuit, upon receipt of a report filed under section 353(c) –

(A) may conduct any additional investigation which it considers to be necessary;
(B) may dismiss the complaint; and
(C) if the complaint is not dismissed, shall take such action as is appropriate to assure the effective and expeditious administration of the business of the courts within the circuit. [...]

§ 354. Action by Judicial Council.

(a) Actions upon receipt of report.

(1) Actions. The judicial council of a circuit, upon receipt of a report filed under section 353(c) –

(A) may conduct any additional investigation which it considers to be necessary;
(B) may dismiss the complaint; and
(C) if the complaint is not dismissed, shall take such action as is appropriate to assure the effective and expeditious administration of the business of the courts within the circuit. [...]

(b) Referral to Judicial Conference.

(1) In general. In addition to the authority granted under subsection (a), the judicial council may, in its discretion, refer any complaint under section 351, together with the record of any associated proceedings and its recommendations for appropriate action, to the Judicial Conference of the United States ...

§ 355. Action by Judicial Conference.

(a) In general. Upon referral or certification of any matter under section 354(b), the Judicial Conference, after consideration of the prior proceedings and such additional investigation as it considers appropriate, shall by majority vote take such action ... as it considers appropriate.
(b) If impeachment warranted.

(1) In general. If the Judicial Conference concurs in the determination of the judicial council, or makes its own determination, that consideration of impeachment may be warranted, it shall so certify and transmit the determination and the record of proceedings to the House of Representatives for whatever action the House of Representatives considers to be necessary.

Source: Judicial Councils Reform and Judicial Conduct and Disability Act (1980), 28 U.S.C. §§ 351–364, https://www.senate.gov/about/resources/pdf/judicial-councils-reform-disability-act.pdf.

Document 20

Nixon v. United States (1993)

(a) A controversy is nonjusticiable where there is 'a textually demonstrable constitutional commitment of the issue to a coordinate political department; or a lack of judicially discoverable and manageable standards for resolving it ...' *Baker* v. *Carr* .... These two concepts are not completely separate; the lack of judicially manageable standards may strengthen the conclusion that there is a textually demonstrable commitment to a coordinate branch.

(b) The language and structure of [the Constitution's Article I, Section 3, Clause 6] demonstrate a textual commitment of impeachment to the Senate. Nixon's argument that the use of the word 'try' in the Clause's first sentence impliedly requires a judicial-style trial by the full Senate that is subject to judicial review is rejected. The conclusion that 'try' lacks sufficient precision to afford any judicially manageable standard of review is compelled by older and modern dictionary definitions, and is fortified by the existence of the three very specific requirements that the Clause's second and third sentences do impose—that the Senate's Members must be under oath or affirmation, that a two-thirds vote is required to convict, and that the Chief Justice presides when the President is tried—the precise nature of which suggests that the Framers did not intend to impose additional limitations on the form of the Senate proceedings. The Clause's first sentence must instead be read as a grant of authority to the Senate to determine whether an individual should be acquitted or convicted, and the commonsense and dictionary meanings of the word 'sole' indicate that this authority is reposed in the Senate alone. ... A review of the Constitutional Convention's history and the contemporary commentary supports a reading of the constitutional language as deliberately placing the impeachment power in the Legislature, with no judicial involvement, even for the limited purpose of judicial review.

(c) Justiciability is also refuted by (1) the lack of finality inherent in exposing the country's political life—particularly if the President were impeached—to months, or perhaps years, of chaos during judicial review of Senate impeachment proceedings, or during any retrial that a differently constituted Senate might conduct if its first judgment of conviction were invalidated, and by (2) the difficulty of fashioning judicial relief other than simply setting aside the Senate's judgment of conviction.

(d) A holding of nonjusticiability is consistent with this Court's opinion in *Powell* v. *McCormack* ....

Source: Nixon v. United States, 506 U.S. 224 (1993), https://supreme.justia.com/cases/federal/us/506/224/#tab-opinion-1959127.

Document 21

Justices White and Blackmun on* Nixon v. United States *(1993)

Justice White, with whom Justice Blackmun joins, concurring in the judgment.

Petitioner contends that the method by which the Senate convicted him on two articles of impeachment violates ... the Constitution, which mandates that the Senate 'try' impeachments. The Court is of the view that the Constitution forbids us even to consider his contention. I find no such prohibition and would therefore reach the merits of the claim. I concur in the judgment because the Senate fulfilled its constitutional obligation to 'try' petitioner.

[...]

The majority also claims support in the history and early interpretations of the Impeachment Clauses, noting the various arguments in support of the current system made at the Constitutional Convention and expressed powerfully by Hamilton in The Federalist Nos. 65 and 66. In light of these materials there can be little doubt that the Framers came to the view at the Convention that the trial of officials' public misdeeds should be conducted by representatives of the people; that the fledgling Judiciary lacked the wherewithal to adjudicate political intrigues; that the Judiciary ought not to try both impeachments and subsequent criminal cases emanating from them; and that the impeachment power must reside in the Legislative Branch to provide a check on the largely unaccountable Judiciary.

The majority's review of the historical record thus explains why the power to try impeachments properly resides with the Senate. It does not explain, however, the sweeping statement that the Judiciary was 'not chosen to have any role in impeachments'. Not a single word in the historical materials cited by the majority addresses judicial review of the Impeachment Trial Clause. And a glance at the arguments surrounding the Impeachment Clauses negates the majority's attempt to infer nonjusticiability from the Framers' arguments in support of the Senate's power to try impeachments.

Source: Nixon v. United States, 506 U.S. 224 (1993), https://supreme.justia.com/cases/federal/us/506/224/#tab-opinion-1959127.

Document 22

Clinton v. Jones (1997)

The principal rationale for affording certain public servants immunity from suits for money damages arising out of their official acts is inapplicable to unofficial conduct. In cases involving prosecutors, legislators, and judges we have repeatedly explained that the immunity serves the public interest in enabling such officials to perform their designated functions effectively without fear that a particular decision may give rise to personal liability. We explained in *Ferri v. Ackerman*, 444 U.S. 193 (1979):

> 'As public servants, the prosecutor and the judge represent the interest of society as a whole. The conduct of their official duties may adversely affect a wide variety of different individuals, each of whom may be a potential source of future controversy. The societal interest in providing such public officials with the maximum ability to deal fearlessly and impartially with the public at large has long been recognized as an acceptable justification for official immunity. The point of immunity for such officials is to forestall an atmosphere of intimidation that would

> conflict with their resolve to perform their designated functions in a principled fashion.'

That rationale provided the principal basis for our holding that a former President of the United States was 'entitled to absolute immunity from damages liability predicated on his official acts' ....

This reasoning provides no support for an immunity for unofficial conduct. ... [W]e have never suggested that the President, or any other official, has an immunity that extends beyond the scope of any action taken in an official capacity.

Source: *Clinton v. Jones*, 520 U.S. 681 (1997), https://supreme.justia.com/cases/federal/us/520/681/#tab-opinion-1960129.

Document 23

Trump v. United States (2024)

Chief Justice Roberts delivering the opinion of the Court.

This case is the first criminal prosecution in our Nation's history of a former President for actions taken during his Presidency. We are called upon to consider whether and under what circumstances such a prosecution may proceed. Doing so requires careful assessment of the scope of Presidential power under the Constitution.

[...]

The parties before us do not dispute that a former President can be subject to criminal prosecution for unofficial acts committed while in office. They also agree that some of the conduct described in the indictment includes actions taken by Trump in his unofficial capacity.

They disagree, however, about whether a former President can be prosecuted for his official actions. Trump contends that just as a President is absolutely immune from civil damages liability for acts within the outer perimeter of his official responsibilities, he must be absolutely immune from criminal prosecution for such acts. And Trump argues that the bulk of the indictment's allegations involve conduct in his official capacity as President. Although the Government agrees that some official actions are included in the indictment's allegations, it maintains that a former President does not enjoy immunity from criminal prosecution for any actions, regardless of how they are characterized.

We conclude that under our constitutional structure of separated powers, the nature of Presidential power requires that a former President have some immunity from criminal prosecution for official acts during his tenure in office. At least with respect to the President's exercise of his core constitutional powers, this immunity must be absolute. As for his remaining official actions, he is also entitled to immunity. At the current stage of proceedings in this case, however, we need not and do not decide whether that immunity must be absolute, or instead whether a presumptive immunity is sufficient.

[...]

Congress cannot act on, and courts cannot examine, the President's actions on subjects within his 'conclusive and preclusive' constitutional authority. It follows that an Act 9 of Congress—either a specific one targeted at the President or a generally applicable one—may not criminalize the President's actions within his exclusive constitutional power. Neither may the courts adjudicate a criminal prosecution that examines such Presidential actions. We thus conclude that the President is absolutely immune from criminal prosecution for conduct within his exclusive sphere of constitutional authority.

[...]

As for a President's unofficial acts, there is no immunity. The principles we set out in *Clinton v. Jones* confirm as much.

[...]

Trump asserts a far broader immunity than the limited one we have recognized. He contends that the indictment must be dismissed because the Impeachment Judgment Clause requires that impeachment and Senate conviction precede a President's criminal prosecution.

[...]

The implication of Trump's theory is that a President who evades impeachment for one reason or another during his term in office can never be held accountable for his criminal acts in the ordinary course of law. So if a President manages to conceal certain crimes throughout his Presidency, or if Congress is unable to muster the political will to impeach the President for his crimes, then they must forever remain impervious to prosecution.

Source: Trump v. United States, 603 U.S. ___ (2024), https://supreme.justia.com/cases/federal/us/603/23-939/#tab-opinion-4913924.

Glossary

Antifederalist: Those individuals who opposed ratification of the Constitution, believing it gave the federal government too much power. Their numbers included Patrick Henry and George Mason.

Communism: A form of socialism, communism is a social and political ideology in which there are no social classes and key means of production, such as industry, are controlled by the state. It is the opposite of capitalism.

Credibility gap: A difference between what government officials say and what is true.

Deposition: The taking of sworn testimony outside of court.

Federal Reserve Board: In 1913, Congress passed and President Woodrow Wilson signed the Federal Reserve Act, which created a new banking system that included twelve regional federal reserve banks. This purpose of this new banking system was to prevent financial panics that had taken place in the past. The Federal Reserve Board manages this banking system.

Federalist: A person who supported ratification of the Constitution. They included Alexander Hamilton, James Madison, and John Jay. Later, 'Federalist' referred to a member of the Federalist Party, one of America's first political parties.

Great Depression: A worldwide economic downturn that began in the United States in 1929 and continued until World War II.

Great Society: President Lyndon Johnson's domestic program aimed at eliminating poverty in America.

Impeachment: The process by which Congress charges a federal official with misconduct.

Iran–Contra scandal: A political scandal that took place during the presidency of Ronald Reagan. It involved illegal arms sales to Iran in return for that country's help to free U.S. hostages held by Iranian-backed terrorists in Lebanon. In another violation of the law, the money from the arms sales went to the Contras, a U.S.-backed rebel group in Nicaragua that was then fighting Nicaragua's leftist Sandinista government.

Interstate Commerce Commission: A federal agency established in 1887 that originally focused on regulating the railroad industry but later included all interstate transportation. The federal government abolished the Commission in 1995.

Judicial Conference of the United States: A body created in 1922 that is headed by the chief justice of the Supreme Court. The Judicial Conference establishes guidelines for federal courts, and has the power both to investigate judges and to recommend their impeachment by Congress.

Judicial review: The process by which the judicial branch of government determines the constitutionality of actions taken by the legislative or executive branches.

New Deal: President Franklin Roosevelt's domestic program to help the United States escape the Great Depression.

Office of Legal Counsel (OLC): Founded in 1934, the Office of Legal Counsel provides legal advice to all of the federal government's executive-branch agencies.

Political question doctrine: A rule by which federal courts will refuse to hear a case if it centers on a question of a political rather than a legal nature.

Progressivism: A broad political, social, and economic reform movement that appeared in the United States in the 1890s and continued through the first two decades of the twentieth century. Progressives sought to make the nation more receptive to the needs of average Americans by eliminating political corruption and having the government regulate corporations.

Receiver: An individual appointed by a court to supervise the finances of a person or company that has declared bankruptcy.

Rule XI: A Senate rule adopted in 1935 that allows a committee of twelve senators rather than the full Senate to take evidence and hear testimony in an impeachment trial. Since then, the rule has been challenged in court and upheld by the U.S. Supreme Court.

Securities and Exchange Commission (SEC): As a response to the stock market crash of 1929 that led to the Great Depression, Congress passed and President Franklin Roosevelt signed the Securities Exchange Act of 1933. That law regulates the sale of stocks and bonds. It also requires transparency by companies that sell stock so that buyers understand what they are purchasing. The SEC enforces the Securities Exchange Act's rules.

Socialism: An economic ideology that calls for having all key means of production, such as factories, run by the government as opposed to being in private hands. It is the opposite of capitalism.

U.S. Commerce Court: A court established in 1910 that heard appeals of decisions made by the Interstate Commerce Commission. In 1913, the U.S. government abolished the Commerce Court.

U.S. Court of Claims: A court established in 1855 that heard claims for monetary payment made against the federal government. The government eliminated the Court of Claims in 1982.

Watergate: A building in Washington, D.C. that housed the Democratic Party's headquarters in 1972. A break-in at that party's office became the start of a scandal (also called Watergate) that forced President Richard Nixon to resign in 1974.

Guide to Further Reading

Historiography

Anyone who is interested in learning more about the history of impeachment will want to begin with Michael Gerhardt's books. Considered by legal scholars as the 'dean' of impeachment studies, Gerhardt has not only written extensively on the subject but has also testified before Congress during both President Bill Clinton's impeachment and the first attempt to remove President Donald Trump from office. Particularly important is his *The Federal Impeachment Process: A Constitutional and Historical Analysis*, 3rd ed. (Princeton, N.J.: Princeton University Press, 2019). Starting with the origins of the process of impeachment in the United States, he addresses changes to the way in which the House and Senate conduct that process, and possible reforms to it. In 2024, Gerhardt published a shorter but equally incisive study, titled *The Law of Presidential Impeachment: A Guide for the Engaged Citizen* (New York: New York University Press), that included Trump's two impeachments and what the author foresaw as the future for impeachments in the United States.

While *The Federal Impeachment Process* and the *Law of Presidential Impeachment* are accessible to a general audience, those who feel they need a primer may find it best to start with Gerhardt's *Impeachment: What Everyone Needs to Know* (New York: Oxford University Press, 2018). In an easy-to-follow question-and-answer format, the author explains what impeachment is, the history of the impeachment process, who can be impeached and for what, and what types of penalties the Senate can impose. While Gerhardt's work is by far newer, readers may still want to consult Supreme Court Justice Hugo Black's classic work, *Impeachment: A Handbook* (New Haven, Conn.: Yale University Press, 1974). In a concise 80 pages, Black covers the roles of the House and Senate in impeachment proceedings, the types of malfeasance that justify removal from office, and the inapplicability of judicial review to Senate convictions.

Other general studies readers may wish to consult are *British Origins and American Practice of Impeachment* (New York: Routledge, 2023), edited by Chris Monaghan and Matthew Flinders; Keith E. Whittington's *The*

Impeachment Power: The Law, Politics, and Purpose of an Extraordinary Constitutional Tool (Princeton, N.J.: Princeton University Press, 2024); and both editions of Frank O. Bowman III's *High Crimes and Misdemeanors: A History of Impeachment for the Age of Trump* (New York: Cambridge University Press, 2019 and 2024). All address the British underpinnings of impeachment as practiced in the United States—indeed, more than half the essays in *British Origins* relate to that subject—how the process has changed, and how political partisanship has entered into it. Michael de la Pole, one of the first people in England to be impeached, is the subject of John Smith Roskell's *The Impeachment of Michael de la Pole, Earl of Suffolk, in 1386: In the Context of the Reign of Richard II* (Manchester, U.K.: Manchester University Press, 1984). Though fifty years old, Raoul Berger's *Impeachment: The Constitutional Problems* (Cambridge, Mass.: Harvard University Press, 1973) is an important source for examining such questions as to whether: a president can be indicted only for criminal malfeasance, the impeachment process is by its nature criminal or political, senators who have expressed opinions on one's removal from office should be permitted to partake in an impeachment trial, and judicial review is legal. To get a better understanding of how the Founding Fathers intended for the Senate to avoid the partisan quarrels that might infuse impeachment proceedings in the House, readers should consult Jonathan Turley's 'Senate Trials and Factional Disputes: Impeachment as a Madisonian Device', in the *Duke Law Journal*, 49 (1999): 1–146.

To get a fuller grasp as to why impeachment is a process that affects only members of the executive and judicial branches, a good place to begin is Buckner F. Melton Jr.'s *The First Impeachment: The Constitution's Framers and the Case of Senator William Blount* (Macon, Ga.: Mercer University Press, 1998). In reaching a nonpartisan decision to expel him from the Senate, Blount's colleagues concluded that their hearings were not akin to a criminal proceeding, but rather an endeavor to uncover and punish political misdeeds.

The Presidency

Most of those works that have been on impeachment focus on the presidency. This is not surprising, given how few presidents have served the nation and how well-publicized efforts to remove them from office have been. In studying the first chief executive whose impeachment case reached the Senate, Andrew Johnson, readers will want to consult Hans L. Trefousse's *Impeachment of a President: Andrew Johnson, the Blacks, and Reconstruction* (Knoxville: University of Tennessee Press, 1975). Trefousse contends that Johnson's racist views placed him on a collision course with Radical Republicans, who wanted to do more to defend African American rights. The failure of the Radicals to remove from him office, though, prevented their vision for Reconstruction from achieving fruition. Similarly, Robert S. Levine connects

President Johnson's failure to support the rights of African Americans to his impeachment in *The Failed Promise: Reconstruction, Frederick Douglass, and the Impeachment of Andrew Johnson* (New York: Norton, 2021).

Those who want a front-row seat to Johnson's impeachment as presented though the eyes of the participants will want to consult Brenda Wineapple's *The Impeachers: The Trial of Andrew Johnson and the Dream of a Just Nation* (New York: Random House, 2019). The author focuses on members of Congress who wanted him out of the Oval Office. One of those lawmakers, Charles Sumner, is a main character—the other being Johnson—for Gene Smith, who authored *High Crimes and Misdemeanors: The Impeachment and Trial of Andrew Johnson* (New York: McGraw-Hill, 1976). Michael Les Benedict blames congressional ineptitude for the failure to convict the nation's seventeenth president in *The Impeachment and Trial of Andrew Johnson* (New York: Norton, 1973). Readers may also wish to consult David O. Stewart's *Impeached: The Trial of President Andrew Johnson and the Fight for Lincoln's Legacy* (New York: Simon & Schuster, 2009) and Chester G. Hearn's *The Impeachment of Andrew Johnson* (Jefferson, N.C.: McFarland, 2000).

Though not impeached, Richard Nixon has received extensive attention for his role in the Watergate scandal, which certainly would have led to his conviction by the Senate. While it focuses heavily on the machinations of Nixon and his inner circle between January and April 1973, readers will get a good sense of the decisions that ultimately led to the president's downfall through Michael Dobbs' *King Richard: Nixon and Watergate: An American Tragedy* (New York: Knopf, 2021). *All the President's Men* (New York: Simon & Schuster, 1974) is a classic. Written by *Washington Post* reporters Carl Bernstein and Bob Woodward, it recounts their investigation that helped unravel Watergate. Bernstein and Woodward also co-wrote *The Final Days* (New York: Simon & Schuster, 1976). It serves as a sequel to *All the President's Men*, taking the reader through Nixon's last days in office.

Elizabeth Drew, who wrote for the magazine *New Yorker*, presents readers with a near-daily account of what happened in the year leading up to Nixon's resignation in *Washington Journal: The Events of 1973–1974* (New York: Random House, 1975). An early study that relied on what were then recently released documents from the Nixon administration is Stanley Kutler's *The Wars of Watergate: The Last Crisis of Richard Nixon* (New York: Knopf, 1990). Fred Emery also turns to the documentary record, as well as interviews with the participants, in his *Watergate: The Corruption of American Politics and the Fall of Richard Nixon* (New York: Times Books, 1994). A recent recounting that examines the scandal from the perspective of myriad of individuals involved in it (including politicians, investigators, and journalists) is Garrett M. Graff's *Watergate: A New History* (New York: Avid Reader, 2023). To learn more about the effects of that scandal on American politics, on law, and on the relationship between the government and the U.S. public, readers will want to consult *Watergate Remembered: The Legacy for*

American Politics (New York: Palgrave Macmillan, 2012), edited by Michael A. Genovese and Iwan W. Morgan.

Bipartisanship was the word in what would have been Nixon's impeachment. By the time Bill Clinton faced his Senate trial a generation later, partisan politics had entered the mainstream. Indeed, argue Peter Baker in *The Breach: Inside the Impeachment and Trial of William Jefferson Clinton* (New York: Berkley, 2001) and Nicol C. Rae and Colton C. Campbell in *Impeaching Clinton: Partisan Strife on Capitol Hill* (Lawrence: University Press of Kansas, 2004), political partisanship was the key factor in the effort to kick Clinton out of the Oval Office. Placing Clinton's impeachment in the broader history of the use of that weapon, Frank O. Bowman and Stephen L. Sepinuck reaffirm in '"High Crimes and Misdemeanors": Defining the Constitutional Limits on Presidential Impeachment', in the *Southern California Law Review*, 72 (1999): 1517–1600, that removing a president from office via impeachment requires meeting a high bar.

Whether or not Clinton committed criminal acts deserving of impeachment has divided experts. Judge Richard A. Posner writes in *An Affair of State: The Investigation, Impeachment, and Trial of President Clinton* (Cambridge, Mass.: Harvard University Press, 1999) that party politics was essential to acquitting Clinton on what were potentially impeachable crimes that included perjury and obstruction of justice. Likewise, Charles J. Cooper charges Clinton with committing criminal acts, in 'A Perjurer in the White House? The Constitutional Case for Perjury and Obstruction of Justice as High Crimes and Misdemeanors', in the *Harvard Journal of Law and Public Policy*, 22 (1999): 619–46. Peter Tiersma disagrees with the claim of perjury in 'Did Clinton Lie? Defining "Sexual Relations"', in the *Chicago-Kent Law Review*, 79 (2004): 927–58.

Some authors have compared Clinton's impeachment with those of Johnson and Nixon. On this score, readers may wish to consult Keith E. Whittington's 'Bill Clinton Was No Andrew Johnson: Comparing Two Impeachments', in the *University of Pennsylvania Journal of Constitutional Law*, 2 (2000): 422–65; and Fred H. Altshuler's 'Comparing the Nixon and Clinton Impeachments', in *Hastings Law Journal*, 51 (2000): 745–52.

Individuals may also wish to peruse *The Clinton Impeachment and the Presidency in the Age of Political Spectacle* (New York: New York University Press, 2021), edited by Leonard V. Kaplan and Beverly Moran. In nearly two dozen essays, contributors assess the effort to impeach Clinton from political, religious, legal, and public opinion perspectives. Another potentially useful set of essays can be found in *The Clinton Scandal and the Future of American Government* (Washington, D.C.: Georgetown University Press, 2000), edited by Mark J. Rozell and Clyde Wilcox. Michael R. Kagay addresses the extent to which public opinion played a role in Clinton's acquittal in 'Public Opinion and Polling during Presidential Scandal and Impeachment', in *Public Opinion Quarterly*, 63 (1999): 449–63. In looking at Clinton's impeachment, Neal Katyal contends in 'Impeachment as Congressional Constitutional

Interpretation', in *Law and Contemporary Problems*, 63 (2000): 169–91, that the way one believes the judiciary should apply an originalist interpretation of the Constitution does not mean members of the legislature should define originalism similarly.

Talk of impeaching President Donald Trump began even before his inauguration and contributed to a new wave of literature that tried to place his potential removal from office with past efforts to do the same. J. Richard Broughton warned against the Senate becoming bogged down in partisanship should Trump (or any president) be impeached, in 'Conviction, Nullification, and the Limits of Impeachment as Politics', in the *Case Western Law Review*, 68 (2017): 275–315. Laurence Tribe—who had urged Congress to impeach the president-elect the moment he took the oath of office—and Joshua Matz make clear in *To End a Presidency: The Power of Impeachment* (New York: Basic Books, 2018) that they are no fans of Trump. However, by examining the history of impeachment, they offer a balanced argument that leaves the reader understanding that attempting to remove a president should not be taken lightly. Before pursuing such a course, lawmakers must ask themselves if doing so is constitutional, has a good chance of success, and is worth the potential impact it will have on the country.

Cass Sunstein and Alan Hirsch second the need for cautiousness. In *Impeachment: A Citizen's Guide* (Cambridge, Mass.: Harvard University Press, 2017), Sunstein examines not just the history of impeachment in the United States but how the Constitution's Second Article on impeachment differs from the 25th Amendment, even though both relate to the president's removal. Additionally, he asserts that partisan politics need to be kept out of any serious proposal to oust the country's highest political officer. In *Impeaching the President: Past, Present and Future* (San Francisco: City Light Books, 2018), Hirsh builds his argument by focusing heavily on the cases of Andrew Johnson, Richard Nixon, and Bill Clinton. He finds that members of Congress appeared to be much more careful about impeachment after their failed bid against Johnson, and that Nixon deserved both impeachment and conviction. Republicans' determination to impeach Clinton, though, is proof that partisan politics has led those who sit on Capitol Hill to throw to the wind the caution that Hirsh urges. Yet Hirsch concludes that the evidence of Trump's collusion with Russia during the 2016 election and that he obstructed justice were strong enough to consider impeachment proceedings against him.

In *Impeachment: An American History* (New York: Modern Library, 2018), Jeffrey Engel, Jon Meacham, Timothy Naftali, and Peter Baker also devote their attention primarily to Johnson, Nixon, and Clinton. Engel writes in the concluding essay that these three case studies illustrate how rare presidential impeachments are. That said, they provide valuable lessons for the present. Engel suggests that, based on those lessons, Trump committed impeachable offenses. Using comparisons with Johnson, Nixon, and Clinton, as well as Vice President Spiro Agnew, Lawrence J. Trautman spells out the allegations against Trump that could justify his impeachment in 'Presidential Impeachment: A Contemporary Analysis', in the *University of Dayton Law Review*, 44 (2019): 529–94. At the same time, he expresses doubt that the Senate would convict, and concern that trying to remove him from office would only deepen the nation's political polarization. Matthew Hansen argues that Trump is why it is important to enhance the powers of the special counsel established under the Ethics in Government Act, in 'All the President's Lawyers: Problems and Potential Solutions in Prosecuting Presidential Criminal Conduct', in the *Arizona Law Review*, 61 (2019): 231–52. Joel Goldstein laments the failure of the Senate to convict Trump in 2019, in 'The Senate, the Trump Impeachment Trial and Constitutional Morality', in the *Chicago-Kent Law Review*, 95 (2020): 475–95.

Trump supporters declared that Congress's impeachment of him in 2019 represented a violation of his right to due process and an attempt at a 'coup'. These claims are rejected by Brian Owsley in 'Due Process and the Impeachment of President Donald Trump', in the *University of Illinois Law Review*, 67 (2020): 67–80, and by Keith Whittington in 'Is Presidential Impeachment Like a Coup?', in the *Georgetown Journal of Law and Public Policy*, 18 (2020): 669–92. For J. Richard Broughton, in 'The Second Article and Congressional Self-Defense,' in the *Houston Law Review*, 59 (2021): 259–311, impeachment was a justified response to the Trump administration's efforts to obstruct Congress.

In 2020, a year after Trump went through his first impeachment, Daniel P. Franklin, Stanley M. Caress, Robert M. Sanders, and Cole D. Taratoot published *The Politics of Presidential Impeachment* (Albany: SUNY Press). Using four case studies, two of them of presidents who were impeached (Johnson and Clinton) and two about whom impeachment came up (Nixon and Reagan), the authors develop a model for impeachments that revolves around structural and ideological factors—such as how close the president and Congress are—and the accusations leveled against the Oval Office's occupant. They find that the partisanship infusing Washington made inevitable the attempt to remove Trump from office. Moreover, had Trump's 2016 opponent, Hillary Clinton, won, partisan politics would have seen efforts to impeach her as well. Whether Trump could be impeached after he left office in 2021—a question that indeed appeared as a result of the events of 6 January 2021—is the subject of Harold J. Krent's 'Can President Trump Be Impeached as Mr. Trump? Exploring the Temporal Dimension of Impeachments', in the *Chicago-Kent Law Review*, 95 (2020): 537–49. He concludes that it is only possible to impeach a federal officer while that person holds a government post. Michael Gerhardt challenges that assertion in 'Impeachment and Trial After Officials Leave Office', *Missouri Law Review*, 87 (2022): 793–817.

James C. Phillips and John C. Yoo in 'You're Fired: The Original Meaning of Presidential Impeachment', in the *Southern California Law Review*, 94 (2021): 1191–1277, take issue with those who sought Trump's impeachments in 2019 and 2021. The authors question many of the arguments Democrats used to justify removing the president in 2019, and reject the suggestion made by those in 2021 that Trump could be convicted by the Senate even though he no longer held public office. One of Trump's claims was that he was immune from criminal prosecution while in the White House, an argument refuted by Claire O. Finkelstein and Richard W. Painter in 'Presidential Accountability and the Rule of Law: Can the President Claim Immunity If He Shoots Someone on Fifth Avenue?', in the *University of Pennsylvania Journal of Constitutional Law*, 24 (2022): 93–210.

Placing Trump's two impeachments within a broader historical context, Michael Gerhardt considers whether the process of removing presidents from office is broken. In 'The Trump Impeachments: Lessons for the Constitution, Presidents, Congress, Justice, Lawyers, and the Public', in the *William & Mary Law Review*, 64 (2023): 1309–44, he admits that the impeachment process has serious problems but still offers an effective means of controlling a president's worst intentions. Similarly, in *The Law of Presidential Impeachment*, Gerhardt laments that partisanship has so weakened the impeachment process that it will be difficult to prevent a president from abusing their power. That said, he feels that while the process is bent, it is not broken.

Frank O. Bowman, in his second edition of *High Crimes and Misdemeanors*, also expresses concern. Indeed, he devotes nearly half of the text to Trump's two impeachments, spelling out in great detail the president's offenses that, the author concludes, justified both impeachment and conviction. That the Senate refused to find the president guilty based solely on partisan political grounds, though, has placed the country's democratic system in jeopardy. In *Unchecked: The Untold Story Behind Congress' s Botched Impeachments of Donald Trump* (New York: Morrow, 2022), authors Rachael Bade and Karoun Demirjian place the blame for Trump's political survival not only on Republicans but also on Democrats. Despite the deep partisan divide in Washington, they write, Trump faced a very real possibility the second time around of conviction by the Senate for his malfeasance. Yet, largely because of Democratic Party infighting, the president escaped punishment.

The Judiciary

Less has been written on judicial impeachments. Though older, two good studies include John D. Feerick, 'Impeaching Federal Judges: A Study of the Constitutional Provisions', in the *Fordham Law Review*, 39 (1970): 1–53, and Frank Thompson, Jr. and Daniel H. Pollitt, 'Impeachment of Federal Judges: An Historical Overview', in the *North Carolina Law Review*, 39 (1970): 87–121.

Interest in the impeachment of jurists increased significantly with the removal of judges Harry Claiborne, Walter Nixon, and Alcee Hastings in the 1980s. Here, one may want to start with Eleanore Bushnell's *Crimes, Follies, and Misfortunes: The Federal Impeachment Trials* (Urbana: University of Illinois Press, 1992). While she includes attempts to remove presidents, Bushnell dives into each of the other impeachment cases that had reached the Senate by the time her book came out. Hence, one learns not just about Andrew

Johnson but also about William Blount, John Pickering, Samuel Chase, and others, ending with the trials of judges Claiborne, Nixon, and Hastings. In so doing, Bushnell explains how members of Congress has grappled with what constitutes an impeachable offense, emphasizes that criminality is not required for removal from office, and recounts not only the Senate's adoption of Rule XI but also challenges to that rule. In 'The Revival of Impeachment as a Partisan Political Weapon', *Hastings Constitutional Law Quarterly*, 34 (Winter 2007): 161–327, Richard K. Neumann, Jr. describes how partisan politics was a key factor in efforts to remove from office executive and judicial branch officials in the first eighty so or years of the republic, declined for the next century, and then returned starting around 1968.

Though he focuses on the period since 1960, David Kyvig also looks at both presidential and judicial impeachments in *The Age of Impeachment: American Constitutional Culture since 1960* (Lawrence: University Press of Kansas, 2008). He argues convincingly that impeachment prior to 1960 was used rarely. Since then, however, its employment has become more common, for it is viewed as a weapon to force political rivals from office. Robert Welch's determination to impeach Supreme Court Justice Earl Warren is covered by Brett Bethune in 'Influence Without Impeachment: How the Impeach Earl Warren Movement Began, Faltered, but Avoided Irrelevance', in the *Journal of Supreme Court History*, 47 (2022): 142–61. Though focused strictly on the impeachments of judges Claiborne, Nixon, and Hastings, readers might wish to consult Mary L. Volcansek's *Judicial Impeachment: None Called for Justice* (Champaign: University of Illinois Press, 1993).

The attempts by judges Nixon and Hastings to demand judicial review of their Senate convictions generated a wave of interest in the question of the justiciability of impeachment. Hence, readers may want to consult Brendan C. Fox's 'The Justiciability of Challenges to the Senate Rules of Procedure for Impeachment Trials', in the *George Washington Law Review*, 60 (1992): 1275–310; Lisa A. Kainec's 'Judicial Review of Senate Impeachment Proceedings: Is a Hands Off Approach Appropriate?', in the *Case Western Reserve Law Review*, 43 (1993): 1499–527; Rebecca Brown's 'When Political Questions Affect Individual Rights: The Other *Nixon v. United States*', in the *Supreme Court Review*, 1993 (1993): 125–55; Peter M. Shane's 'Who May Discipline or Remove Federal Judges? A Constitutional Analysis', in the *University of Pennsylvania Law Review*, 142 (1993): 209–242; David Todd Smith's 'Constitutional Law-Impeachment Trial Clause: A Claim That Senate Impeachment Rule XI Violates the Impeachment Trial Clause is a Nonjusticiable Political Question. *Nixon v. United States*, - U.S. -, 113 S.Ct. 732, 122 L.Ed.2d 1 (1993)', in *Saint Mary's Law Journal*, 25 (1994): https://commons.stmarytx.edu/thestmaryslawjournal/vol25/iss2/10; Michael J. Gerhardt, 'Rediscovering Nonjusticiability: Judicial Review of Impeachments after *Nixon*', *Duke Law Journal*, 44 (1994): 231–76; Alan I. Baron, 'The Curious Case of Alcee Hastings', *Nova Law Review*, 18 (1994–1995): 873–908; and Alexa J. Smith, 'Federal Judicial Impeachment: Defining Process Due', *Hastings Law Journal*, 46 (1995): 639–74.

References

Adams, Charles F. ed. 1874–1877. *Memoirs of John Quincy Adams*, 12 vols. Philadelphia: J. B. Lippincott.
Albert, Carl, with Danney Goble. 1990. *Little Giant: The Life and Times of Speaker Carl Albert*. Norman: University of Oklahoma Press.
Alschuler, Albert W. 2021. 'Limiting the Pardon Power'. *Arizona Law Review* 63: 545–607.
Amar, Akhil Reed. 1999. 'On Impeaching Presidents'. *Hofstra Law Review* 28: 291–341.
Ames, Herbert V. 1897. *The Proposed Amendments to the Constitution During the First Century of its History*. Washington, D.C.: American Historical Association.
Annals of Congress. 1795–1796. 4th Cong., 1st sess.
Annals of Congress. 1803–1804. 8th Cong., 1st sess.
Annals of Congress. 1804–1805. 8th Cong., 2nd sess.
Annals of Congress. 1805–1805. 9th Cong., 1st sess.
'Archbald Guilty on Five Counts'. 1913, January 14. *New York Times*, 1.
'Article Seven'. 1937, January 30. *Literary Digest* 123: 7–8.
Bade, Rachel, and Karoun Demirjian. 2022. *Unchecked: The Untold Story Behind Congress' Botched Impeachments of Donald Trump*. New York: Morrow.
Baker, Peter. 2001. *The Breach: Inside the Impeachment and Trial of William Jefferson Clinton*. New York: Berkley.
Baker, Peter. 2018. 'Bill Clinton'. *Impeachment: An American History*, Jeffrey A. Engel, Jon Meacham, Timothy Naftali, and Peter Baker. New York: Modern Library, 155–204.
Bemis, Samuel Flagg. 1956. *John Quincy Adams and the Union*. New York: Knopf.
Berger, Raoul. 1973. *Impeachment: The Constitutional Problems*. Cambridge, Mass.: Harvard University Press.
Bethune, Brett. 2022. 'Influence Without Impeachment: How the Impeach Earl Warren Movement Began, Faltered, But Avoided Irrelevance'. *Journal of Supreme Court History* 47: 142–60.
Black, Charles L., Jr., and Philip Bobbitt. 2018. *Impeachment: A Handbook*, new ed. New Haven, Conn.: Yale University Press.
Bloch, Susan Low. 2000. 'A Report Card on Impeachment: Judging the Institutions that Judged President Clinton'. *Law and Contemporary Problems* 63: 143–67.
Bowman, Frank O., III. 2019. *High Crimes and Misdemeanors: A History of Impeachment in the Age of Trump*. New York: Cambridge University Press.

Bowman, Frank O., III. 2024. *High Crimes and Misdemeanors: A History of Impeachment in the Age of Trump*, 2nd ed. New York: Cambridge University Press.
Boyd, Julian P., ed. 1950–. *The Papers of Thomas Jefferson*, 45 vols. Princeton, N.J.: Princeton University Press.
Bresnahan, John. 2013, November 14. 'GOP to Call for Holder Impeachment', Politico, https://www.politico.com/story/2013/11/house-republicans-eric-holder-impeachment-099845.
Broughton, J. Richard. 2021. 'The Second Article and Congressional Self-Defense'. *Houston Law Review* 59: 259–311.
Brown, Rebecca L. 1993. 'When Political Questions Affect Individual Rights: The Other *Nixon v. United States*'. *Supreme Court Review* 1993: 125–55.
Bushnell, Eleanore 1992. *Crimes, Follies, and Misfortunes: The Federal Impeachment Trials*. Urbana: University of Illinois Press.
Byas, Steve. 2021, March 22. 'Belknap Trial was a Precedent against Second Trump Trial'. *New American* 37: 36–38.
Cannandine, David. 2007. *Mellon: An American Life*. New York: Knopf.
Castel, Albert. 1979. *The Presidency of Andrew Johnson*. Lawrence: University Press of Kansas.
Charlton, Linda. 1977, February 3. 'Dixon Writes an Apology to Nader for "Derogatory" Ethnic Remark'. *New York Times*, 18.
Clayton, Andrew R. L. 1996. 'When Shall We Cease to Have Judases? The Blount Conspiracy and the Limits of the 'Extended Republic'. *Launching the 'Extended Republic': The Federalist Era*, edited by Ronald Hoffman and Peter J. Albert. Charlottesville: University of Virginia Press.
Congressional Globe. 1859–1860. 36th Cong., 1st sess.
Congressional Globe. 1867–1868. 40th Cong., 2nd sess.
Congressional Globe. 1871–1872. 42nd Cong., 3rd sess.
Congressional Record. 1877–1879. 44th Cong., 1st sess.
Congressional Record. 1933–1934. 73rd Cong., 2nd sess.
Congressional Record. 1935–1936. 74th Cong., 1st sess.
Cooke, Jacob E., ed. 1961. *The Federalist*. Cleveland: World Publishing.
Coon, Mark E. 2017–2018. 'Vice Presidential Immunity in the Age of Impeachment: A Fresh Look at the Agnew Precedent'. *ConLawNOW* 9: 209–25.
Cooper, Charles J. 1999. 'A Perjurer in the White House? The Constitutional Case for Perjury and Obstruction of Justice as High Crimes and Misdemeanors'. *Harvard Journal of Law and Public Policy* 22: 619–46.
Cooper, Edmund S. 2003. *William Worth Belknap: An American Disgrace*. Madison, N.J.: Fairleigh Dickinson University Press.
Covarrubias, Rey, Jr. 2025, February 13. 'Rep. Eli Crane Wants Congress to Impeach This US Judge After DOGE-Treasury Standoff'. *Arizona Republic*, https://www.azcentral.com/story/news/politics/nation/2025/02/13/why-rep-eli-crane-wants-congress-to-impeach-judge-paul-engelmayer/78460235007/.
Drutman, Lee. 2020, October 5. 'How Hatred Came to Dominate American Politics'. FiveThirtyEight, https://fivethirtyeight.com/features/how-hatred-negative-partisanship-came-to-dominate-american-politics/.
Duram, James C. 1981. *Justice William O. Douglas*. Boston: Twayne.
Eisen, Norman. 2018, August 13. 'Unpacked: Can a President Pardon Himself?', Brookings Institution, https://www.brookings.edu/articles/unpacked-can-a-president-pardon-himself/.

Elliot, Jonathan 1836–1845. *The Debates in the Several State Conventions on the Adoption of the Federal Constitution*, 5 vols. Philadelphia: Lippincott.

Ellis, Richard E. 1971. *The Jeffersonian Crisis: Courts and Politics in the Young Republic*. New York: Oxford University Press.

Engel, Jeffrey. 2018. 'Conclusion'. *Impeachment: An American History*, Jeffrey A. Engel, Jon Meacham, Timothy Naftali, and Peter Baker. New York: Modern Library, 205–23.

Farrand, Max, ed. 1966. *The Records of the Federal Convention of 1787*, 4 vols. New Haven, Conn.: Yale University Press.

Feerick, John D. 1970. 'Impeaching Federal Judges: A Study of the Constitutional Provisions'. *Fordham Law Review* 39: 1–58.

Fenton, Paul S. 1970. 'The Scope of the Impeachment Power'. *Northwestern University Law Review* 65: 719–57.

Finkelstein, Claire O., and Richard W. Painter. 2022. 'Presidential Accountability and the Rule of Law: Can the President Claim Immunity If He Shoots Someone on Fifth Avenue?' *University of Pennsylvania Journal of Constitutional Law* 24: 93–210.

Firmage, Edwin Brown. 1973. 'The Law of Political Impeachment'. *Utah Law Review* 4: 681–704.

Firmage, Edwin Brown, and R. Collin Mangrum. 1974. 'Removal of the President: Resignation and the Procedural Law of Impeachment'. *Duke Law Journal* 1974: 1023–116.

Ford, Paul Leicester, ed. 1888. *Pamphlets on the Constitution of the United States, Published During its Discussion by the People, 1787–1788*. Brooklyn, N.Y.

Fox, Brendan C. 1992. 'The Justiciability of Challenges to the Senate Rules of Procedure for Impeachment Trials'. *George Washington Law Review* 60: 1275–1310.

Fritze, John, Tierney Sneed, Hannah Rabinowitz, and Holmes Lybrand. 2024, April 25. 'Supreme Court Hears Arguments on Trump Immunity Case. CNN, https://www.cnn.com/politics/live-news/supreme-court-trump-immunity-04-25-24/index.html.

Gerhardt, Michael J. 1994. 'Rediscovering Nonjusticiability: Judicial Review of Impeachments after *Nixon*'. *Duke Law Journal* 44: 231–76.

Gerhardt, Michael J. 2000. *The Federal Impeachment Process: A Constitutional and Historical Analysis*, 2nd ed. Chicago: University of Chicago Press.

Gerhardt, Michael J. 2019. *The Federal Impeachment Process: A Constitutional and Historical Analysis*, 3rd ed. Chicago: University of Chicago Press, 2019.

Gerhardt, Michael J. 2022a. 'How Impeachment Works'. *Missouri Law Review* 87: 743–67.

Gerhardt, Michael J. 2022b. 'Impeachment and Trial After Officials Leave Office'. *Missouri Law Review* 87: 793–817.

Gerhardt, Michael J. 2023. 'The Trump Impeachments: Lessons for the Constitution, Presidents, Congress, Justice, Lawyers, and the Public'. *William and Mary Law Review* 64: 1309–44.

Gerhardt, Michael J. 2024. *The Law of Presidential Impeachment: A Guide for the Engaged Citizen*. New York: New York University Press.

Gonzales, Alberto R. 2019. 'Presidential Pardons, Immunities, and Pardons'. *Washington University Law Review* 96: 905–40.

Gould, Lewis L. 2003. *The Modern American Presidency*. Lawrence: University Press of Kansas.

Groves, Stephen, and Farnoush Amiri. 2023, June 28. 'Threats of Impeachment and Censure Used to Be Rare. In This Congress, They're Becoming Routine'. Associated Press, https://apnews.com/article/impeachment-house-censure-schiff-biden-boebert-70a2206fc0c543a307fc3ec63d5287e9.

Hall, Kermit L. 1975. 'West H. Humphreys and the Crisis of the Union'. *Tennessee Historical Quarterly* 34: 48–69.

Harrington, Clodagh, and Alex Waddan. 2024. 'The U.S. Impeachment Process: Fit for Purpose in a Hyper-Partisan Era?' *British Origins and American Practice of Impeachment*, edited by Chris Monaghan and Matthew Flinders. Abingdon, Oxon: Routledge, 238–57.

Healy, Gene. 2022. 'Be Careful What You Wish For: Impeachment in the Trump Era'. *Missouri Law Review* 87: 769–79.

Heflin, Howell Heflin. 1990. 'Impeaching Federal Judges: Making the Case for Change'. *Trial* 71: 32–34.

Hirsch, Alan. 2018. *Impeaching the President: Past, Present, and Future*. San Francisco: City Light Books.

Hollis-Brusky, Amanda. 2020. 'Impeachment as a "Madisonian Device" Reconsidered'. *Chicago-Kent Law Review* 95: 497–517.

Holmes, Kristen, and Paula Reid. 2024, July 1. 'Trump Calls Immunity Ruling a "Big Win" as His Legal Team Says Decision Could Also Help Him in Other Cases'. CNN, https://www.cnn.com/politics/live-news/trump-immunity-supreme-court-decision-07-01-24.

Hopkins, James, ed. 1959–1992. *The Papers of Henry Clay*, 11 vols. Lexington: University of Kentucky Press.

Howe, Amy. 2024, July 1. 'Justices Rule Trump Has Some Immunity from Prosecution'. SCOTUSblog, https://www.scotusblog.com/2024/07/justices-rule-trump-has-some-immunity-from-prosecution/.

'Impeachment No. 13'. 1936, March 16. *Time* 27: 18–19.

Isenbergh, Joseph. 1998. 'Impeachment and Presidential Immunity from Judicial Process'. *University of Chicago Law Occasional Paper*, No. 39: 1–40.

'Judge Archbald's Conviction'. 1913, January 25. *Literary Digest* 46: 169–70.

'Judge English Defends Actions on Bench'. 1925, April 1. *New York Times*, 18.

'Judge on Trial'. 1936, April 20. *Time* 27: 16–17.

Kainec, Lisa A. 1993. 'Judicial Review of Senate Impeachment Proceedings: Is a Hands Off Approach Appropriate?' *Case Western Reserve Law Review* 43: 1499–527.

Kanstroom, Daniel. 2007. *Deportation Nation: Outsiders in American History*. Cambridge, Mass.: Harvard University Press.

Katyal, Neal, with Sam Koppelman. 2019. *Impeach: The Case against Donald Trump*. Boston: Mariner.

Kaufman, Scott. 2017. *Ambition, Pragmatism, and Party: A Political Biography of Gerald R. Ford*. Lawrence: University Press of Kansas.

Krent, Harold J. 2020. 'Can President Trump Be Impeached as Mr. Trump? Exploring the Temporal Dimension of Impeachments'. *Chicago-Kent Law Review* 95: 541–49.

Kyvig, David E. 2008. *The Age of Impeachment: American Constitutional Culture since 1960*. Lawrence: University Press of Kansas.

Lambert, William. 1969, May 9. 'The Stock Manipulator'. *Life* 66: 32–37.

'A Lame and Impotent Conclusion'. 1867, 4 June. *National Intelligencer*.

Lilienthal, David E. 1926, June 5. 'For "High Crimes and Misdemeanors"'. *The Independent* 116: 653–54, 669.

Lindberg, Tod. 2000, February 1. 'Necessary Impeachments, Necessary Acquittals'. *Policy Review*: 3–26, https://www.hoover.org/research/necessary-impeachments-necessary-acquittals.

Ling, Peter J. 2021. 'Why Reagan Was Not Impeached'. *European Journal of American Culture* 40: 201–14.

'Louderback Trial Roils Democrats'. 1933, May 17. *New York Times*, 11.

Low, A. Maurice. 1913, February 15. 'The Ethics of the Bench', *Harper's Weekly* 57: 9.

Maier, Pauline. 2010. *Ratification: The People Debate the Constitution, 1787–1788* New York: Simon & Schuster.

Mannweiler, Laura, Aidan Pittman, and Alan Kronenberg. 2024, July 1. '"Simply Frightening" v. a "Massive Win": Congress Reacts to Presidential Immunity Ruling'. US News and World Report, https://www.usnews.com/news/national-news/articles/2024-07-01/simply-frightening-v-a-massive-win-congress-reacts-to-presidential-immunity-ruling.

McConnell, Michael W. 2022. 'Impeachment and Trial after Officials Leave Office', *Missouri Law Review* 87: 793–817.

McDonald, Forrest. 1965. *E Pluribus Unum: The Formation of the American Republic, 1776–1790*. Boston: Houghton Mifflin.

McNulty, Paul J. 2019. 'Passions, Politics and the Removal of the President: Lessons Learned from the Impeachment of President Clinton'. *Grove City College Journal of Law and Public Policy* 10: 1–18.

Melton, Buckner F., Jr. *The First Impeachment: The Constitution's Framers and the Case of Senator William Blount*. Macon, Ga.: Mercer University Press, 1998.

Meriwether, Robert L. ed. 1959–2003. *The Papers of John C. Calhoun*, 28 vols. Columbia: University of South Carolina Press.

Mohr, Lillian Holman. 1979. *Frances Perkins: 'That Woman in FDR's Cabinet!'* Croton-on-Hudson, N.Y.: North River Press.

Monaghan, Chris. 2024. 'Impeachment During the Fourteenth and Fifteenth Centuries and Its Abeyance in the Sixteenth Century'. *British Origins and American Practice of Impeachment*, edited by Chris Monaghan and Matthew Flinders. Abingdon, Oxon: Routledge.

Morgan, Charles, Jr., Hope Eastman, Mary Ellen Gale, and Judith Areen. 1974. 'Impeachment: An Historical Overview', *Seton Hall Law Review* 5: 689–719.

Most, Doug. 2023, September 14. 'Does Impeachment Mean Anything Anymore?' *BU Today*, https://www.bu.edu/articles/2023/impeachment-meaning-and-impact/.

Mueller, Robert. 2019, May 29. 'Charging Trump Was Not an Option'. BBC, https://www.bbc.com/news/world-us-canada-48450534.

Neumann, Richard K., Jr. 2007. 'The Revival of Impeachment as a Partisan Political Weapon'. *Hastings Constitutional Law Quarterly* 34: 161–327.

Oberg, Barbara B., ed. 1950–. *The Papers of Thomas Jefferson*, 48 vols. Princeton, N.J.: Princeton University Press.

Palmer, Beverly Wilson, and Holly Byers Ochoa, eds. 1997–1998. *The Selected Papers of Thaddeus Stevens*, 2 vols. Pittsburgh: University of Pittsburgh Press.

Parlatore, Timothy C. 2024, July 3. 'Opinion: The Presidential Immunity Ruling Is Good for Trump—and for Biden, Too'. CNN, https://www.cnn.com/2024/07/03/opinions/trump-biden-scotus-presidential-immunity-parlatore/index.html.

Parton, James. 1860. *Life of Andrew Jackson*, 3 vols. New York: Mason Brothers.

Peck, James Randolph. 2000. 'Restoring the Balance of Power: Impeachment and the Twenty-Second Amendment'. *William and Mary Bill of Rights Journal* 8: 759–94.

Peterson, Merrill D. 1970. *Thomas Jefferson and the New Nation: A Biography*. New York: Oxford University Press.

Peterson, Todd D. 1993. 'The Role of the Executive Branch in the Discipline and Removal of Federal Judges'. *University of Illinois Law Review* 4: 809–96.

Phillips, James C., and John C. Yoo, 2021. 'You're Fired: The Original Meaning of Impeachment'. *Southern California Law Review* 94: 1191–277.

Posner, Richard A. 1999. *An Affair of State: The Investigation, Impeachment, and Trial of President Clinton*. Cambridge, Mass.: Harvard University Press.

'The Proposed Impeachment of the President'. 1866, 19 November. *Bangor Daily Whig and Courier*.

Rae, Nicol C., and Colton C. Campbell. 2004. *Impeaching Clinton: Partisan Strife on Capitol Hill*. Lawrence: University Press of Kansas.

Rakove, Jack N. 2024. 'Impeachment, Responsibility and Constitutional Failure: From Watergate to January 6'. *British Origins and American Practice of Impeachment*, edited by Chris Monaghan and Matthew Flinders. Abingdon, Oxon: Routledge, 206–37.

Rattey, Justin D. 2021. 'Impartial Justice: Restoring Integrity to Impeachment Trials'. *Pepperdine Law Review* 49: 123–94.

Remini, Robert V. 1981. *Andrew Jackson: The Course of American Freedom, 1822–1832*. New York: Harper & Row.

Report of the National Commission on Judicial Discipline and Removal. 2003. Washington, D.C.: National Commission on Judicial Discipline and Removal.

Rossetti, Michael, and Tauhid Zaman. 2023. 'Bots, Disinformation, and the First Impeachment of U.S. President Donald Trump'. *Plos One* 17: 1–27.

Schleifer, Theodore, and Tom LoBianco. 2015, October 27. 'House Republicans Move to Impeach IRS Head'. CNN, https://www.cnn.com/2015/10/27/politics/john-koskinen-irs-impeach/index.html.

Schmidli, William Michael. 2013. *The Fate of Freedom Elsewhere: Human Rights and U.S. Cold War Policy toward Argentina*. Ithaca, N.Y.: Cornell University Press.

Smith, Alexa J. 1995. 'Federal Judicial Impeachment: Defining Process Due'. *Hastings Law Journal* 46: 639–74.

Smith, David Todd. 1994. 'Impeachment Trial Clause: A Claim that Senate Impeachment Rule XI Violates the Impeachment Trial Clause Is a Nonjusticiable Political Question'. *St. Mary's Law Journal* 25 (1994): 855–83.

Solender, Andrew. 2025, February 15. 'Republicans Move to Impeach Judges Who Blocked Trump'. Axios, https://www.axios.com/2025/02/16/impeachment-judges-republicans-trump.

Sollenberger, Michael A. 2008. *The President Shall Nominate: How Congress Trumps Executive Power*. Lawrence: University Press of Kansas.

Stephens, Harold M. 1952. 'The Administrative Affairs of the U.S. Courts: A Report to the Bar'. *American Bar Association Journal* 38: 555–60, 621–22.

Summers, Mark W. 1987. *The Plundering Generation: Corruption and the Crisis of the Union, 1849–1861*. New York: Oxford University Press.

Sumner, Charles. 1870–1873. *Works of Charles Sumner*, 15 vols. Boston: Lee and Shepard.

Sumrall, Allen. C. 2020. 'Incongruous Ideas of Impeachment: "Impeachable Offenses" and the Constitutional Order'. *Presidential Studies Quarterly* 50: 948–67.

Sunstein, Cass R. 1998. 'Impeaching the President'. *University of Pennsylvania Law Review* 147: 279–315, https://scholarship.law.upenn.edu/penn_law_review/vol147/iss2/1.

Sunstein, Cass R. 2017. *Impeachment: A Citizen's Guide*. Cambridge, Mass.: Harvard University Press.

Sweeney, J. P. 1974. 'Presidential Impeachment and Judicial Review'. *American University Law Review* 23: 959–93.

Tarinelli, Ryan. 2024, July 1. 'Historians, Legal Experts Express Dismay at Trump Immunity Ruling'. Roll Call, https://rollcall.com/2024/07/01/historians-legal-experts-express-dismay-at-trump-immunity-ruling/.

TenBroek, Jacobus. 1939. 'Partisan Politics and Federal Judgeship Impeachment since 1903'. *Minnesota Law Review* 23: 185–204.

Thompson, Frank Jr., and Daniel H. Pollitt. 1970. 'Impeachment of Federal Judges: An Historical Overview'. *North Carolina Law Review* 49: 87–121.

Trefousse, Hans L. 1963. *Benjamin Franklin Wade: Radical Republican from* Ohio. New York: Twayne.

Trefousse, Hans L. 1975. *Impeachment of a President: Andrew Johnson, the Blacks, and Reconstruction*. Knoxville: University of Tennessee Press.

Trefousse, Hans L. 1989. *Andrew Johnson: A Biography*. New York: Norton.

Trefousse, Hans L. 1997. *Thaddeus Stevens: Nineteenth-Century Egalitarian*. Chapel Hill: University of North Carolina Press.

Tribe, Laurence, and Joshua Matz. 2018. *To End a Presidency: The Power of Impeachment*. New York: Basic Books, 2018.

Turley, Jonathan. 1999. 'Senate Trials and Factional Disputes: Impeachment as a Madisonian Device'. *Duke Law Journal* 49: 1–146.

U.S. Congress, House of Representatives. 2022. *Impeaching Merrick Brian Garland, Attorney General of the United States, for Endangering, Compromising, and Undermining the Justice System of the United States by Facilitating the Persecution of President Joseph R. Biden, Jr.'s, Political Rival, Donald J. Trump, the 45th President of the United States*, 117th Cong., 2nd sess, https://www.congress.gov/bill/117th-congress/house-resolution/1318/text.

U.S. Congress, Senate. 1868. *Trial of Andrew Johnson, President of the United States, before the Senate of the United States, on Impeachment by the House of Representatives for High Crimes and Misdemeanors*, 3 vols., 40th Cong., 2nd sess.

U.S. Congress, Senate. 1876. *Proceedings of the Senate Sitting for the Trial of William W. Belknap, Late Secretary of War, on the Articles of Impeachment Exhibited by the House of Representatives*, 44th Cong., 1st sess.

U.S. Congress, Senate. 1905. *Proceedings in the Senate of the United States in the Matter of the Impeachment of Charles Swayne, Judge of the District Court of the United States in and for the Northern District of Florida*, 58th Cong., 3rd sess.

Van Tassel, Emily, and Paul Finkelman. 1999. *Impeachable Offenses: A Documentary History from 1787 to the Present*. Washington, D.C.: CQ Press.

'The Week'. 1913, January 16. *The Nation* 96: 45.

Wegmann, Philip. 2106, January 25. 'Jason Chaffetz Wants to Use "Atrophied" Muscle of Impeachment against IRS Commissioner', *Daily Signal*, https://www.dailysignal.com/2016/04/19/jason-chaffetz-wants-to-use-atrophied-muscle-of-impeachment-against-irs-commissioner/.

Wehle, Kimberley L. 2020. '"Law" and the OLC's Article II Immunity Memos'. *Stanford Law and Policy Review* 32: 1–58.
Whitman, C. M. 1884. *American Orators and Oratory: Comprising Biographical Sketches of the Representative Men of America*. Chicago: Fairbanks, Palmer.
Whittington, Keith E. 2020a. 'A Formidable Weapon of Faction? The Law and Politics of Impeachment'. *Wake Forest Law Review* 55: 381–413.
Whittington, Keith E. 2020b. 'Is Presidential Impeachment Like a Coup?' *Georgetown Journal of Law and Public Policy* 18: 669–92.
Wiltse, Charles M., ed. 1974–1989. *The Papers of Daniel Webster*, 3 vols. Hanover, N.H.: University Press of New England.
Wood, Gordon S. 1969. *The Creation of the American Republic, 1776–1787*. Chapel Hill: University of North Carolina Press.

Index

For Product Safety Concerns and Information please contact our EU
representative GPSR@taylorandfrancis.com
Taylor & Francis Verlag GmbH, Kaufingerstraße 24, 80331 München, Germany

www.ingramcontent.com/pod-product-compliance
Ingram Content Group UK Ltd.
Pitfield, Milton Keynes, MK11 3LW, UK
UKHW020003200926
475702UK00015B/2450

* 9 7 8 1 0 3 2 9 3 3 9 1 7 *